THE ORGANIZED
EXECUTIVE

THE ORGANIZED

EXECUTIVE

New ways to manage
time, paper, people, and
the electronic office

Updated and revised for the nineties

STEPHANIE WINSTON

W · W · NORTON & COMPANY · NEW YORK · LONDON

The text of this book is composed in Monotype Bodoni Book
with the display set in Frutiger and Futura Light Condensed.
Composition and manufacturing by The Haddon Craftsmen, Inc.
Book design by Jack Meserole

ACKNOWLEDGMENT IS DUE TO THE FOLLOWING: Cartoon from *The Wall Street Journal* (p. 38) reprinted by permission of Cartoon Features Syndicate; the card "How to Get Ready to Instruct," "How to Instruct," (p. 255) reprinted by permission of The Goodyear Tire & Rubber Company.

Library of Congress Cataloging-in-Publication Data
Winston, Stephanie.
 The organized executive : new ways to manage time, paper, people,
and the electronic office / Stephanie Winston.—Updated and revised
for the nineties.
  p. cm.
Includes bibliographical references and index.
 1. Paperwork (office practice)—Management. 2. Executives—Time
management. 3. Office management. I. Title.
HF5547.15.W56 1994
658.4′093—dc20   93-7537

ISBN 0-393-03567-0

W. W. Norton & Company, Inc., 500 Fifth Avenue, New York, N.Y. 10110
W. W. Norton & Company Ltd., 10 Coptic Street, London WC1A 1PU

To my family

Contents

Preface

This book answers two kinds of questions about getting organized. The first are nuts-and-bolts questions: How do I take control of paperwork, manage a hectic schedule, get more done in less time, set up an effective filing system, use my computer to enhance my productivity, delegate effectively to my staff? What are some innovative ideas for making the most of available resources? For these purposes, *The Organized Executive* is a straightforward reference, a source of "how to" information.

The second and more fundamental question is "How can I conduct my daily professional life so as to achieve maximum productivity in a way that is consistent with long-term goals?" While the answer partly involves practicing and changing habits, the issue is also one of personal values. *The Organized Executive* explains why many managers feel out of control and the basic attitudes contributing to this perception. Equally important, the book offers new ways to think about time, paper, and people so that potential productivity can be translated into a coherent program.

My own experience as director of the firm The Organizing Principle forms the background for the book. Our diverse experience in areas relating to managerial productivity has made it possible to pinpoint the specific areas in which organizing is crucial, and to recognize the steps toward effective management in a variety of situations, whether personal or professional.

In turn, I would welcome planning or organizing counsel from the experience of my readers. If you will write to me c/o W. W. Norton, 500 Fifth Avenue, New York, NY 10110, all correspondence will be forwarded to me.

Many people have cooperated during the process of translating a collection of ideas into this book. Marnie Winston-Macauley, Norma Fox, and Nancy L. Lane were always "on call" to provide guidance and criticism. The publication *Boardroom Reports* was a fertile source of ideas, and I am grateful to *Boardroom*'s publisher, Martin Edelston, for his encouragement and support.

Special thanks go to these individuals who were kind enough to offer advice, comments, or information: Carlton D. Burtt, Dorothy M. Cook, Roger Griffith, Peter Jablon, Martin H. Jaffe, Debra Klein, Nina Liebman, Jean Meyer, Charles J. Moxley, Jr., Amanda Murray, Karen Olson, and Lewis Wunderlich. A private acknowledgment is offered to family and close friends for their indulgence and goodwill during the writing.

The chapter "Getting Organized the Electronic Way" could not have been written without the able contribution of Toni L. Kamins, whose generously shared knowledge informs all of this material. Copy editor Ted Johnson's emendations were extremely helpful, and valuable direction was offered by George Pickett.

To my editor, Carol Houck Smith, grateful appreciation as

always for patience, a fine eye, a firm hand, and unwavering faith that it would all come right. My agent, Susan Ann Protter, for the second time around, is an ally and friend. Most particular thanks go to Sharon Morgan, editor/consultant, who blasted out, shaped, organized, rewrote, and clarified the ideas expressed here, and whose generous contribution enhanced this book in every way. Thanks and appreciation are due my editor at Warner Books, Susan Suffes.

And finally, thanks to my clients for sharing their questions and concerns with me. This book is, in large part, the distillation of their experience.

STEPHANIE WINSTON

THE ORGANIZED
EXECUTIVE

1

The Organizing Principle

Sometimes it seems that the day-to-day organization of America rests in very uncertain hands. For example:

- Two airline executives were under consideration for a senior post. One was capable, the other was brilliant. But the brilliant manager was a kind of black hole: memos, phone messages, etc. went into his office and never came out again. So the capable manager, not the brilliant one, won the position.
- A technology-company marketing manager declared rather proudly that she often didn't bother returning phone calls until someone finally penetrated her attention after three, four, or five attempts. She learned later that her company had lost the services of an important spokesperson because she hadn't returned the spokesperson's representative's two calls.
- According to the Conference on Law Office Management,

the majority of malpractice suits against lawyers result from failure to file papers by required due dates.

• It is quite possible—even likely—that the nuclear melt-down crisis at Three Mile Island might have been avoided if the manufacturers of the nuclear reactor had handled their paperwork in a more organized manner. According to the *New York Times*, officials of that company conceded that "they had failed to take proper heed of warnings . . . contained in memorandums written by assistants, [which] had been sent to the wrong people, and had been subordinated to more pressing matters."

These incidents represent an undercurrent that is astonishingly prevalent throughout American business. Perhaps as many as half the people whose work consists of dealing with paper, time, and other people are not certain how to organize their operations on the most fundamental level.

This is the way it goes: Craig Bradley is a bright, talented group manager for a marketing firm. It is 3:45 P.M.—which finds him sifting hurriedly through the debris on his desk for the plans that were promised to the client by 4:00. Meanwhile, a staffer hovers anxiously at his elbow, trying to explain why the budget hasn't yet been completed. The sales training program review—which must be ready for tomorrow's meeting—is only half done because the time set aside for it has evaporated in a stream of phone calls, meetings, and emergencies. As usual, Bradley will have to stay late tonight to finish it. In short, just another day.

Bradley's story is a story of waste: the squandering of time, money, and talent. He symbolizes a costly bleeding of resources that has two faces: the company face and the individual face. The company face of managerial disorder is lost productivity dollars. If Bradley, who earns $75,000 per year, loses one hour per day to disorder (a very conservative estimate!), the company loses more than $9,000 per year. Multiply Bradley by fifty managers, or by a hundred, and the numbers become awesome.

Furthermore, how do you assign a dollar value to projects undone or half-finished; to sales calls not made; to initiatives not pursued; to lost opportunities? Looked at in these terms, a manager's personal inefficiency turns out to be an operating inefficiency for the company, and restoring that performance is a key factor in getting the highest productivity return on the managerial dollar.

The personal face of disorder is all too familiar—either because you have suffered from it yourself or have borne the brunt of the disorder of colleagues and associates. The symptoms are clear: an edgy feeling that there's not enough time to do it all; multiplying stacks of paper; constant interruption; seemingly incompetent staff; blunted competence; and loss of confidence. Time and again, basic skills are compromised by what appears to be an inability to organize the environment.

MANAGERIAL PRODUCTIVITY DOLLAR DRAIN

One manager who loses one hour per day to disorder costs:

ANNUAL SALARY	YEARLY DRAIN PER MANAGER
$200,000	$25,000
105,000	13,125
95,000	11,875
85,000	10,625
65,000	8,125
55,000	6,874
45,000	5,625

The yearly drain averages over 10 percent of the manager's salary.

The process of regaining (or gaining) control by getting organized begins with defining what organization is (and is not). Misconceptions on this subject are rife. The most common assumptions, some of which are contradictory, are:

- Order is a question of neat desks, straight rows of razor-sharp pencils, and precisely aligned stacks of paper.
- Orderliness is next to godliness. Disorganization indicates weakness and lack of moral fiber.
- To be sloppy and disorganized is to be creative.
- Disorganization is destiny.
- Organization requires an inflexible regimen.
- Organization is bureaucratic, related to nitpicking, and unworthy of people who are capable of thinking more grandly.
- Your secretary should be able to organize you.
- Your computer should be able to organize you.

Not only are none of the above true, but these persistent notions often get in the way of genuine organization. In fact:

- Neatness and organization do not necessarily go together—it is a matter of style.
- Disorganization is neither in your fate nor in your genes. The ability to make sense of random data is a fundamental human attribute.
- Whether you are a good or bad person is not in question, and therefore guilt over disorganization is not appropriate. The propensity to disorder often reflects leftover traces of childhood rebellion to parental authority.
- Organization liberates, it does not constrict. The "assembly-line" misconception descends from old time/motion studies in factories and a lingering "artist-in-the-garret"

notion that chaos is a hallmark of creativity. However, intensely creative people as varied as Saul Bellow and Martha Stewart and innovative business executives such as John Welch at General Electric reveal a strict personal discipline far beyond that of even the average "organized" person.

- Personal organization is a key trait of many successful people.
- Your secretary is potentially your key organizing aide. Only you, however, can define the needs and set the priorities that organizing requires.
- Your computer and other office technologies can enhance your productivity if they are harnessed to the service of an organized structure. Otherwise, they can just make things more chaotic.
- Organizing *is*, quite simply, a learned skill—a set of methods and tools with which to arrange your time and workload to meet your goals.

How do you recognize organization when you see it? Let's take a look at the day of Jacob Johnson, organized manager.

Johnson is with Allied Foods, a Michigan firm that prepares and sells canned foods to restaurants, hotels, and institutions. Johnson and his people run the canning operation. This is a rundown of one particular day:

8:45   Mail. Johnson sorts his opened mail, quickly jotting notes, and places each piece in the appropriate receptacle. He leaves three items on the desk for further consideration.

9:15   Johnson meets with his secretary, May Ritten. He gives her the day's assignments and yesterday's dictation tapes, and they discuss various items of business. Ritten hands Johnson a folder containing the papers and documents he'll need for the day's meetings and events.

9:45   Johnson reviews one of the items put aside during the mail sorting and taps three brief E-mail messages into his computer.

10:00   Weekly staff meeting. The five managers reporting to Johnson gather in his office. Questions and assignments from last week's meeting are updated, and current business is discussed. May Ritten sits in, noting assignments and due dates. Immediately after the meeting she prepares a "meeting memo" and E-mails it to all participants for follow-up next week.

11:30   Phone, drop-ins, brief meetings.

12:00   Johnson greets the members of a Japanese trade delegation who are there for lunch and a tour of the canning operation. The tour is interrupted by a staff member, who whispers that the computer has gone down in the middle of the costing cycle.

Johnson turns the tour over to a staffer and checks that appropriate repair action is in progress—returning in time to see the delegation off.

2:30   Johnson slips into an empty conference room to snatch some time for a major project: his proposal to increase productivity by buying new equipment. He jots a calendar note to call his boss tomorrow to review some cost guidelines.

3:45   "Available" time. For the rest of the day, Johnson sees visitors, makes and takes calls, handles paperwork, dictates letters, etc., and has a ten-minute wrap-up with Ritten to review the day's events and get a start on tomorrow.

The single most striking characteristic of Jacob Johnson's day is his command of his environment. He is generously accessible to others, but not disrupted except in a crisis. And when a crisis *does* arise, he has the resources to deal with it. The Japanese believe, rightly, that frequent crisis represents a failure in business management. And if frequent crisis is a chief diagnostic clue to disorganization, then the ability to limit crisis—and cope with it when it occurs with relative lack of disruption—marks an organized system.

Control does not necessarily, by the way, mean calm. Different businesses have different "beats." The frenzy of a newspaper city desk or the floor of the Stock Exchange may appear chaotic to an untrained eye, but both are in fact highly controlled operations.

Being organized is not an end in itself—it is a vehicle to take you from where you are to where you want to be. A good system expresses the organization of your mind in the environment. This book is designed to place in your hands the tools and techniques that will enable you to achieve your goals through skillful management of time, paper, and people. It does for the individual manager what management consultants have been doing for the company for years.

Specific methods can largely be tailored to your temperament and needs. The place to start is to find out where you are now. Your score on the Organizing Audit that follows will suggest the best way to use *The Organized Executive* for maximum benefit.

Organizing Audit

	YES	NO
1 Can you retrieve any paper from your desktop within one minute?	☐	☐
2 Can your secretary retrieve papers from the office files within five minutes of your request?	☐	☐
3 When you walk into your office in the morning, do you know what your two or three primary tasks are?	☐	☐
4 Do you usually accomplish those tasks by the end of the day?	☐	☐
5 Do you meet daily with your secretary? Weekly with your staff?	☐	☐
6 Does your staff typically receive clear-cut assignments that outline the range of their authority, the overall purpose, and the due date?	☐	☐
7 Do you always monitor staff to ensure that tasks are completed on time?	☐	☐
8 Are there some papers on your desk, other than reference materials, that you haven't looked through for a week or more?	☐	☐
9 During the last three months have you failed to reply to an important letter because it got lost on your desk?	☐	☐
10 Do you regularly receive letters or calls that begin: "You haven't gotten back to me yet, so . . ."?	☐	☐

	YES	NO

11 Within the last three months have you forgotten any scheduled appointment or meeting, or any special date that you wanted to acknowledge? □ □

12 Do you carry home a loaded briefcase more than once a week? □ □

13 Are you harassed by frequent interruptions—whether phone calls or visitors—that affect your ability to concentrate? □ □

14 Do you frequently procrastinate on an assignment until it becomes an emergency or panic situation? □ □

15 Do you receive long reports from which you have to extract a few key points? □ □

16 Do your own reports tend to be wordy or excessively detailed? □ □

17 Do magazines and newspapers pile up unread? □ □

18 Do you often wind up doing a little bit of your staff's jobs in addition to your own? □ □

19 Are you so busy with details that you are ignoring opportunities for new business or promotional activities? □ □

Scoring   Questions 1–7: 1 point for each "no."
           Questions 8–19: 1 point for each "yes."

Which Reorganizing Program Fits Your Needs?

Score of 1–5   *Organizing reference source.* You are well organized. Many of the tips in this book can further enhance your efficiency and productivity, however. Read the book through, select the most helpful techniques, and keep it handy for easy reference.

Score of 6–8   *Problem-solving method 1.* The current disorder is annoying, and confusion causes difficulty. Pick from the audit the most critical "wrong" answer. Then check the table of contents for the appropriate chapter and implement the solutions described there. Choose the next-most-critical "mistake" and continue this process until each problem has been solved.

Score of 9–12   *Problem-solving method 2.* You feel distinctly hampered in your work. Disorder is often debilitating. Try the nine-step process outlined below.

1 List your three or four primary responsibilities: managing staff, selling, improving products, and so on.
2 List the three most significant challenges facing your firm: for example, improving cash flow, expanding markets, developing new products.

3 Decide which responsibilities connect most directly to your firm's goals. If your firm is committed to enlarging product lines, zero in on product improvement, research, or marketing efforts.

4 List the daily impediments that preclude smooth handling of these responsibilities. For instance: "Constant interruptions leave no time for research"; "Daily emergencies keep me from getting out into the field."

5 Set up a regular organizing session: an hour a week, a half hour twice a week, fifteen minutes a day—whatever seems most comfortable. Enter this appointment on your calendar and keep it as strictly as a doctor's appointment.

6 During the first session, select the most aggravating problem on your impediments list, turn to the appropriate chapter, and follow it through. If all problems seem equally troublesome, begin with the first.

7 Use as many sessions as needed to implement solutions, then continue down the list until you've covered everything.

8 Turn back to the audit and follow problem-solving method 1 for any "wrong" answers still outstanding.

9 Set up a fixed monthly appointment for reviewing your new procedures and ensuring that you haven't returned to old habits.

Score of 13–19   *Full-fledged reorganization.* You are seriously disorganized. Your ability to function
is significantly impaired. Getting organized
could change your life. Pull yourself out of
the mire—more quickly than you might
think—by following the Organizing Program below. It is, in effect, a retraining program to help you take control of your work,
perhaps for the first time in your life. You
can expect to see light within three days.
Major changes on your desk and in your office will be visible within a month. Within
three months, more subtle changes in control and reliability will be apparent; within
eight months, with steady application, you
will have assimilated even the finer points of
organizing.

Will the "new you" last? You may have to struggle for a
time against the forces of inertia that caused you to be disorganized in the first place. But this book is designed to help you
make the transition to new systems in easy, manageable steps.
Then, once the tools of organizing are in your hands, the
choice of whether or not to use them is yours.

Organizing Program

PRELIMINARIES

Read the book straight through. Schedule a
starting date and regular organizing sessions on

your calendar. Photocopy the Five Steps to End Paper Buildup on page 62 and tape it up in an easily visible spot.

THE FIRST TWO WORKWEEKS:

Putting the Basic System into Practice

On the starting date, process that day's correspondence. Do this for three days. Use the "calendar/holding" method for follow-up.

pp. 42–55

On the fourth day, start a Master List. Schedule a Saturday within the next week or so for reorganizing the paper backlog. (*Note:* Keep processing daily papers. This is the root of your organizing system.)

pp. 121–24

Three days later, start the Daily List. Look for opportunities to break large tasks into segments, justify tasks, and delegate.

pp. 124–29

On the same day, set a basic "prime time" schedule. Start recording interruptions.

pp. 129–32

Record interruptions for three days. Put antiinterruption strategies into effect. Start saying no.

pp. 141–52

THE SECOND THREE WORKWEEKS:

Consolidating the Basic System

You have now initiated radical changes in your way of working. Spend the next three weeks getting comfortable with the new system.

If you slip back, just pick up where you left off. Before moving on to the third period, however, give yourself one solid week of uninterrupted daily paperwork processing. This is one facet of your work that can never be ignored.

Have two "reorganizing" Saturdays under your belt by the end of this period. Schedule additional ones if needed. During this time, also reread the sections in Chapters 7 and 10 on procrastination, time-savers, and delegation. Incorporate only those ideas that don't require a special effort. pp. 59–62

Do you work regularly with a personal computer? See Chapter 12 for suggestions on computerizing all or part of your organizing program. pp. 293–320

THE THIRD PERIOD:

Becoming Thoroughly Organized

Review the section in Chapter 5 on schedules, and design a more detailed schedule if you think it would be helpful. Otherwise, stick to the simple one. pp. 136–37

On the same day, schedule a Saturday within the next week or so to begin file reorganization. pp. 95–103

Carefully reread the sections in Chapter 7 on procrastination and efficiency techniques. Select and integrate the techniques that apply to you. pp. 167–83

One week later, reread Chapters 10 and 11 on staff management and secretaries. Select and integrate techniques that appear useful. pp. 237–89

One week later, reread Chapter 2 on daily pp. 37–64 paperwork. Enter on your Master List any tasks or techniques that were not instituted when you set up the basic system. For example, you may now wish to set up a tickler file.

One week later, begin rereading each chapter, with the exception of Chapter 9. Give yourself at least a week to integrate into your routine the tips and pointers in each one. Also finish reorganizing your files during this period.

Don't hesitate to turn back to read and reread pp. 42–58 the basic sections on paper and time. They are pp. 119–33 meant to serve as action guides. Tab the references you turn to most often.

If you find a more effective way of doing things, one that differs from the methods in this book, do it your way. Whatever works is the name of the game.

THE FOURTH PERIOD:

Over the Long Haul

The techniques of organizing are simply a vehi- pp. 209–34 cle to get from Point A to Point B. But where is Point B? Where do you want to go? Now that you have mastered the tools of organizing and have day-to-day affairs under control, you are in a position to benefit from the long-term analyses and strategies outlined in Chapter 9, "Time Evaluation: From Objective to Reality."

Part I

PAPERWORK

2

The Paperwork Crisis: A Solution in Five Stages

*Man's best friend, aside from
the dog, is the wastebasket.*
—Business Week

The architect's desk was a disaster. "The papers were stacked eight inches high," he said. "The desk was invisible. *I* was invisible behind the stacks. I spent so much time looking for things that nothing got out on time. The situation was out of control."

Paper mismanagement can cripple your ability to function effectively. The executive who is perversely proud of the "busy" look of his stacked-up desk is not considering the information lost, opportunities missed, tasks undone, or decisions unmade that those papers represent. On the other hand, the executive who confuses neatness with order—periodically sweeping papers into folders and drawers to clear the decks—is missing the point as well. Neatness is not the name of this particular game, as one manager discovered who insisted that staffers clear their desks at the end of each day. They began

stuffing papers into drawers and then spent an hour every morning retrieving them—with the predictable sharp drop in productivity.

Neither neatness nor sloppiness is the key to paper management, nor is quantity the root cause of a paper glut. The real cause of a paperwork crisis is a problem with decision-making: picking up the same piece of paper five times and putting it down again because you can't decide what to do with it. It is curious but true that many executives who are experienced in making major decisions feel stymied by individual pieces of paper.

The key to paper management is *processing:* that is, channeling each piece from your in-box to its appropriate destination. But channel it where? What are your alternatives?

Peter Jenks: A Case Study in Handling Paper

Peter Jenks is the publisher of a film trade magazine. Every day he receives about fifteen pieces of mail, faxes, printed-out

E-mail, and interoffice memos. And every day, with his secretary's help, he moves those papers from his desk "into work." We will look at his processing technique—how decisions are made and the physical disposition of each piece—and then crystallize his procedure into the simple components that will enable you, with or without an executive secretary, to do the same.

At 9:30, Jenks' secretary, Joan Willis, arrives with the paper stack, which she's read and prepared for rapid decision-making. Jenks looks over each item and gives Joan instructions, which she records on her pad. Today's stack brings the following items:

Fax from a West Coast sales rep, advising Jenks about a minor problem with an account: Jenks dictates a brief reply, and turns the fax back to Joan.

Procedural memo from Julie, the associate publisher: Jenks skims the memo, dictates some notes to Joan, and asks her to add the notes and Julie's memo to Julie's referral folder for discussion during their regular Friday meeting.

Complaint letter from a subscriber: Jenks jots the advertising manager's name on the letter and drops it into his outbox.

Cash-flow report from the accounting department: Jenks reviews the report, noting several delinquent accounts. He asks Joan to set up a meeting with the controller to discuss the cash-flow problem and a more stringent payment policy.

Subscription renewal notice for the magazine High Technology: This kind of decision usually gets made by default—when the subscription runs out. Key question: Is the magazine useful? If yes, renew. If not, let it lapse. Jenks asks Joan to handle the routine renewal.

Invitation to a screening: Jenks decides to attend, marks the date and time on his calendar, and puts the invitation in his "hold" file.

Check request from Julie to join a professional trade association: Jenks okays the request and drops it into the out-box for the bookkeeper.

Letter from company attorney requesting information on a legal matter: Jenks instructs Joan to ask his assistant, Sam, to compile the materials. Joan will type up a list for Sam, with a due date, which Jenks notes on his calendar. Joan will also put a copy of the list in Sam's referral folder as a control.

Copy of the January issue's lead story: Jenks skims it quickly and asks Joan to file it.

Announcement of an upcoming magazine publishing seminar: Key issues: Will seminar benefits—information and contacts—outweigh the cost of time and money? Does its timing conflict with the busy season? Jenks anticipates having a clearer picture of his schedule in mid-March, so he jots a calendar reminder for March 15 and puts the announcement in his "hold" file.

Memo from the advertising department on sales for the January issue: Jenks skims the memo, noting that the West Coast sales force hasn't met its ad space quota. Before writing to the regional sales manager, he asks Joan to set up a meeting for tomorrow morning with the sales director. He also asks her to pull relevant files. Jenks places the memo and some notes he's made in "hold."

Repertory theater schedule: To go or not to go? If not, toss the notice. If yes, add to action stack. If maybe, set a deadline for a deferred decision. Jenks can't say yes or no until checking with his wife, who's out of town on business. So he marks a calendar reminder a week before the order's due date and puts the schedule in "hold."

When the mail has been sorted, Jenks gives Joan other assignments, as well as dictation tapes from the preceding day. Joan reports on the status of previously assigned projects and checks the status of the papers that Jenks has been holding. Joan then leaves Jenks to work on the four items he's retained:

Proposal from the sales department to compile an equipment directory—cameras, video equipment, and so on—for subscribers: Is the investment justified? Jenks calls both the sales director and the editorial director to get their reactions. The upshot: More data are necessary. Jenks asks the sales director to gather the information and schedules a "decision" meeting one week hence, noting time and date on his calendar. He puts the proposal in the "hold" file.

Art department memo and layouts for a projected design change: Deciding he'll need at least two solid hours to go over the memo and layouts, Jenks checks his calendar and schedules two one-hour work sessions over the next two days. In the meantime, he jots down a few ideas and places notes and memo in "hold."

"Hold" file reminder to compile budget figures for afternoon meeting with accountant: Jenks gathers the figures and adds them to a folder with other materials needed for the meeting.

Article referred by Sam concerning film industry trends: Jenks puts the article on his reading shelf to get to later.

The TRAF Technique

Jenks' paper-processing flow illustrates the uncelebrated fact that there are only four and a half things you can do with a piece of paper. You can throw it away, refer it, act on it, file it, or (the "one-half") read it. The trick of paper mastery is to make *each piece*, whether or not it is intrinsically important, yield an action. On this point, I disagree with some colleagues who advise putting "lower priority" papers aside until they die of old age. The time spent processing every paper is so negligible, while the costs of not doing so can be so high, that there is no contest. Your four and a half choices crystallize into the simple acronym: TRAF. (Think of "traffic"—paper flowing from one point to another.) To enlarge a bit on these alternatives:

1. *Toss.* "Man's best friend, aside from the dog," says *Business Week*, "is the wastebasket." Challenge the papers you are loath to discard by asking: What is the worst thing that could happen if I threw this out? Would someone call me on it later? If so, are duplicates available?

Examples of typical discardables: FYI weekly reports, notices of seminars you won't attend, most advertising circulars.* When you are genuinely unsure about a paper's future value, don't agonize over it. Keep it with other papers to be filed.

---

*When circulars and other "junk mail" become more of a burden than a diversion, write to the various companies and ask to be removed from their mailing lists. Or write: Mail Preference Service, c/o Direct Marketing Association, Post Office Box 9008, Farmingdale, NY 11735, and request a free "mail preference" form, which will enable you to have your name removed from any or all lists. You can also use this form to get *on* selected lists by checking your particular areas of interest.

Certain papers have to be held for a few days only. Set aside a temporary holding pen for such short-life papers. One food distributor keeps daily price-change sheets in a desk drawer, and discards last week's sheets every Friday.

2. *Refer.* Delegate paperwork when possible to a secretary or staffer, or send it on to a colleague with greater knowledge or expertise in that area. Jenks, for example, referred a complaint letter to the advertising manager, and a legal matter to his executive assistant.

Drop routine referrable papers and "please handle" notes into your out-box. Track more significant referrals by making up a set of labeled folders: one folder per reporting staff member; a folder for your secretary, for your boss, and for any colleagues with whom you consult regularly. Drop a copy of any assignment, idea, or query that you wish to follow up into that person's folder. For example: Send a staffer a note asking him to bring his draft of the new brochure to your Tuesday meeting, and drop a copy of the note into his folder as a reminder. Once a week or so, review each folder and ask for progress reports.

Keep the folders in a desk-top rack, or toward the front of your file drawer. Also make up folders for regular meetings—the weekly staff meeting, the monthly board meeting—and collect discussion items as they come up, providing an instant agenda.

One executive assigns a notebook page to everyone with whom she does business on a regular basis: "As I think of what I want to discuss with them, I jot it down on their page. Then, if they walk by my office or call me, I can flip to their page and take care of several issues at once."

Also see Chapter 12, "Using Your Computer to Get Organized," page 293, for ideas on computerizing the referral process.

3. *Act.* Place all papers requiring personal action on your part—dictating a letter, composing a report, analyzing the budget, researching data—into an "action" box or folder, or on one predesignated spot on your desk. Include all those ambiguous "I'm not sure what to do with it" papers that you tend to put aside to "think about tomorrow." Decisions have to be made, and decisions are actions. Pinpoint top-priority tasks with a red check mark or sticker. As a general rule, don't pin action papers to the bulletin board to "get to later." Papers pinned to the board on the theory that seeing means doing usually wind up as part of the decor.

4. *File.* Set up a box or folder marked "to file" for your deskside files. Use the out-box for papers that are slated for the general office files. If you can assign an immediate file heading to the papers, fine. If not, *don't spend time during the sorting process thinking about how to file them.* Mark a discard date—three months, six months, a year—on each paper that will eventually outlive its usefulness.

Some examples of papers to be filed: the "new member" pamphlet from the professional organization you just joined; the "hope to see you again soon" note from a man you met at a recent industry conference (he might be a good contact); a *Harvard Business Review* article germane to a paper you might write; a *Wall Street Journal* roundup of recommended hotels in a city you visit frequently. In contrast, a discount coupon for a new calculator is not a thing to file. If you might use it, it's an "action." If not, throw it away. Any paper requiring a decision is an "action," not a "to file." See Chapter 4, "The Fine Art of Filing," for more information on this topic.

4½. *Read.* Why this "half" designation for reading, which is, after all, an action? Because any paper that requires more than five to ten minutes of reading time should be handled separately. TRAF short articles as you would any other paper, but set aside a separate box or shelf space for lengthy reports, trade journals, and other publications. See Chapter 3 (p. 80) for a discussion of how to read expeditiously.

> **Action Step 1**   Sort all incoming papers through the TRAF system, moving them from your desk to wastebasket, referral folder, action box, file box, or reading stack.

The Daily Routine: With Secretary and Without

To translate the TRAF technique into action, first assemble the basics: action box, file box, out-box, and referral folders. Then, here's how to establish a daily routine and regain control of your paperwork.

With an Executive Secretary

Perhaps the single most valuable service your secretary can perform is to process the day's mail with you. The dual, instant paper- and task-processing technique described below has been a boon to all who've tried it. Routine tasks are dispatched promptly and efficiently, and in the process your secretary becomes thoroughly acquainted with your goals and requirements. Schedule half an hour to forty-five minutes for this daily session. The five-step procedure is as follows:

1 *Mail preparation.* Your secretary opens the mail, collects faxes and E-mail, reads each item, and prepares them for prompt decision-making. If a letter, fax, or E-mail is in reply to one of yours, your secretary attaches your file copy and any relevant documents. When information is requested, your secretary obtains it in advance if possible.

When possible, your secretary recommends a course of action, drafts a response, or summarizes a lengthy report. Your secretary should also collect, to process with the daily paperwork, any pending papers or tasks that have become current (material you've been holding for further information before replying, calls or notes due today, etc.).

2 *Preliminary sorting.* Your secretary sits by your desk with pad and calendar, and hands you each piece of mail with a one-line description: for example, "This is a fax from Stan Rodner about some trouble on the West Coast," "These are the sales figures for Thursday's meeting," "Here's a summary of Julie's marketing report."

3 *Decision-making.* Glance at each item and return most of them to your secretary with an instruction: "Call Rodner and set up a conference call for Monday," "Ask Sam to check these figures and get back to me tomorrow," "Put this summary in Julie's referral folder." Retain only those papers requiring complex action or further reflection. Out of, say, fifteen items, it is rare to keep more than three or four—often not that many. If you can't get to these tasks right away, schedule time for them on your calendar. Your secretary should list all papers retained as well as all your instructions.

4 *Additional assignments.* Give your secretary assignments and dictation tapes from the day before; review your phone messages for calls your secretary can make on your behalf; check the contents of his or her referral folder and follow up on previously assigned tasks.

5 *Wrap-up.* Your secretary reviews the list of the papers that you retained on previous days and haven't yet cycled back, coordinates his or her appointment calendar with yours, makes sure you have materials for any meetings or

appointments, and discusses any business of his or her own.

When you both become familiar with this routine, you might invite your secretary to take a more active role by screening all mail and dealing with much of it directly. For more about this partnership, see Chapter 11.

> **Action Step 2** If you process the mail with your secretary, turn back most papers to him or her with instructions, retaining only those items requiring further thought or complex action.

Without an Executive Secretary

When you share or otherwise don't fully control your secretary's time, you will have to sort and process most papers yourself. Set aside about forty-five minutes a day, preferably right after the morning mail delivery, and follow this procedure:

Mail preparation. Your secretary brings in the mail, opened and loosely sorted—junk mail on the bottom, correspondence and contracts on top.

Decision-making. Look over each piece and decide its TRAF category. Put a personal task in the action box, a policy memo about health coverage in the file box, an assignment for a staffer in his or her referral folder. Glance at and discard this month's FYI budget summary. There are plenty more where that came from.

"Instant" actions. Whenever possible, handle routine requests or tasks immediately. Okay staffer's suggested new

deadline for a status report on the bottom of her memo and return it to her. Drop a slip of paper noting the new deadline into her referral folder as a control.

When every piece of paper on your desk has found a home, you're ready for the second half of the daily processing routine: acting on the "actions."

This is the paperflow distribution chart for a financial analyst and consultant who does not have a private secretary. You might find it interesting to design such a flowchart for yourself.

PAPERFLOW CHART

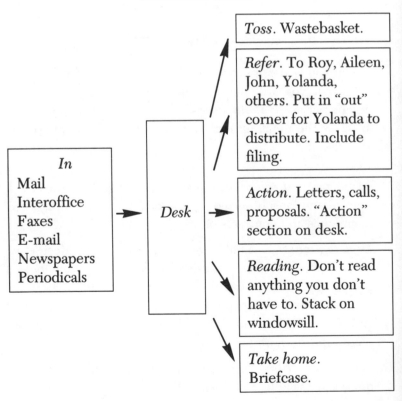

Begin by moving all follow-ups scheduled for today into your action stack. Then riffle through the box or folder, pulling the two or three most urgent tasks. After dispatching these, *work straight through the rest of the box as it falls. Do not shuffle pieces of paper around.* Take each piece as far as you can go with it, or until it is ready to be passed on to colleagues or assistants. Handle each piece only once. When you can't sign off on a task or paper right away (you need more information, it has to be discussed with a colleague who's out of town, etc.), arrange to follow it up in several days. Follow-up systems will be discussed shortly.

With so many managers using computers, two schools of thought have emerged as to whether or not it is appropriate for professionals to do their own typing, rather than turn typing over to a secretary in the traditional way.

One view was expressed by Dana Peck, an economic development specialist quoted in *Inc.* magazine, who said that sending revisions of reports back and forth to a secretary used to waste a day and a half. Said Peck, "I'd rather have my secretary buffering me from the corporate side or tracking down something I need in order to do the next report [myself]."

Other professionals take the opposite position, believing that time spent preparing their own reports is time that would have been better spent in other activities. These managers are more apt to define their priorities as interacting with other people rather than preparing materials. This probably explains why most corporate CEOs, whose work consists largely of interaction, rarely use computers. Even executives such as Andrew Grove, CEO of the microprocessor manufacturer Intel, does not personally employ a PC because he spends most of his time in personal interaction.

Both views have strong arguments in their favor. In order to help determine which approach suits you best, consider your personal temperament. Are you more oriented toward "production" or toward "interaction"? What is your present position, and what kind of position do you aspire to?

Make some decision about every piece of paper you pick up. If, despite your resolution to act, a decision doesn't seem possible, perhaps you have insufficient information. One manager, for example, put off a purchasing decision for three days—until he realized he couldn't make it without comparative cost figures. So his first step was to call purchasing for the figures, then make the decision. On the other hand, when your "head just isn't there," don't fiddle around with a document. Put a red dot on the paper and return it to the box. An accumulation of three red dots puts a paper on priority status, to be handled immediately. Also watch for referrable tasks that may have slipped into the action box during the sorting stage. (*Tip:* Keep your briefcase open by your desk to receive nightly "homework." Empty all papers the next morning and re-sort through the TRAF system. Your briefcase is a mode of transport, not a long-term storage facility.)

Avoid the "low-priority trap." The trap commences with putting a piece of paper to the side of your desk "because it's not important." It may not be important in itself, but to ignore it is to start to build a paper cage around yourself. One thorn or bramble might not make much of a difference, but enough of them put together makes quite a thicket.

In a study of twenty-five chief executives who had climbed to the top of their corporations, every single one felt so strong a need to process all papers and clear their desks down to the shine that one executive termed it "pathological." This is one pathology we could all use a little bit of. These executives had followed this pattern from the beginnings of their careers. So do as the CEOs do: Deal with the piece of paper, whatever it might be, and move on.

When your time is up, stop. It is rarely possible to work through an entire action stack of paper in one session. Tomorrow, tackle the stack from the bottom up, and alternate thereafter every day to make sure no papers lie fallow on the bottom.

This daily session is limited to daily, routine paperwork. Demanding or time-consuming tasks like lengthy reports, analyses, or complicated contracts require a planned approach.

You'll recall that Peter Jenks received a memo and layouts from the art department for a projected design change that he estimated would take over two hours to review. A good way to handle a complex task of this kind is to apply a five-point review:

1 *Delegate.* Can someone besides yourself do all or part of this task?
2 *Time frame or priority.* When should the task be done? (*Tip:* If there is no specific due date, create one.)
3 *Estimate.* About how long will it take? (*Tip:* Add half again the amount of your first estimate. Things always take longer than you expect.)
4 *Allocate.* Block out enough time on your calendar to do the task. Make an appointment or appointments with yourself. If the task isn't due for several weeks, you might want to schedule your working appointment(s) a few weeks hence, rather than feel pressured to do it right away.

   Be sure to give yourself plenty of time and space, avoiding a panicky time crunch by spacing tasks as evenly as possible.
5 *Recall.* Mark the task for follow-up (see the next section, "Following Up and Following Through"), and have the

task back on your desk the day before or the morning of the day you've scheduled to start work.

> **Action Step 3** Schedule about an hour each day for processing routine paperwork, dividing the time as needed between TRAFing and "doing." Select two or three priority tasks first, then work through the action box as it falls. Schedule more demanding tasks into separate work periods.

Following Up and Following Through

Patrick Hayes is a landmarks preservation specialist whose fledgling consulting firm almost went out of business before it got started. "I was invited to bid on a major job—replacing the windows in a landmark building," Hayes recalls, "but I wasn't sure whether it was going to be profitable for me. I hired a contractor to draw up some estimates and told him I needed the information in two weeks. Almost a month later, after a conversation with the State Preservation Office on another matter, I suddenly awoke to the fact that the bid deadline was only a week away—and I'd never heard from my contractor. By the time I got his estimates and made my decision, I had two days to put the whole package together. I made it—just barely—and since then I've become an absolute fanatic about monitoring every detail."

Keeping track of yourself and others is the essential flip side of the action process. There is no other way to be sure that commitments are honored, deadlines met, calls returned, and long-term projects tracked through their various stages. Failure to keep track can result in any number of serious consequences, ranging from personal embarrassment, to resentment on the part of others, to diminution of your professional credibility, to complete disasters.

With so much riding on effective follow-up, why run the risk of relying on memory, especially since there are three very effective means of keeping track? One is the simple "calendar/holding file" technique, for use when follow-ups average no more than five or six a day; the second is the somewhat more elaborate "tickler file," appropriate for offices in which a higher volume of reminders is produced; and the third technique, which applies to people who use a computer or hand-held organizer for personal organization, is to type in the follow-up notice and set it to pop up on the appropriate day.

The *calendar/holding file* method requires only your regular appointment calendar and a manila folder labeled "holding." Here's how it works:

On February 9, you write to contractor Richard Ellis, requesting an estimate on a new office wing. Allotting two weeks for a response, you jot a reminder—"Ellis"—on your calendar for February 23, and put your file copy of the letter in the holding file. It's that simple. Had Patrick Hayes used this method to monitor *his* contractor, he could have saved himself a lot of last-minute aggravation.

Suppose, instead of writing Ellis you phone him on the 9th, requesting that he return your call. Allowing three days for a callback, you mark a reminder on your calendar for the 12th. Now, giving the process another spin, suppose he calls on the 12th to ask for another few days. Forward the reminder on your calendar to the 16th. Keep jotting fresh reminders until you've received the estimates or written Ellis off as unreliable. Once a transaction is complete, TRAF all papers.

Use this method for a variety of reminders. For example:

- *Meeting materials.* List on your calendar or computer calendar the papers you'll need for a meeting, and collect them in the holding file until meeting day. *Tip:* Ask your secretary to assemble all papers needed for that day's meetings and appointments in a color-coded folder headed "Daily Events." A list of the day's engagements can be stapled to the front.

- *Deferred actions.* These are tasks or decisions, like Patrick Hayes' bid proposal, that must be postponed pending further information or because time is not available now. Example: You have to prepare figures for a meeting three weeks hence. You decide to do this task next week, and enter a reminder on your calendar.

- *Staff follow-ups.* Example: Your boss requests information on computer maintenance costs. You forward his memo to Smith, the resident expert, with a due date, and jot a reminder on your calendar. If Smith is delayed, find out why and advise your boss accordingly, instead of waiting until he demands the information and having to admit that you (and Smith) forgot about it.

- *Task due dates.* Enter due dates on your calendar and, when a project is lengthy or complex, choose a starting date generous enough to allow for contingencies. Jog yourself with interim dates.

- *Paper-tracking.* Example: Your boss has asked for a rewrite on a technical report. This involves several steps: turn your report over to your secretary for retyping (referral); send the draft to your boss (referral); schedule a meeting with him to discuss it (deferred action); meet with him (action); revise it again (action); and, finally, file a copy of the approved version. If you're not on top of the whole process, you can easily lose control. So enter deadline dates on your calendar for each step, and follow up as appropriate.

- *Long-term follow-ups.* Push future follow-ups through your calendar year by year. Suppose a keyman insurance policy comes up for renewal in July 1997. On December 31 of this year's calendar, write "Renew keyman insurance July 1997." Rewrite the same reminder on December 31, 1995, on December 31, 1996, and finally on July 1, 1997.

- *Repetitive tasks.* For example, ask your secretary to note "monthly marketing report" on the first Monday of every month, with a reminder on the last Monday of the year to enter the task on next year's calendar.

A *tickler file,* which fulfills the same monitoring function as the calendar/holding method, is appropriate when follow-ups are so numerous that a holding file becomes unwieldy. To set up this system, number a set of manila folders 1 through 31 (corresponding to the days of the month). Also label a folder "next month," or, if long-term follow-ups are common, label twelve folders "January," "February," "March," and so on. Your secretary keeps the tickler file at her desk.

You write to Ellis on February 9 as before. Your secretary puts your file copy of the letter into the tickler file folder numbered "23." On February 23, she pulls all papers and reminders in that folder, which you TRAF as part of the day's paperwork, following up with Ellis as necessary. If, on the 23rd, Ellis promises the estimates in four days, return the letter to the tickler file—to folder number "27."

Every reminder goes into one or another of the thirty-one tickler folders, depending on its assigned "call-up" date. Your secretary empties a folder every day and includes the contents with your daily paperwork.

When you can't sign off on a task until the following month, place the paper in the "next month" folder and assign it a specific completion date. For example: On January 15, you receive a letter requesting certain information by February 25.

Tickler Checklist

Here is a checklist of reminders and materials that can be called up through calendar/holding or tickler systems.

- ☐ Letters, memos, E-mail to which you expect a response

- ☐ Phone callbacks

- ☐ Responses to proposals or ideas from the boss or colleagues

- ☐ Staff follow-ups

- ☐ Deferred tasks (e.g., a reminder to begin a project next week)

- ☐ Task start and due dates

- ☐ Repetitive tasks (e.g., the monthly sales report)

- ☐ Papers and other materials for meetings

- ☐ Airline tickets, theater tickets, invitations

- ☐ Items for long-term follow-up

Place it in the "next month" folder, marked for February 18, to give you some leeway in compiling the information. On January 31, empty the "next month" folder and distribute all papers into specific daily folders, putting the letter in folder "18." On that day, collect the information, attach it to the letter, and ask your secretary to put both papers into folder "25." Alternatively, you might wish to compile the materials as soon as you receive the letter, placing both papers in the "next month" folder, marked for February 25.

The twelve monthly folders can be used in much the same way. Suppose that in January you receive a renewal notice for a health insurance policy that needs to be mailed on approximately April 15. Put the papers in the "April" folder, marked for the 15th. On March 31, the "April" folder is emptied and the renewal enters daily folder "15."

People who spend much time away from their desks, such as sales representatives and consultants, often use a weekly tickler system, labeling folders "first week," "second week," and so on. Although less exact, this variation offers greater flexibility to those who can't attend to paperwork every day.

The tickler method is quite versatile: you can store airline tickets until departure, hold meeting materials until meeting day, or jot reminders about repetitive tasks on index cards and move them through the folders. However, since simplicity is the key to effective follow-up, the calendar/holding system is the method of choice when you don't have a high volume of reminders.

> **Action Step 4** Keep track of complex, deferred, and referred actions with a calendar/holding or tickler file. Calendar/holding method: Jot a reminder on your calendar and put papers in a holding file. Tickler: Place papers in a numbered folder that corresponds to the call-up date.

Although you can use a calendar or tickler system—or referral folders—to keep track of staff assignments, many managers prefer to employ special follow-up methods for staffers. These and more complex project-monitoring techniques are discussed in Chapters 8 and 10.

If you've TRAFed all incoming papers throughout the day, no papers should be beached at the side of your desk at day's end. But with human nature being what it is, to forestall any new accumulations, run through this quick desk check at the end of each day:

> Are all "action" papers in the action box? Put any homeless papers in this box for decision-making tomorrow.
>
> Are all papers that are to be filed in the file box?
>
> Are all papers destined for your secretary or colleagues in the out-box or referral folders?
>
> Are all follow-ups in the holding or tickler files?

One day I had to leave my office unexpectedly at midday, abandoning my desk in considerable disarray. When I returned the next morning, I simply couldn't "see" anything on my desk for the jumble. So, even though I was still working with the papers that were out on the desk, I put everything away as if it were the end of the day, and then pulled out the materials I needed to recommence work. This was a telling example of how visual confusion can confuse one's direction, and a strong recommendation for an end-of-the-day brush-up.

> **Action Step 5**   Quick desk check. At the end of each day, run your eye over your desk to make sure all papers are properly channeled into their TRAF receptacles.

Digging Out from Under

Once daily mail and paperwork are under control, you're ready for a full-scale reorganization: clearing out all the papers piled up in your office over days, months, even years. If your backlog is considerable, you'll probably need at least two or three Saturdays for the job—and lots of trash bags as well. Rigorous use of the wastebasket is highly recommended during this process. Also useful to have on hand is a spiral-bound notebook in which to record those random jottings—ideas, notes to yourself, old "to do" lists—that you're likely to unearth.

The four-step "dig out" procedure is as follows:

1 *Desk surface.* In your mind's eye, block your desk into four rough quadrants. Select a starting pile within the right quadrant closest to you—either one containing critical materials or the one closest to hand. If papers are scattered rather than stacked in piles, block out a square foot of space and begin there. TRAF each paper, *moving down the stack until you hit desk bottom.* Don't shift from stack to stack. Once you clear an area, leave it clear, creating a widening pool of open space. Return files to the file cabinet; take extra supplies back to the supply room. Rewrite loose jottings into your notebook, and discard the original scraps. Complete one quadrant before moving on to the next. Also TRAF any papers that are jammed into desktop racks.

2 *Desk drawers.* Divide drawers into "thirds" and work on one section at a time, sorting, consolidating, and discarding dog-eared index cards and antique packets of sugar.

> *Exception:* Bypass file drawers. Filing is covered in Chapter 4.

3 *Visible surfaces.* TRAF all papers that have accumulated on windowsills, shelves, credenza, bulletin board, and so on. Tackle one stack at a time, down to the bottom, working clockwise around the room from your desk. TRAF odd-sized papers—catalogs, computer printouts, photos —as you would other papers, and store those you wish to save on a shelf or bookcase.

4 *Integration of "action" papers.* Often, this sort of "dig out" uncovers a mass of "action" papers. How should you handle them? Integrate them gradually into your daily processing routine. Pull any that require your personal attention, and delegate the remainder to your secretary, requesting that he or she handle at least three or four a day. Divide your own stack into high-priority "A's" and lesser-priority "B's." Incorporate the "A's" into your daily action stack, and extend your paperwork session for fifteen minutes or so until you've caught up. Tackle several "B's" a day, or reserve two or three hours a week for the "B's."

If there are numerous publications, divide them into "must reads" and "would like to reads." Toss as many of the latter as possible—certainly any periodical more than three months old. Schedule reading time for the remainder over the next weeks. See also Chapter 3.

Setting Up Your Office: Tips for Ease of Performance

Paper processing, perhaps more than any other office function, depends on a responsive physical environment: easy access to files and equipment. When your working surfaces are pristine (relatively speaking), adapt them for maximum efficiency according to the following deployment tips:

- *Positioning.* Are you right-handed or left-handed? Do you tend to turn one way rather than another? Run through your typical movements—reaching for the phone or the files, turning to your computer or calculator—to determine what feels natural. Then position the equipment accordingly.

  If you're right-handed, keep your phone to your left, leaving your right hand free for note-taking. Keep a small message box next to the phone and, perhaps, a small desktop file rack for "working" papers and files. Place other equipment—computer, calculator, dictation machine—to your right, and keep TRAF boxes in front of you, along the outer edge of your desk.

- *Work space.* Clear some open space in front of you—about the dimensions of a small desk blotter—and maintain some space to the side for working papers. If desk space is a problem, move your phone, computer, and other equipment, as well as the most often consulted references, to a side extension or rear credenza within swiveling range of your desk. (A good swivel chair, in fact, is a very useful convenience.)

- *Accessibility.* Place the most frequently used items in "fingertip storage": prime, immediately accessible space. Store the items used less often, and group items that are used together. Keep decorative objects and personal mementos in a spot where they won't get in your way or distract you.

- *Office layout.* Keep guest chairs in front of, or to the side of, your desk. Avoid choosing a couch or club chairs that are too low or soft.

For more information on furniture and office supplies, see the Office Supplies Checklist and Office Deployment Checklist at the end of this book. The Bibliography also lists several books on office design and arrangement.

Summary: Five Steps to End Paper Buildup

STEP 1   Sort incoming papers through TRAF system. See Easy Reference TRAFing Chart on page 64.

STEP 2   If you process paperwork with your secretary, turn back most papers to him or her with instructions, retaining only those items requiring further thought or complex action.

STEP 3   If you solo at paper processing, schedule about an hour each day for processing routine paperwork, dividing the time as needed between "TRAFing" and "doing." Select two or three priority tasks first, then work through the action box as it falls. Schedule more demanding tasks into separate work periods.

STEP 4   Keep track of complex, deferred, and referred actions with calendar/holding or tickler files. Calendar/holding method: Jot a reminder in your calendar and put papers in a holding file. Tickler: Place each paper in the numbered folder that corresponds to the call-up date.

STEP 5   Quick desk check. At the end of each day, run your eye over your desk to make sure all papers have been properly channeled into their TRAF receptacles.

THE PAPER GAME

Once you've sorted through your backlog, amuse yourself by monitoring your efficiency in handling current paperwork with "the paper game." Every day for a week, before leaving the office, check each piece of paper or file folder sitting on or near your desk and assign it a point value as follows:

Each piece homeless because you "don't know what to do with it" or haven't moved it to its appropriate receptacle	+5
Each piece in your action box that should have been completed already	+3
Each piece that should have been referred elsewhere	+2
Each piece in the file box *in excess of* twenty pieces	+1
Each piece in the file box *up to* twenty pieces	−½
Each piece in tomorrow's tickler file or noted on the calendar for follow-up	−1
Each piece appropriately placed in the action box	−½

Total up each day's score. Your object for the *first go-round* is to end up with a daily score, for one week, no higher than 30. *Second go-round:* A score no higher than 15 points a day for a week. *Third go-round:* A score no higher than 30 points *total for the week*. Now you're organized.

EASY REFERENCE TRAFING CHART

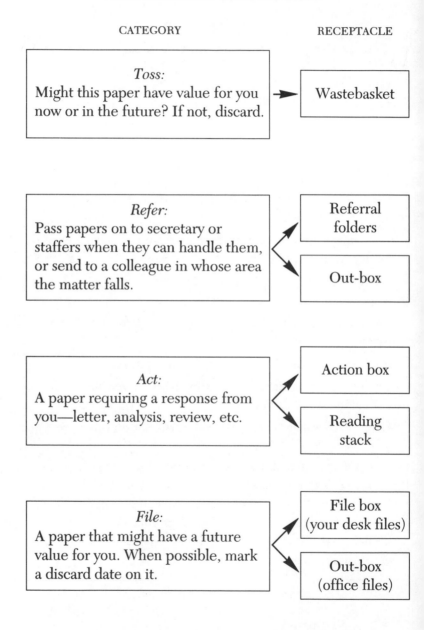

CATEGORY   RECEPTACLE

Toss:
Might this paper have value for you
now or in the future? If not, discard.

Wastebasket

Refer:
Pass papers on to secretary or
staffers when they can handle them,
or send to a colleague in whose area
the matter falls.

Referral
folders

Out-box

Act:
A paper requiring a response from
you—letter, analysis, review, etc.

Action box

Reading
stack

File:
A paper that might have a future
value for you. When possible, mark
a discard date on it.

File box
(your desk files)

Out-box
(office files)

3

Streamlining Paper: Shortcuts for Overload

*Pray let me have by this evening,
on one page, the status of
our tank deployment. . . .*
—Winston Churchill

When the ancient Sumerian scribes sat down with clay tablets and cuneiform wedges to tally up their accounts, you can bet your high-speed copier that they didn't turn out an original plus five for the department. But with the advent of easy duplication, production of written materials has bloomed exponentially—to the point where paper has become an active impediment to the work process. The "paperless office" that was supposed to emerge as a result of office technology has turned out to be not only a myth, but a laugh.

While the paper-processing techniques described in the preceding chapter will help you cope much more effectively with the written word in its many incarnations, the sheer quantity of paper flowing in and out of many offices remains a serious problem. This chapter is designed to help you cut down on the volume by reducing, streamlining, and standard-izing many procedures connected with paper.

Reports Overload

A corporate vice president who once counted up the number of periodic reports she received in one month found that the total came to twenty—nearly one hundred pages. And this tally did not include the many special-purpose reports and general memos. Many less-than-productive hours were spent extracting the nuggets of relevant information from this mass of paper.

Certainly, effective management is predicated on the timely receipt of full information—up to a point. However, reporting every possible fact without regard to its relative value or ap-propriate presentation, and disseminating such information to practically everyone in the hope that some will reach its mark, is a wasteful and misguided procedure. Unfortunately, it's also quite common. How, then, to handle reports overload? The solution depends on whether you are on the receiving or gener-ating end.

Incoming Reports

How many interoffice reports do you routinely receive be-cause "you are on the routing list"? Your name isn't inscribed there in stone, and you do have the option of removing it. The key to stemming the tide of incoming reports is to eliminate the unnecessary ones, and excerpt or refer the remainder. To begin, collect a month's worth of reports and analyze them according to the following criteria:

1 *Eliminate.* Identify unnecessary or unimportant reports by asking: What is the worst thing that could happen if I stopped receiving this? Are the data relevant to my job? Is the information available elsewhere? Best question: Which reports would I do without if I were charged for them?

Ask the originator of the report to remove your name from the routing list or, perhaps more politic, ask your secretary to discard these reports automatically.

2 *Excerpt.* Do you need the entire document, or just one part? Can you ask the originator to send only the relevant section? Could your secretary or assistant summarize or flag pertinent material, or tear off the pages that you need and toss the rest? One senior executive inundated with staff FYI reports sent the following memo to the five managers reporting to him:

> I think we would all be better served if I spent less time reading detailed reports. In the future, please send me a one-page summary of any relevant points and let me request more details if I need them. If the report itself contains a summary, duplicate that or, if you prefer, duplicate any relevant pages. Thanks.

3 *Delegate.* Can you refer certain reports directly to staffers? One airline executive restricted reports by redirecting them. Audit reports, equipment reports, weekly gross intake reports, and résumés were referred to subordinates and brought to his attention only if questions arose, if they contained information of more than usual interest, or when figures dropped below a certain level (referral "by exception").

Outgoing Reports: An Evaluation Method

A report should not simply be a compendium of facts, but a judgment tool for management: the right information presented in the right way to the right people. Does every report produced by you and your staff meet this standard? Are any of them excessively detailed, wordy, poorly structured, burdened with extraneous facts, or even unnecessary? In order to produce fewer—and shorter—reports, collect a month's worth, and use the following six-step procedure to analyze their necessity, brevity, frequency, and format:

1 *Eliminate.* Is this report necessary? Assume, in a procedure derived from zero-based budgeting, that all reports have been wiped out and you must justify reinstating each one. What is the rationale for reporting a given piece of information? What objectives does the report forward? What questions does it answer? What would be the consequences if it were discontinued? Which reports would you dispense with if you were charged for them?

   Are you generating certain reports merely out of habit, or because you believe they offer you a power base? Fourteen of fifteen managers in one company said they needed a particular report. But when distribution was purposely delayed, only two asked about their copies. And the information they needed was available elsewhere. The report was eliminated.

2 *Reduce.* How many people really need a particular report? A religious foundation cut the number of its internal reports by close to one-third, largely by reducing the number of people receiving them. They divided the routing list into two groups: those who used the report as a working document, and an "FYI" group. Managers in the

latter group who could conduct their business just as effectively without the report were eliminated from the list. A copy was *circulated* to the remaining FYI group. As a result, distribution of one report dropped from twelve copies to five. The four managers who used it received individual copies, and a fifth copy was circulated among the five for whom it was an FYI.

When materials routinely circulate among the same people, print up a routing slip: a list of everyone's names, plus a few extra blank lines for adding more names if necessary. To guarantee that the report completes the circuit, put your own initials at the bottom of the list, jot a return date on your calendar, and follow up if the report hasn't come home to roost by the due date.

Sometimes it is sufficient simply to post one copy of a general memo on a central bulletin board for all to see.

P.S.: It may seem tempting to E-mail reports to everyone on the list, but long reports on E-mail are even more bothersome than paper copies.

3 *Consolidate.* Do any reports duplicate each other? Does information overlap? Could several reports be combined into one more concise document?

4 *Highlight.* Are key facts in prominent relief? Frame a question or series of questions that the report is to address. For example: Should sales efforts be increased, reduced, or maintained as they are? What criteria should be developed to measure ourselves against competitors?

Are the facts supporting these questions accessible? Are conclusions articulated? A small import/export firm that made a killing shipping Colombian coffee into the United States came perilously close to bankruptcy because of poorly designed reports. Although reports noted that coffee imports from other countries were on the rise, the most important information was buried in the text. And when the bottom suddenly fell out of the Colombian market, the company was unprepared.

5 *Simplify.* Are reports concise and to the point? Is the text clear and sharp, minus locutions like "impacted on" and "interface with"? Fight the tendency to tell readers more than they need to know. Is there too much background information, technical material, or statistics? Could an outline, summary, graph, or chart convey the same information more sharply than a narrative?

Ideally, a report should meet the diverse information requirements of everyone receiving it, which might range from simple overview to full documentation. Solve this problem by bringing important points into relief by organizing reports longer than two or three pages according to the following structure:

I *Summary:* a one-page covering statement presenting the objective of the report, a summary or recap of the data, conclusions, and recommendations. Actions to be taken, if any, should be specific and clear. For many people, the summary is all that's required.

II *Body:* greater development of the data, and the reasoning behind the conclusions.

III *Backup* (when relevant): raw data, references, bibliography.

To hone your ability to focus on the heart of a report, you might try to restructure an already existing report using these guidelines.

6 *Issue.* Would timely decision-making be crippled if a weekly report were distributed twice a month? If a

monthly report came out bimonthly? On the other hand, reports occasionally need to be issued more frequently.

Involve colleagues and staff in the reports evaluation process. Use the reports evaluation form on page 72 as a guide to developing your own form for assessing departmental or company reports policy.

Here are some additional tips for writing reports:

- When possible, develop a standard report format. Use "fill-in" forms or a checklist, or formulate several standard paragraphs and add summary or interpretive narrative as needed.
- Enter a yearly schedule for periodic reports, including *start* days, on your calendar or on a reports chart (see example on p. 198).
- Pace yourself. Spread the work as evenly as possible over the week. Draft material quickly, with the expectation of reviewing and revising later. Try to leave an interval of a day or two between writing and review.
- Prepare calculations, graphs, and so on separately, after you've finished the writing.
- When compiling a report for your boss that summarizes reports from your subordinates, ask staff to flag the elements that they consider most important. Ask your secretary to compile the checked items into a draft report, from which you can prepare the final version. *By-product:* You'll get a good feel for your subordinates' judgment.

Forms and Standardization Procedures

One of the most effective methods for cutting paper down to size is the form. In one research foundation, grants administra-

Evaluation of Departmental Reports*

The proliferation of internal reports has begun to cost more—in terms of time, expense, and paper—than the benefits warrant. To aid in cutting back on the number produced, please evaluate each report received according to the following criteria:

NAME	DO YOU RECEIVE?	IS REPORT, OR PART OF IT, OF VALUE?	WOULD CIRCULATION COPY SUFFICE?	TOO MUCH DETAIL?	FORMAT CLEAR?	KEY IDEAS HIGHLIGHTED?	FREQUENCY: CUT BACK, INCREASE, OR OK AS IS?	COMMENTS
New hire								
Outplacement								
Affirmative action								
Compensation								
Unemployment								
Payroll								

*Form used by one company's personnel department.

tors routinely produced four- or five-page reports on applicants who were seeking research funds. By simply condensing this information into a one-page questionnaire, these managers reduced monthly paper output by close to 25 percent. Although the word "form" often elicits visions of complicated packets filled out in triplicate, a form is in fact an efficient and simple means of ensuring that repetitive tasks are handled correctly and with dispatch. A surprisingly large number of office procedures are susceptible to standardization. Specific examples might include certain types of correspondence, conference planning, speaking engagements, publishing and design procedures, client questionnaires, and merchandising and order information.

Form Letters

Leon Stein, head of a real estate management concern, had been considering hiring part-time help because his secretary was so busy answering tenants' queries and routine complaints that she had no time for other work. But when Stein analyzed her output, it was clear that most of her letters were providing the same information. With a standard form letter, she was able to produce ten letters in the time it used to take her to do one.

Form letters, which utilize a standard text and require only the addition of address, date, name, or a specific insert, can be utilized for much routine correspondence, including inquiries, rejection letters, confirmation or acceptance letters, solicitations, and monthly sales reports.

To organize a form-letter system, determine the types of letters you produce that are suitable for forms, and then draft a "base" letter for each or select an appropriate example from your files. Paste each letter into a notebook, or keep the letters in a folder. Assign each letter a heading, such as "Sales letter I," "Thanks for the inquiry," "Order can't be filled," and so on. Duplicate the entire set for your secretary.

When you process the mail each day, simply indicate at the top of a letter the appropriate form to send in response, and drop it into your out-box. Or ask your secretary to prescreen, pulling all correspondence that can be answered with a form and handling it independently.

A variation on form letters are "mix-and-match" letters, created by mixing standardized paragraphs with original material. To establish a mix-and-match system, collect samples of four or five previously successful letters of the same broad type: real estate evaluations, sales solicitations, letters of agreement, client reports, and so forth. Assign each letter a number, and each paragraph a letter. Thus, dictating a mix-and-match might consist of "Letter 3, Paragraph G," then some original material, then "Letter 2, Paragraph B," and so on.

"Homemade" Forms

Many professionals make up their own forms to streamline routine procedures. Career counselor Laura Hass, for example, designed a "workshop checklist" to help her keep track of the various seminars she was organizing simultaneously. Edward Taylor, a busy physician who was often asked to speak to various groups, designed a "request to speak" form for his secretary to ensure that all arrangements were handled smoothly and quickly.

To create your own homemade forms, identify tasks or procedures susceptible to standardization. Then, walk through each procedure in your mind—with your secretary if he or she is involved in it—listing each step as you go. Ask your secretary to type up the list, adding boxes or lines for checking off

Workshop Checklist

Name of workshop_____   Date(s) _____
Instructor _____   Room number _____
Address _____   Phone _____
City/state/zip _____   Fee _____

Notification to prospective participants

Mailing: Ad:
To printer _____   To printer _____
Sample returned_____   Sample returned_____
Mailed_____   In what publications
                           & dates: _____
Number responses ____   Number responses ___

Postings: Other:
To printer _____
Sample returned_____
Number posted_____
Date_____
Number responses____

Total number participants_____

Logistics

Room: Food:
Reservation sent____   Order sent _____
Contact_____   Contact _____
Acceptance
received_____   Reconfirmed_____

REQUEST TO SPEAK FORM

Date _____

Name _____

Address _____

City/state/zip _____

Phone _____

Representative _____

Type of group _____

Format (lecture, panel, workshop) _____

Topic _____

Dates desired _____

Information to be given to group
making request

Honorarium is $1,750 _____

Speaker to be accompanied by staff member,
all expenses paid _____

Plane tickets to be sent in advance to Dr.
Taylor's home (500 East 66th Street, New
York, N.Y. 10021) _____

Are terms acceptable? _____

If yes, will Dr. Taylor accept engagement? __

Has group been informed of Dr. Taylor's response? _____

If acceptance

Who makes travel and hotel reservations? ___

Reservations made? Put on doctor's calendar.

_____

Tickets received? _____

After trip, any reimbursements to be billed?

_____

Reimbursements received? _____

or filling in pertinent information. Duplicate a supply, and *voilà*, a form.

Mini-forms—half a page or smaller—are particularly useful for minor procedures. An MIS professional, for example, was frequently distracted from statistical analysis by colleagues requesting an immediate check of information on the mainframe. She made up a small "Mainframe Reservation" form, listing name, nature of task, and due date and added the following legend: "Please turn in all mainframe requests at least two days before due date. In cases of emergency, please check 'emergency' box below." Her colleagues, she discovered, were too embarrassed to check "emergency" very often and were, thereafter, much more considerate about timing their requests.

A checklist—a list with check-off boxes—is another simple and useful form. Some examples:

Make up a "supply requisition" form listing all supplies in alphabetical order. Add a check-off box for each item, and a space for filling in quantity.

Follow a routine. An engineering consultant developed an eight-point checklist used to follow client reports from point of initial presentation through receipt of payment.

Maintain records of warehouse inventories with a weekly checklist.

Acknowledge mail inquiries with a variation of this form, used by a catalogue operation:

☐ Your order will be filled within 21 days.
☐ We are out of the color you selected. Please select two alternative colors.

☐ Due to heavy demand, we are temporarily out of stock. Your order will be filled in 60 days.

☐ We are out of stock on this item, and are unable to fulfill your order. Please accept our apologies. Your refund check is enclosed.

☐ Other _____

Time-Saving Tips

- Preprint postcards or labels for repetitive correspondence such as acknowledgments, hotel reservations, and appointment confirmations. Examples: When you send FYI materials frequently, enclose a preprinted card saying, "I think you will find this of interest. No acknowledgment expected." Respond to frequent requests for materials with a standard card: "This comes to you at your request." Leave space for a short message.

- Preprint self-stick labels listing standard inquiry information like prices and terms, and attach each label to an acknowledgment postcard.

- Preprint or hand-stamp envelopes with the names of anyone to whom you regularly send material, such as a branch office or major supplier. Accumulate send-outs in the envelope and, at regular intervals, seal and mail.

- Make up *referral slips* for your department or group. These, as distinct from routing slips, are attached to materials being sent to one person only. Preprint these slips with the names of people you deal with regularly, include a list of routine actions ("let's discuss," "call me," and so on), and leave space for a brief message. A sample is provided here:

TO:

☐ Ellie Michaels ☐ Lucille Taylor

☐ Chris Muscat ☐ Henry Wagner

☐ Jim Petrie ☐ George Welsh

☐ Renee Roberts ☐ Jack Wilson

☐ Steve Ryder ☐ Carol Wood

☐ Gary Savarin ☐ _____

FROM: N. L. Street   Date: _____

☐ For your information/interest

☐ Let's discuss

☐ Please handle

☐ Note and return by _____

☐ Please call me

- If your office regularly sends out memos, invoices, or announcements to the same people, type each individual's name and address on an index card, superimpose the card on the appropriate form, and run a supply through the copier. Or create a set of "ready" labels for recurring mailings by typing names and addresses into your computer. Produce labels as needed by printing them out onto blank labels.
- Use a rubber signature stamp on memos and letters that don't require a personalized signature. Make up a letterhead stamp for routine mail, saving expensive letterhead stationery for expensive occasions.
- Conserve your secretary's time—and enhance his or her efficiency—with these tips: use window envelopes to save

typing time. To reduce your secretary's typing load, reply to some letters by jotting a note on the bottom of the letter itself.

Reading Expeditiously

High on the list of office irritants is the accumulation of trade magazines, newspapers, professional journals—and the certain knowledge that even if you spent a week doing nothing but reading, you'd never catch up. But you can manage business reading if: you select what you read, how much you read, and when you read.

Evaluate each publication you now receive by asking yourself: Do I really need this? What would happen if I didn't get it? How often does it offer something genuinely useful, interesting, or absorbing? Would I be willing to pay for the subscription myself if I had to? Which periodicals offer most information or value for the least reading time?

Star the more valuable publications and eliminate the rest. If your starred list is fairly extensive, you might choose two or three magazines for annual renewal and rotate the rest on a less frequent basis.

Make the *rip and read* technique a habit. Pull articles you wish to read, put them in a "reading" folder, and toss the publication. An articles folder is much less intimidating than a stack of unread magazines. Try to flip through each publication as soon as it arrives and pull appropriate articles.

Flag articles that can't be removed (because the publication is a departmental or library copy) for duplication. Bend or tear page corners, or put a Post-It listing article pages on the front cover. Or mark articles you want to read on the contents page, and flip from contents to article to avoid the temptation to read everything else.

You might indicate your selection guidelines to your secretary or assistant, and ask that person to pull or duplicate articles for your reading folder for you. One manager passed most publications on to a staffer with the query "Anything I should know about?"

Process all articles, once read, through the TRAF system as you would any other document. Assign each publication a reasonable toss-out date, perhaps a month or two after receipt, and discard it on that date, read or unread. When you wish to save entire editions of magazines or journals, note on the front cover the articles of particular interest, and then store the publications in bookcases. Some magazines offer special binders or boxes for storage.

Here's a valuable axiom: "Don't read it till you need it." A member of the Small Business Administration, for example, received a sixty-page document in connection with a conference to be held in three months. Normally he would have read the report upon receipt, and then been forced to read it again before the conference.

Instead, this time he skimmed the report to see if there was anything of current need, made some notes on the cover page, and then passed the report to his secretary requesting that it be brought to his attention three weeks before the conference.

Newspapers present a special problem because they accumulate so quickly. One executive solved the problem by asking her secretary to give her only the first and editorial pages of the *Wall Street Journal* each morning. Others consult news summaries and index pages to pinpoint articles of interest. Several services offer abstracts of important business books and articles. (See Bibliography, "Digests of business books and articles.")

Many people *schedule* reading sessions for late afternoon or early evening—the "low" part of their day. Others set aside fifteen minutes every morning, either with coffee or right after their paperwork session. You might also schedule a "reading hour" once or twice a week, giving your secretary a list of the articles you wish to read on a particular day. One manager has "reading and lunch" sessions twice a week, while another enjoys a monthly "catch-up" day at the library.

Tuck your reading folder or several articles into your briefcase or handbag to read during taxi rides, during plane trips, or while waiting in line. One training director keeps a reading drawer containing trade magazines. She pulls these out for trips or when she's on the phone, flipping through them quickly and then tossing or passing them on. When the drawer fills, she discards the oldest materials, read or not.

Catch up on reading while commuting. Keep your reading folder near your desk, on top of your briefcase, and add articles you wish to read on the trip home.

If a sizable backlog of reading matter continues to take up shelf space, there are unfortunately only two solutions: throw out the entire stack and start fresh, or toss most publications more than three months old, retaining only those directly related to your work.

Additional Efficiency Tips

- Learn to skim. Read headlines, check the newspaper index, and read in full only articles of particular interest. Get the gist of a story by skimming the headline, the first few paragraphs, and the conclusion. To extract the kernel of a report, check the section headings, then skim the relevant parts for key ideas. Highlight with a marker as you read.

- Consider a rapid reading course. One administrator found a "rapid reading" drill extremely useful in identifying key ideas. However: *Speedreading is not a substitute for rigorous selection.* There is no point in speedreading information that has no value to you.
- Read slowly when appropriate. Obviously, not everything should be read quickly. Some documents reward close study. Much more typical, however, is the magazine article that calls for a two-and-a-half-minute hop-and-skip and receives instead fifteen minutes of undeservedly close attention.
- Ask the sender of a book or thick report for your review to indicate specific sections or chapters for your attention.
- Flag and circulate articles of interest to your staff. Ask them to do the same for you.

Summary: Reducing Paper Overload

Reports Evaluation Guide

Collect a month's worth of reports, incoming and outgoing, and size up each report against the following checklist:

INCOMING	*Eliminate* yourself from routing list.
	Block. Secretary or staffer tosses or refers before report reaches you.
	Excerpt. Secretary or staffers excerpt relevant parts, or provide summary.
	Delegate "by exception."
OUTGOING	*Eliminate,* using "zero-based budgeting" justification.

Reduce number of people receiving report, either by eliminating from routing list, circulating, or posting centrally.

Consolidate with other reports.

Highlight key questions answered in report, key facts, and conclusions.

Simplify by means of literate text, charts, check-lists, summaries.

Design. Is a building-block structure appropriate?

Issue. Cutback possible?

Forms

STRATEGY	DESCRIPTION
Form letters	Draft a "base" letter for all correspondence that can be standardized, assign each letter a heading, and note that heading on any letters to which your secretary should respond with a form letter.
Mix-and-match letters	Collect several successful letters of the same broad type, and assign each letter a number and each paragraph a letter. Then dictate letters by combining original material with appropriate material from these letters.
Homemade forms	Identify tasks and procedures susceptible to standardization, and list all steps involved. Have your secretary type up and duplicate this list, adding lines or boxes for "fill-ins" and "check-offs."

Reading

STRATEGY	DESCRIPTION
Eliminate	Discontinue subscriptions on all periodicals that are no longer useful or sufficiently interesting.
"Rip/Read"	Pull articles you wish to read, keep in a "reading" folder, and discard or refer the publication. Give selection guidelines to secretary or staffers and ask them to pull articles for you.
Skim	Skim headlines, the first few paragraphs, and conclusions of news stories. Consult indexes and abstracts to pinpoint articles of interest.
TRAF	Prevent reading buildup by TRAFing all articles: tossing, referring, acting on, or filing, once read. Assign journals a toss-out date and discard, read or not.
Schedule reading time	Schedule specific reading sessions once or twice a week. Tuck reading folder or articles in briefcase to read while commuting, traveling, or waiting in lines.

4

The Fine Art
of Filing

Until recently, Lee Johnson, like most managers, would have agreed that filing was a clerical activity. But after a near-crisis caused by a "minor" filing error, his perspective has changed. Says Johnson:

> I was preparing a report recommending implementation of a direct marketing campaign for one of our products, and I asked my secretary to pull out a consultant's study I'd commissioned several months ago. She checked every logical file—direct mail, marketing, product information, even the consultant's name—with no luck. The day before my report was due, she finally found it: under "F" for the title "A Feasibility Study of Telemarketing Methods." Her detective work saved my neck because the study contradicted several points I'd made. I spent the night revising my report, and the next day my secretary and I reorganized our files from scratch. Never again will I belittle the importance of a workable filing system, or ignore my responsibility in formulating usable file guidelines.

Easy access to information is the point of filing. If you don't know where a document is, it might as well not exist. Yet, there is valuable material, ideas, concepts, information, and the potential for new business buried in your files. If you know where it is, you have an important resource at hand. In many offices, however, filing is haphazard at best, and retrieval virtually a guessing game. The reason is not, as one executive put it, "too damned many files and too few people who know how to file." Rather, the culprit is almost always an ambiguous or ill-defined classification system. How a document is filed (under what heading) depends on how and when you intend to use it, and what else it might relate to—decisions you are best equipped to make. Which brings us to the heart of a common management misconception: equating the physical act of putting papers into folders with the conceptual act of classifying information into practical, usable categories. The former is, quite properly, a clerical activity. The latter is a judgment call for which a manager is ultimately responsible. In fact, developing an effective system is best handled as a team effort. The more direction you can provide, the better able your secretary will be to manage the system efficiently.

What constitutes an effective system? At least one successful executive got a leg up on his career by answering that question. While a student, former Securities Exchange Commission chairman Roderick Hills took a summer job as a file clerk in the personnel department of an aircraft plant. "The system had been set up to make filing *all* information easy, with the predictable result that retrieving any of it was almost impossible. Hills determined which data would be useful in day-to-day management decisions and rearranged the system to make that *specific* information automatically retrievable. . . ." In other words, *usage*—not storage—determined how information was categorized. And when Hills returned the following summer, it was as assistant personnel manager.

More specifically, an effective filing system should: (1) group information into clear and simple categories that reflect your concerns; (2) permit retrieval of any paper within three minutes or less; (3) facilitate the orderly incorporation of new files; and (4) provide a simple, consistent method for clearing out obsolete files. How do your files stack up against this definition? The following quiz will enable you to rate your system and pinpoint any special trouble spots.

File Audit

	YES	NO
1 Can you retrieve any paper from your deskside files within three minutes?	☐	☐
2 Can your secretary or clerical assistants retrieve papers from the office files within five minutes of your request?	☐	☐
3 Are backup materials for a report generally stored compactly in a few folders, or scattered randomly in many folders?	☐	☐
4 Have you ever "winged" a report because backup materials were lost in the files?	☐	☐
5 Do you often keep papers longer than two years "just in case" you might need them someday?	☐	☐
6 Do any file headings, other than proper or "tag" names, start with a date or adjective (e.g., "1997 Reports" or "Old Plans")?	☐	☐

YES   NO

7 Other than cross-reference copies, are duplicates of one document likely to be found in several different files? □ □

8 Would it take more than half an hour to file the papers in your "to file" box or folder? □ □

9 Are broad categories (travel, for instance) broken down into many minor subdivisions (travel agents, hotels, restaurants, client addresses, car services, etc.)? □ □

Scoring   Questions 1–3: 7 points for each "no."
               Questions 4–9: 5 points for each "yes."

Score of 0–10   Your system is efficient, although the numerous tips in this chapter may facilitate additional fine-tuning.

Score of 11–25   Missing papers have probably caused anxiety more than once. File review and reorganization may be advisable. The section on "file logic," below, should be especially helpful in reducing the incidence of misfiling.

Score of 26–51   Your system is chaotic. Reorganization is a high priority, and this chapter is designed to guide you and/or your assistants through the mechanics of a large-scale overhaul.

File Logic: The Classification Process

Labeling file folders appropriately—putting the right heading on each label—is the key to rapid retrieval. The simplest method, of course, is to file in straight alphabetical sequence by correspondent's name or company affiliation. A letter from John Jones of Avebury & Art goes into the "J" file if Jones himself is your focus of interest, or the "A" file if Avebury & Art is the focus. Alternatively, if you exchange a sizable amount of correspondence, you might have a separate "Jones" (or "Avebury") file made up.

But strict "who" or "what" alphabetizing has its limitations, as witnessed by Lee Johnson's lost feasibility study. In fact, such overprecision is precisely why so many filing systems have minimal retrieval capability. Often, a heading that reflects too specifically the title or contents of a document is simply too hard to remember. How then to classify the myriad reports, memos, and brochures that have either no connection to a particular individual or company, or a connection that isn't germane to retrieval? The key is to analyze their purpose and function: what a paper relates to and how it might be used. Three rules of classification follow:

1. *Use broad, generic headings.* Had Lee Johnson's study been filed by function—"Direct Selling" or "Marketing" or "Telemarketing"—retrieval would have been instantaneous. The idea, in other words, is to substitute broad, inclusive labels for overly specific, hard-to-remember headings. What about a brief "let's get together soon" note from a new business acquaintance? Ask yourself why you are keeping the note. If the writer is a potential client or customer, file it under "Prospects." Otherwise, add the note to a "Contacts" file.

Other examples: Scratch "Time Management," "Paperwork Tips," and "Efficiency" in favor of one general "Organizing" file. Blend "Venture Capital," "Getting Loans," and "Going Public" into one easily retrievable "Capitalization" or "Financing" file. Merge "Chimpanzees," "Cell Division," and

"San Andreas Fault" into a single "Science" folder. Collect information about management seminars and technical instruction in one inclusive "Education" file. The result: Your information-retrieval rate soars. Other typical headings might include "Competitors," "Marketing," "Personnel," "Sales," and "Travel."

As a general rule of thumb, everyone who uses a file should be able to make a meaningful association between the heading and the file's contents. When you are the sole user, however, you have greater latitude in choosing vivid or idiosyncratic labels. Writer Ralph Keyes, for example, collected material for an article on the public display of emotion by politicians in a "Muskie" folder because he associated the project with the 1972 incident when Edmund Muskie cried in public. Although only a few papers concerned Muskie himself, the heading was legitimate since it had a special meaning for Keyes. For one businesswoman, "Memorabilia" was the appropriate label for a file of souvenirs like the airline ticket to Pittsburgh commemorating her first trip paid for by a client.

2. *Use headings comprehensive enough to absorb a substantial quantity of papers.* A file drawer containing numerous thin folders almost invariably indicates too many headings to keep track of. One property owner, for instance, subdivided her papers by location, contractor, lawyer, and so on, and wasted a lot of time searching various files when she needed a particular document. In discussing the problem with me, she kept mentioning the word "property," which was, of course, the obvious heading for *all* the material. Finding something in a bulky folder may take an extra minute or two, but at least you know it's there. The idea, therefore, is to merge similar materials into relatively few "fat" files, subdividing only when the folder becomes physically unwieldy—about two or more inches thick. Some examples:

- *Mailings from your professional organization.* Make a separate folder for the organization *only* if you save a lot of its material. Otherwise, incorporate its mailings with other professional materials, such as magazine articles and newspaper clippings, in a folder labeled "Industry Information" or "Semiconductor Trends."
- Harvard Business Review *article pertaining to a paper you plan to write.* If you're actively collecting information for the paper, make a separate folder labeled "Northeast Industrial Recovery," "REIT, Pro & Con"—whatever the piece will be about. But if the project is just a gleam in your eye, combine the material with other project ideas in a folder labeled "Future Projects" or "Ideas."
- *Camera store notice.* "Photography" is the obvious heading *if* there's a fair amount of additional material to accompany it. Otherwise, subsume the notice in a general "Stores" or "Hobbies" folder.
- *Letter from boss excusing you from jury duty.* Integrate with other personal office materials—insurance programs, pension benefits, and so on—in a "Personal," "Office—Personal," or "Benefits" file. Again, the particular heading that you choose doesn't have to reflect the precise contents of the file as long as it is meaningful to you.

3. *Head folders with a noun. Rarely use an adjective, adverb, date, or number as the first word (unless it's a proper name or "tag" name).* A direct mail firm filed a set of "hot" mailing lists under the heading "New Lists." Three weeks later, the word "new" had been forgotten—and the material remained lost in the files for over three years. The company got the message. Now all lists are filed under "Lists," which is *followed* by a secondary heading: "New," "1998," "Advertis-

ing," "Regional," and so on. Similarly, turn "Old Plans" into "Plans—Old," and "1998 Reports" into "Reports—1998."

Easy-to-retrieve subdivision headings are important when a bulky folder is broken up. If the focus of the material remains unchanged, keep the present heading and add a secondary label. For example: A "Travel" folder might break down into "Travel—U.S.," "Travel—Foreign," "Travel—Metropolitan Area," or perhaps "Travel—Restaurants" if eateries are a special focus of interest. Alternatively, you might label the latter folder "Restaurants—Out of Town." Which term should you choose? Simply the one you're more likely to remember. To avoid confusion, you can also put a cross-reference folder at the other location. So if restaurant information is filed under "R," add a "Travel—Restaurants" folder to the "T" section and attach a note saying "See 'Restaurant' file."

A subdivision that changes the focus or function of a file should be renamed. A cosmetics company production unit for example, broke down an oversized "Suppliers" file into "Binders," "Printers," and "Production Houses," interfiling them with the other "B" and "P" folders. For easy reference, a list of the new folders was clipped to the front of the original "Suppliers" folder.

Filing Pointers

Once files are properly named, you need only mark an "F" on papers you want to save, jot an appropriate heading, and place them in your out-box or "to file" folder. Depending on quantity, your secretary should spend fifteen to thirty minutes once or twice a week filing these papers. Although I recommend that you handle deskside filing yourself, you can, if you prefer, turn that task over to your secretary as well. However, ask him or her to check with you before subdividing any folder or making up new ones.

Take advantage of these practical filing tips:

- *Alphabetization.* Common practice is to alphabetize folders into one continuous sequence: a general "A" folder followed by, say, files for "Actuarial Information," "Paul Aller," "American Industries," "Asset Management," and "Avebury & Art." Some people like to keep a small batch of "frequent use" folders right at the front of the file drawer. Filing by date is appropriate for bills and other date-related materials.

- *Articles filed by subject.* File magazine or newspaper clippings by subject, not under "Articles" or "Clippings," since their content—not their physical form—is what's relevant.

- *Cross-reference.* When a document relates to more than one category, make a copy for the second file or put a "See thus-and-so" note in one of the folders. If, for example, Joe Smith's pension papers are in the "Pension Fund" file, add a note to the Joe Smith file: "See Pension Fund for Smith's pension papers."

- *Easy access.* Add the most recent materials to the front of a folder. Avoid paper clips, which slip off easily and catch on other papers, and staple papers instead. Always unfold letters before filing. Maintain several inches of play in each file drawer. When drawers get tight, weed them out.

- *Planned obsolescence.* Whenever possible, mark a discard date on each item. Every time you or your secretary looks through a file, toss these "expired" documents, along with any other old or unnecessary papers.

- *Quantity filing.* When there are masses of papers to be filed, presort them into the letter slots of an alphabetical expanding folder. If a desk or office reorganization produces a sizable filing accumulation, include small filing batches—ten to twenty pieces per week—with your secretary's "current filing" stack until the mass is absorbed.
- *Quick location of vital documents.* Keep in your deskside files a list of the locations of contracts, deeds, insurance policies, tax returns, and other important business-related papers. See page 97 for more information about this "vital documents list."
- *Segregation of working files.* As a general rule, separate action files—material in current use—from storage files. Keep working files in a separate caddy or desktop file rack.

Reorganizing a Filing System

When a shortage of file cabinets appears to be the greatest threat to conducting your business; when retrieval consists of guessing which of many possible files contains the papers you need—a thorough reorganization of your system seems due. Why not just buy extra cabinets? Because if the system is out of kilter, new cabinets will simply offer you more space in which to lose more information. And in fact, most users find, post-reorganization, that space is no longer a problem. (But if you do need—or want—to add to or update your equipment, the Glossary of Filing Equipment on pages 111–14 offers some guidelines.)

Before beginning the overhaul process, have the following items on hand:

Manila folders (letter-size for most systems). Use one-third cut if you don't use hanging folders, straight cut if you do.

Hanging folders (Pendaflex), if you use them.

Self-stick labels (Avery brand is standard).

Pendaflex plastic tabs and labels.

Cartons or portable cardboard file boxes if you anticipate transferring files to storage.

Copy of pages 89–95, on file logic.

Optional: trolley for moving portable file boxes.

Stage One: Sorting Out

Choose a starting place: the drawer most in need of attention, the one you consult most often, or the top right drawer of a file bank. Then work through each folder as follows:

1 *What can be tossed?* Can the entire folder be discarded? Why not? Rigorously "show cause" why folders older than a year or two should *not* be thrown out. At least streamline. Keep only two or three copies of a document rather than fifteen. Retain only the major documents generated by a large project, and discard—or store—attendant correspondence after a year. Is the information in infrequently consulted documents available elsewhere? If so, discard. Don't be alarmed if your files shrink by half, or more. That doesn't always happen—it depends on how long papers have been accumulating and on the obsolescence rate—but it's not uncommon.

    Tip: One fundraiser tells a staff assistant, when he goes away for a while, "You go through the stacks of old leads and throw away whatever you'd like, and if I don't see it, it won't kill me."

YOUR COMPANY VITAL DOCUMENTS CHECKLIST

If you're an officer or principal in your firm, store all legal documents, securities, insurance policies, and so forth—any papers whose loss would create great hardship—in a safe-deposit box or fireproof safe. A key question in determining what to save: If there were a fire, which documents would you most hate to lose? List these documents and their whereabouts, keep one copy of the list for yourself, give copies to other officers or principals, and send one to your lawyer. This list should include:

Bank account information. Include account names, numbers, signers, and banks.

Insurance policies. For each policy, list type (fire, liability, etc.), insurer, agent or contact, number and date, key provisions (optional but wise), and expiration or renewal date, if any.

Legal documents. Examples are incorporation or partnership instruments, certifications, licenses, leases, and deeds and titles.

Receivables. Keep a duplicate list of current receivables in a safe place.

Safe-deposit box. Also list other individuals (such as your partner or spouse) who have access to the box in case of emergency.

Securities, such as documents and information on Keogh, IRA, and pension plans.

Tax returns and supporting materials. IRS returns should be kept for seven years. Then discard or store indefinitely, as you wish. Keep backup materials (can-

(Continued)

celed checks, bills, etc.) easily accessible for three years, then store for another four years, after which they can usually be discarded. Confirm with your lawyer or accountant.

Warranties and bills of purchase for major items such as office equipment, computers, and machinery.

Consulting professionals. List names and addresses of attorneys, accountants, brokers, insurance agents, bankers, and so forth.

Personal papers germane to your business (if you are a major stockholder, partner, or sole proprietor), such as your will. Leave the original with your lawyer and keep a copy at home. Don't put the original in a safe-deposit box. *Tip:* It's wise to also maintain a vital-documents checklist for personal papers. Include credit card account numbers. Keep one copy at home, keep one in the office, and send one to your lawyer.

2 *Name the file.* Is the heading broad and clear—a simple noun meaningful to all users? Does it reflect the purpose or function of the contents? Is the heading relevant in terms of day-to-day management decisions? Review the pages on "file logic."

3 *Is cross-referencing necessary?* Do papers in one file also pertain to another category? If so, make an extra copy for the second file, or put a "see also" note in one of the files.

4 *Is the file active, inactive, or referred? Active* files—those used on a regular basis—should be kept in the main file area. When possible, mark a discard or "to storage" date for the entire folder.

Files that haven't been consulted for a year or more,

but have historical or legal significance, can be considered *inactive.* Move these to a less accessible drawer or a central storage area. To facilitate retrieval, list the folders stored in each carton and assign the latter a number. For example: "Carton #1—Personnel Records A–Z"; "Carton #2—Acme Insurance, Advertising Reports, Bowers Realty." Tape a copy of the list to the carton, and keep another in your desk. When the cartons are moved to storage, jot their location—bin number, shelf, and so forth—on your copy of the list and file.

Move *referred* files—those no longer relevant to you— out of your office altogether. Perhaps you've delegated a project to someone else; send all pertinent files to that individual.

Some important tips:

- Work through one folder at a time. Put documents that belong in different folders aside until you get to those files. Similarly, don't thumb through as-yet unchecked files looking for a paper relating to a folder you're working on. *Swinging back and forth between checked and unchecked files will sabotage the entire reorganizing process.* Integrate related materials as you come to them, or after all files have been checked.
- When you've organized an entire drawer, arrange folders alphabetically as described earlier: "A," "Actuarial Information," "Paul Aller," and so forth. Expand your alphabetical system as you go, finally integrating all the drawers: A–E in the top drawer, F–K in the next drawer, and so on. Label the drawers accordingly.
- *Always* make sure bottom drawers are weighted to prevent the cabinets from tipping over.

Stage Two: Capturing Unfiled Materials

Sort all "loose" folders—those sitting in boxes or currently residing on bookshelves, windowsills, or credenza—in the same way, and integrate them into the system. Then go through any loose papers accumulated during the checking process and either discard them, add them to the appropriate folders, or set them up in new folders.

Stage Three: Blocking Out the System

Now analyze the entire filing system as follows:

1 *Special categories.* In general, aim for a single, consolidated alphabetical system. Certain materials, however, either because they are physically different (photos, printouts, catalogs, samples) or because they form a distinct body of material, warrant separation from the main system. A corporate public relations director, for example, set off half a drawer for the president's speeches, organized by topic. Other logical "special" file categories might be client files, press clippings, special project files, financial files, and forms. A special file should contain enough material to take up at least half a drawer. If it doesn't, you're probably overcategorizing.

2 *Physical distribution.* Files consulted by several people should be centrally located—near your secretary's desk, in an alcove or hallway, or in the "open office" area. Store in your desk-side drawers materials that are frequently consulted, of personal interest, or confidential. Your personal-use files should take up no more than two desk drawers, and usually one will suffice. Robert Townsend, author of *Up the Organization,* automatically weeds his

desk drawer back to half when it fills up. If you seem to overflow, you're almost certainly keeping too much material.

One office consultant proposes this "graduated access" policy: keep files consulted weekly in your work area, files consulted monthly on the same floor, and files consulted every two or three months in a general filing room or area no more than a few-minutes walk from your office.

Don't automatically place active files in the top drawers. If cabinets are normally used by a person who is sitting, then store active materials on the bottom. Fill other drawers with inactive files, tax materials, or supplies. Turn folders in lateral files to face users, whether left-to-right, right-to-left, or facing front.

3 *Labels and index.* Ask your secretary to type fresh labels for all folders and drawers and to make up a file index—a listing of all the folders or types of material contained in each cabinet. Keep this index in your computer file directory so it can be easily revised and updated. A simple *drawer plan* suffices for drawers that contain broad categories of material. From one corporate personnel department, for example:

INDEX: FIVE-DRAWER FILE

Drawer 1	Secrecy and inventions/Exit interviews
Drawer 2	Personnel profiles A–M
Drawer 3	Personnel profiles N–Z
Drawer 4	Terminations A–L
Drawer 5	Terminations M–Z

A more elaborate index—listing individual folders as well as cross-references, if any—is appropriate for a subject file. An example from the same department:

INDEX: TWO-DRAWER FILE

Drawer 1   Absence project
            Acquisitions
            Activity reports
            Budgets
                Budget-general
                Monthly comparisons
                Long-range plans
            Check requisitions
            Committees
            Compflash
            Contacts
            Credit Union
            FAFE
            Financial planning
                (See also: Budgets)
            Level comparison study
            Orientation
                (See also: Sales Rep Orientation)
            Projects—Past
            Projects—Potential
            Sales Rep Orientation
            Severance Pay
            Workmen's Comp

Drawer 2   Forms & manuals
            (Forms have yellow tabs)
            (Manuals have green tabs)

Tape the index to the cabinet or keep it on top in a binder. Put one person in charge of recording additions and deletions, as well as updating the index when revisions make it difficult to read. An up-to-date index is a useful backup, even in a very well-organized system, and it's a lifesaver to a system that's not so well organized. Had that direct mail firm maintained an index, their missing "New Lists" file would have been retrieved almost immediately.

4 *Equipment check*. Does your present equipment meet all your filing needs? Review the filing equipment glossary.

File Maintenance and Update

According to office environmental systems designer Robert Propst, 80 percent of the papers put in filing cabinets never need to be retrieved. Unfortunately, it's rarely possible to know in advance which 80 percent that will be, so you do have to retain many papers you'll probably never refer to again. How, then, to keep files in check—and reasonably up to date? Maintenance is a two-part procedure that involves daily upkeep and long-term update. *Upkeep,* which should be handled by one "file monitor," involves the following:

1 Filing. Papers should be filed once a week, or more often if the system is very active. Four or five well-organized file banks can be maintained in about fifteen minutes a day. Keep a box on top of the cabinets as a "drop" for papers to be filed. One theatrical agency uses one drop for general filing, and another for photos and publicity materials.

2 Typing up new labels.

3 Monitoring and, when necessary, regenerating the file index.

4 Keeping track of files "checked out" by office staff. Here are three simple file-control methods:

(a) Keep a supply of tall, brightly colored markers on top of the cabinet. When someone removes a file, he or she inserts a marker in its place. If the files are used by no more than three or four people, assign a different color to each person.

(b) Once a week, the file monitor makes "office rounds," collecting all files no longer in use.

(c) If space permits, set up a table near the cabinets so staffers can use the files there.

In addition to day-to-day upkeep, some form of periodic *updating* is necessary to keep files lean and current—and to check the common tendency to keep papers indefinitely "just in case." Try one or a combination of the following methods:

Perpetual update. As mentioned earlier, write a specific discard or "to storage" date on any document or folder with a limited shelf life. This method eliminates the need for a full-scale search through files for deadwood. Use the perpetual update, or the file audit described below, for general correspondence.

File audit. Whenever files reach a certain size—two or more inches thick—winnow them automatically, retaining active documents, discarding unnecessary items, and moving inactive papers elsewhere.

Oxford Pendaflex suggests a more formal yearly audit, which I have modified slightly: pull every piece of paper in the current files older than one year, and pull from the one-year files, every paper more than two years old. Keep the active files (papers less than one year old) in the front of your cabinet; file inactives (papers one to two years old) separately in the back of the same cabinet or in another drawer; send all files older than two years to storage. *Tip:* If, while checking older files, you find a document you still consult frequently, move it back into the active files.

Category termination. Set expiration dates for major categories: sales and promotional materials, annual reports, SEC reports and other government documents, expense vouchers, and catalogs. Your secretary should discard all expired files the first week of every new year. Different organizations use varying criteria:

The purchasing department of one corporation tosses equipment catalogs after three years, but saves price lists for seven. A securities analyst keeps the annual reports on the five companies he follows most actively for an indefinite period of time, discarding all others after three years. An investment banker keeps SEC 10-K reports for three years only.

A law firm divides client files into two categories: documents (contracts, court papers, etc.) and correspondence (everything else). After five years, documents, unless specially flagged, are stored in a warehouse. Correspondence is put on microfilm, and the originals, unless flagged, are discarded.

Special Filing Problems

Certain filing needs call for specialized solutions. A number of practical methods follow.

Box Files.   Conventional folders may not be adequate for handling numerous active projects that generate a high volume of papers or bulky materials. One busy professional set up a "wall" of boxes on bookshelves, one box per project, and assigned each a letter code. Then she marked that code on all papers entering this system, which enabled her secretary to file a large mass of papers in a few minutes. This method is particularly useful for photographers, editors, artists, and production people who work with oversized materials.

The Chronological File.   The "chron" or "chrono" file is a duplicate set of every piece of paper generated by your office, organized by date rather than subject. To maintain a chron file, set up twelve folders, one for each month. At the end of each year, toss out last January's material, and start a fresh "January" folder—and so on throughout the year. *Tip:* File only the first page of a lengthy report in the chron and write on it: "Full report in thus-and-so file." Remember that a chron file is intended only for backup. If you turn to it often, something is wrong with your main filing system.

Color Coding.   Color coding can be useful to distinguish file categories. A nonprofit research center color-coded contributor files according to level of donations. Another organization interfiled conspicuous green folders for a certain project into the main filing system. Also consider using different-colored labels for different categories. Color-coded cabinets can be useful: beige units for general files, say, and red for employee records. An editor in charge of three magazines shot finished articles into a red, green, or blue bin, depending on the magazine. One company color-coded its supply room shelving: forms were kept on blue shelves, letterhead stationery and envelopes on white shelves, and boxed supplies were stored on red shelves. Be sparing in color-code applications. A rainbow of colors becomes meaningless.

COMMUNAL FILES. Some innovative solutions are possible when active files are used regularly by a number of people. A social welfare agency, for example, stored client folders in a large "lazy susan" around which staff members arranged their desks. A corporate publications department made up a separate "job jacket" for each project in which all materials— proofs, correspondence, computer sheets, estimates, and so forth—were stored. A "job form" was clipped to the front of each jacket, summarizing the project's various steps. As each worker completed a particular task or step, he or she checked it off on the sheet. Not only did this facilitate easy monitoring of a project's progress, but it also gave the department head a ready-made history of each project in its entirety.

LOOSELEAF NOTEBOOK FILING. Some materials can be retrieved more easily from a notebook than a folder. Some examples: A direct mail firm pasted each mailing in a notebook, organizing the materials by date, which made it possible to update ideas from old mailings and avoid duplicating recent mailings.

MICROFILM. Microfilm—photographing documents for extremely long-term retrieval—is recommended only for documents of legal or significant historical interest.

MICROFICHE. This method, which utilizes a film "card," is most appropriate for statistical or reference information, such as sales records. It can be updated regularly. However, since expensive equipment is required, it's generally only recommended for special purposes.

NUMERIC FILING. The tickler system described in Chapter 2 is a classic example of a numeric file, in which papers are organized by number or date. A numeric system is appropriate for date-related materials like bills, invoices, and orders. Other applications: One firm assigned numbers to its many office forms—Form 1, Form 2, and so on—and filed them accordingly. A computer outfit organized sales brochures and related materials into "visit" folders: "First Visit" contained materials for new potential customers, "Second Visit" contained more specific information, and so on.

PRÉCIS. This is a form stapled to the front of an active file that summarizes the folder's contents and/or any action taken. For example, a foundation attaches a précis to each major contributor's file summarizing the results of each phone call or contact. Any planned action—letter, call, follow-up—is underlined in red and checked off when accomplished. A theatrical booking agency keeps a file on every major city it services and staples to each folder a list of the city's major sales prospects. When an agent plans a trip to one of those cities, a glance at the sheet enables him to arrange his business calls quickly and efficiently. The "job form" mentioned earlier is also a précis.

PROGRESSIVE FILING. This system is useful for papers connected with an active project, or for material connected to more than one category or task. In effect, it allows you to physically "move" papers through each category or stage of a project. For example, a salesman, after his first visit to a prospect, shifted the latter's card to the "Visit 2" folder, and so on. A historian writing a book on labor unions, who found that much of his research applied to more than one chapter, set up a folder for each chapter and moved research notes through these files. When one chapter was completed, he would distribute "overlap" materials into the next appropriate folder. Some documents were routed through five or more chapters.

Summary: A Four-Step Filing Program

STEP 1   Label each file according to its function or purpose. Each heading should:

- Be broad and generic
- Be comprehensive enough to absorb a substantial quantity of material
- Begin with a simple noun, meaningful to all users of the file

STEP 2   Reorganize a system by working through each folder as follows:

- Discard obsolete or unnecessary materials.
- Name each file according to the principles stated above.
- Cross-reference when appropriate by making an extra copy or adding a "see also" note to one file.
- Decide whether files are active, inactive, or referred, and move them to appropriate locations.
- Mark an expiration or "to storage" date on each item or folder whenever possible.

When the contents of all cabinets have been checked and alphabetized, sort through loose papers and folders and integrate into the system.

STEP 3   Block out the entire system as follows:

- Place special categories in separate drawers or sections.
- Place files in areas most convenient to all users.
- Have fresh labels and the file index typed.
- Review equipment needs.

STEP 4   Maintenance:

Upkeep. Choose a file monitor to handle all filing, maintain the index, and track the whereabouts of "checked out" files.

Update. For informal maintenance, mark a "toss out" or "to storage" date on as many documents as possible; audit the files yearly; establish storage policies on the main file categories.

A Glossary of Filing Equipment

Manila folders are available in two widths—letter-size and the wider legal-size. Folder tabs—called "cuts"— also vary. One-third cuts (tabs one-third the length of the folder) are best for a conventional (nonhanging) system. They can be staggered so that none are blocked from view. (*Tip:* Your secretary should stagger new boxes of one-third cuts in advance, readying them for immediate use.) For a hanging system, use straight cuts (tabs that stretch the length of the folder).

Hanging folders, often called Pendaflex folders after their chief manufacturer, Oxford Pendaflex, are tough, pliable folders that hang from racks inserted in a standard file drawer. Despite their popularity, they are a mixed blessing. *Disadvantages:* They are expensive, slippery, and hard to handle off the rack. They take up a third again more space than manila folders. *Advantages:* They are easily visible, are easy to manipulate in the drawer, and can expand to hold bulkier materials.

Lateral vs. vertical cabinets. Handsome lateral filing cabinets have become the equipment of choice in virtually every office aspiring to chic. But they have certain drawbacks: designed with a full drawer extension of only thirty-five inches (as compared to about a fifty-four-inch extension on verticals) for use in corridors and narrow spaces, they take up considerably more floor space than verticals, and are definitely inappropriate for a busy system of several file banks. Because you have to stand alongside a side-by-side lateral to check a file, you will be

(*Continued*)

FOLDERS

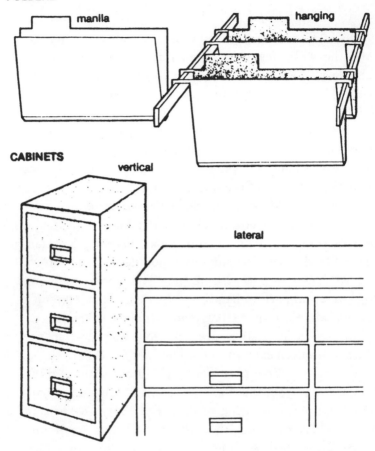

CABINETS

blocking an adjoining cabinet or passageway. Front-filed laterals afford easier access, but they're so shallow that in an active system they require frequent rearrangement. Also, they can only be used with hanging files. In general, laterals are best utilized in narrow spaces, although a two-drawer lateral can double as a room divider and provide some extra counter space as well.

Verticals—the more conventional two-, three-, four-, five-, or six-drawer uprights—remain the most useful cabinets for busy systems. They provide easy access and can be used with either manila or hanging folders. And if you need extra desk-side file space, or want a new desk, put a wood or formica slab on top of two two-drawer verticals and create an "instant" desk.

Whatever type of cabinet you purchase, it's a good idea to stick with recognized brands like Shaw-Walker, Steelcase, or Litton. Cheap cabinets jam easily, and drawers may slip off their tracks or fall out completely. They can also be dangerous because they often have sharp edges and a tendency to tip over. Good cabinets are expensive, but excellent buys are available at stores selling second-hand office supplies.

Mobile and flexible file units. Flexible units include wheeled, open file drawers and a "lazy susan" spinning file. Both are useful in offices where a number of people regularly use the same active files. Portable files range from light, easy-to-carry boxes to "car trunk" files, which are about the size of a standard file drawer. "Transfiles"—the dominant brand name for heavy cardboard files—are used to store or transport file materials.

(Continued)

File cabinet alternatives. Create extra file space by placing free-standing Pendaflex racks on shelves or on top of filing cabinets. Alternatively, bend manila folders vertically to create two creases, forming a stiff spine, and stand them up on shelves like books.

Specialty equipment. Special units are available for art supplies (mechanicals, architectural drawings, portfolios, etc.), cassettes, index cards, computer printouts, floppy disks, maps, newspapers, magazines, and slides. There are also fire and/or burglary-proof cabinets for securities and other valuables, and special shelving for samples and bulky materials.

See the Office Products Guide on page 356 for further source information.

PART II

TIME

AND

TASK

MANAGEMENT

5

Shaping Your Workday: Crisis Management or Cool Control?

I practiced the art of getting more things done rather than getting the really important things done well.

—R. ALEC MACKENZIE

Time is scarce and getting scarcer. Ask any group of managers to describe their most pressing work problem, and you're bound to hear "not enough hours in the day" or "too much to do, no time to do it all." It's not surprising, given the pressures of office life, that so many managers let their days slip through their fingers, losing sight of the larger picture in the crunch of daily demands and interruptions. You have the option, however, of taking the offensive and actively shaping your day. The key is to establish *selective control:* refocus and harness the time you can control, and institute defensive measures to minimize the impact of the demands that you can't control.

If you've been playing a defensive game and reacting to events—putting aside a critical project to take phone calls, juggling four tasks at once, escalating from problem to crisis—

how do you start to regain control? The time-management process can be thought of as three concentric circles reflecting the what/when, how, and why of planning and scheduling, as in the diagram below:

THE CONCENTRIC CIRCLES OF TIME MANAGEMENT

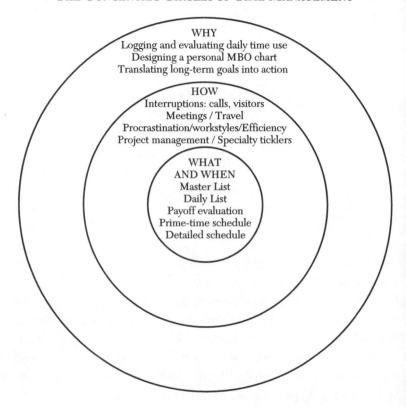

WHY
Logging and evaluating daily time use
Designing a personal MBO chart
Translating long-term goals into action

HOW
Interruptions: calls, visitors
Meetings / Travel
Procrastination/workstyles/Efficiency
Project management / Specialty ticklers

WHAT
AND WHEN
Master List
Daily List
Payoff evaluation
Prime-time schedule
Detailed schedule

What and when: This is the core circle of planning and scheduling, whereby you define what you have to do and when you should be doing it. See Chapter 5.

How: The middle circle of protection and control consists of strategies for defending your schedule against interruptions, time-wasters, and procrastination, and for finding the simplest, most efficient methods for doing what you have to do. See Chapters 6, 7, and 8.

Why: The outer circle of "value" allows you to evaluate your daily activities against overall aspirations, and to organize your time so that long-term goals can be realized. See Chapter 9.

A question arises regarding the reason that "why" comes after "what," "when," and "how." First, the strain that disorganization creates often blocks clear thinking about broader objectives. Second, in order to translate any goal into reality, practical tasks must be undertaken: there are letters and memos to compose, papers to process, phone calls to make, and so forth. Without the organizing channels to render aspirations concrete, your plans will remain no more than blueprints. Thus, learning practical management of the myriad claims on your time is the necessary precondition to your stepping back to take the long view.

The five chapters in Part II will cover these critical aspects of time management. The Time Quotient Self-Report that follows will give you an objective measure of where you stand on the time-management continuum.

What to Do: Identifying Tasks and Priorities

"Yesterday," says research director Mark Jarvis, "I made up four lists: an idea list, a must-do list, a next-week list, and a long-range project list. Now I can't find them, and I know I've forgotten something important. There's got to be a better way."

TIME QUOTIENT SELF-REPORT

	FREQUENCY					SCORE
	ALMOST ALWAYS	USUALLY	SOME- TIMES	SELDOM	ALMOST NEVER	
1. I know when I walk in in the morning what my two or three primary tasks for the day are.						
2. I accomplish my two or three primary tasks.						
3. I complete tasks by the deadline.						
4. I monitor my staff to make sure they complete their tasks by the deadline.						
5. I do my hardest tasks when my energies are at their peak.						
6. I do no task that a subordinate can do.						
7. I allow no more than three unauthorized interruptions a day.						
8. I don't push off difficult tasks or procrastinate.						
9. I return calls when I say I will.						
10. In general, my day-to-day tasks reflect and support my larger goals.						
					TOTAL SCORE	

Scoring   2 points for each "almost always."
               4 points for each "usually."
               6 points for each "sometimes."
               8 points for each "seldom."
            10 points for each "almost never."

If your score is:
        30–46   You are essentially in control. The time-management techniques outlined in this section will, however, enhance your productivity and efficiency.
        47–79   You are racing against the clock. Greater control is advisable.
      80–100   You're on a treadmill. Restructuring time and work habits is vital to productivity.

The planning of your workload is key to productive time use, and for most managers, planning means making lists. Unfortunately, the Jarvis approach to list-making is all too familiar. Notes and reminders show up on the backs of envelopes or on scraps of paper, which are then tucked into pocket or drawer and mislaid. An infinitely more efficient way of solving list overload is to condense those myriad jottings into *two* basic lists: a comprehensive Master List and a specific Daily List.

The Master List

The Master List is a single, continuous list, maintained in a spiral-bound or small looseleaf notebook (or your computer or hand-held organizer—see Chapter 12, "Using Your Computer to Get Organized," for a discussion of how to adapt these time management techniques to computer), of everything you have to do. Let's say you're dictating a letter when a client calls to request estimates by next Wednesday. Then your boss phones: please remember to bring the Steele portfolio to Friday's meeting. Your boss's call sparks the idea of having Steele prepare two further sketches for the portfolio. You reach for the notebook that's with you at all times and jot down these notes. They become your Master List.

> **Action Step I**   Record in a single notebook every idea, assignment, call, project, task, or errand—large or small, minor or important—as it arises. This is your Master List.

Beyond starring an occasional obvious priority, forget about categorizing or assigning priorities at this point. Also include those "someday I'd like to" activities for which you never seem to have time (writing an article for a trade journal, taking a computer course, etc.). Since the Master List is not intended as a daily action list, there are no restrictions on the number or types of entries. One person might add fifteen items in one day; another, three or four. Use the book as a catch-all for every reminder, from ordering champagne for the office Christmas party to the brilliant marketing scheme that came to you in the middle of the night. Some people include personal items on the Master List; others keep a separate notebook or tab a section of the office notebook for personal matters.

A typical Master List might include the following:

Review last year's uncollected accounts.

Plan fall line.

Call Jim re lunch.

Get Steele portfolio for Friday's meeting.

Call Steele re more sketches.

Draft seasonal trends memo.

Call Frank with estimates.

Reschedule date for Sanford presentation.

One executive uses an interesting Master List variation. "In my inside coat pocket," he says, "I keep a special 'action' pad where I make notes, and as soon as I get to a telephone, I read the notes to my secretary to get action started. I never let these notes pile up." Boardroom Inc. publisher Martin Edelston always carries a dictating machine for immediate recording of new ideas or tasks. His secretary later transcribes the notes on distinctive green paper reserved for that purpose. Numerous variations are feasible, so long as all items are recorded in one system.

Think of the Master List as a continuing "to do" record that crystallizes your workload for today, tomorrow, next week, next month, perhaps even next year. As such, it also quantifies the size of your taskload. According to one manager, "Before I began using a Master List, it always seemed as if I had an infinite number of things to do. Now, simply by putting everything down on paper—in one place—I know there's a definite limit, and that I can get it all done in due time."

Another executive offers this colorful analogy: "I think of the Master List as my 'project warehouse'—a facility where I can 'store' and remember all tasks until I'm ready to act on them. Each day I 'move' certain tasks out of the warehouse, distributing some to my staff and adding others to my own daily 'to-do' list." Distribution and scheduling are, in fact, the keys to turning the Master List into a practical planning tool. A reminder to draft a memo isn't going to do you much good if it languishes on the list. Therefore, a daily review of the list is in order:

1 *Delete* any tasks or ideas that upon later reflection seem unnecessary or overzealous.
2 *Break down* large or complex tasks into smaller components or subtasks. The "Plan fall line" entry, for example, could involve numerous subtasks (see chart on page 126), each of which should be included on the Master List. "By segmenting tasks," points out Edwin Bliss in *Getting Things Done*, "you can thus develop that precious habit known as the *compulsion to closure*. It will save time for you every day."

   Establish start dates and deadlines for each subtask by working backward from the project's due date. Set a due date yourself if there isn't one already.
3 *Redistribute* all "referrable" tasks—putting a note in your out-box or delegatee's folder—and cross these off the

list. If follow-up is necessary (for, say, a task due one month hence), use your calendar or tickler file in the usual way.

4 *Schedule* action dates for long-range or date-related projects, transfer them to your calendar, and cross them off the Master List. If the accounts receivable figures must be ready for the accountant by March 15, choose a realistic starting date—perhaps February 25—and enter "Start accounts receivables" on your calendar for that date.

5 *Select* items that demand immediate attention: five phone calls that must be made tomorrow, or editing the final draft of the quarterly sales analysis. Delete these from the Master List and rewrite them on a separate piece of paper, which becomes a source for your daily "to do" list.

> **Action Step 2** Review the Master List daily. Divide large projects into manageable components. Eliminate and delegate the tasks you can, enter deferred tasks on your calendar, immediate tasks on the Daily List. Delete these distributed tasks from the Master List.

When every entry on a page is crossed out, clip a corner of the page or mark it with a red check mark. If a page contains only a few outstanding tasks, rewrite them onto a fresh page and mark the old one completed. Save finished notebooks for a month or two for reference.

The Daily List

If the Master List is your "project warehouse," the Daily List might be compared to a daily distribution allocation or shipment. At the end of each day, after you've gone through the Master List, compile tomorrow's Daily List from these three sources:

Immediate tasks that have evolved during the course of the day (a report revision must be ready by tomorrow afternoon).

Calendar items. These are previously scheduled items that have become current (for example, the February 25 "accounts receivables" project mentioned above).

Master List items. Fill out the Daily List to ten items with those selected from the Master List for immediate action. If you use a double-page calendar, jot the Daily List on one side. It will provide a useful record of each day's accomplishments. Otherwise, use a pad or another notebook—*not* the Master List notebook.

Daily List items should be limited to approximately ten tasks that you can reasonably expect to complete in one day. Consolidate a number of small tasks, such as groups of phone calls, short memos, or errands, into one entry. Break a complex task into components as described earlier. It is the *components* that you enter on to your Daily List. A key to task management is that you selectively either (1) divide and conquer, or (2) consolidate and control. More specifically, limiting the Daily List to ten "one-day" jobs prevents "task paralysis," which can occur when your workload seems unmanageable, or when a particular project involves more subtasks than can be handled in a single day.

A few words about calendars might be in order here. Your calendar is the nerve center of your time-management program. People often ask me to recommend a calendar/planner.

COMPLEX TASKS: FROM MASTER LIST TO DAILY LIST

The three Master List tasks below have been provided by a garment manufacturer, a securities analyst, and a publisher. The components, after being entered on your Master List, are then gradually fed into your Daily List.

PRIMARY MASTER LIST
ENTRY

COMPONENTS

Garment Manufacturer:
Plan fall line.

Review last year's line.
Analyze reasons for success or failure of particular items.
Check materials availability.
Review financing options.
Select designers.
(Note: To reach "Daily List size," some entries might require further breakdown. "Check materials availability" might involve several calls, a letter to the supplier, etc.)
Assemble January–June sales figures.

Securities Analyst:
Conduct year-end survey of agrichemical industry.

Read EPA pesticide report.
Decide survey structure: by topic (financial, marketing) or chronological?

(Continued)

Draft first section.
Draft second section . . .

Publisher:
Decide whether to
continue journal
acquisition program
at same level, expand,
or cut back.

Commission survey about
professional areas not served
or scantily served by
journals.
Request journal advisers to
report on market potential
in those fields.
Ask Marty for list of
important contacts in those
fields.
Ask finance people to
compare value-per-dollar
spent on book program with
that spent on journal
program over last three
years.

I gave up recommending, however, when I realized that one person's calendar/planner is another person's pain in the neck. One's choice of calendar is very personal.

Options range from no calendar at all, but rather a sheet of paper on which the executive's secretary has typed out the day's appointments and itinerary, to a week-at-a-glance calendar such as those manufactured by Letts and Keith Clark, to the legions of Day Timers, to bulging complex calendar/planners.

For people who prefer to travel light, a hefty planner is just too much to deal with, while those who swear by their Filo-

---

QUICK TASK AUDIT

If certain tasks seem to demand considerable time and energy without yielding much in the way of return, take 30 seconds to ask yourself these four questions:

1 Must the job be done at all? What would happen if it were cut?
2 Can the job be delegated? As a whole? Parts? To whom?
3 Is the time expenditure—your own and others'—commensurate with the project's importance?
4 If time expenditure seems excessive, can the task be downscaled: simplified, computerized, made less exhaustive, less detailed, etc.?

---

faxes, Day Runners, Time Designs, and Franklin Planners could not negotiate life without them. So on the question of calendars and planners, I say "to each his or her own."

If you use both a desk and a pocket calendar, coordinate them at the beginning of each year, entering recurring meetings, professional conferences, and other long-range activities. Review both calendars with your secretary daily during the paperwork-processing session to make sure they conform. (Few things are more embarrassing than missing a meeting because you neglected to transfer a note from desk to pocket calendar.) Also transfer pocket calendar notes and reminders to the Master List or your desk calendar for future action. Enter receipts and expense slips daily on a blank expense form, or delegate this task to your secretary.

For long-term planning (monthly, quarterly, etc.), use a wall calendar with large squares for each date. Enter project schedules, staff meetings, vacation dates, and so forth. Note the due dates of staff project assignments (use a different-colored pen for each person); plot start dates for your own long-range projects, and enter those as well. Numerous projects involving many people can be tracked with a wall chart with movable magnetic tabs. Caddylak manufactures such prepackaged systems.

Setting Priorities: The $25,000 Exercise

Since not all tasks are created equal, the organized executive must set priorities: that is, establish a hierarchy of importance, and match the commitment of time and resources to the relative importance of each task. Some cogent practical advice about setting priorities was given some sixty years ago by Ivy Lee, often called the founder of management consulting, to Bethlehem Steel's chief Charles Schwab:

> Number the items [you have to do tomorrow] in the order of their real importance. First thing tomorrow morning, start working on number one and stay with it until it is completed. Next take number two and don't go any further until it is completed. Then proceed to number three, and so on. If you can't complete everything on schedule, don't worry. At least you will have taken care of the most important things without getting distracted by items of lesser importance.

Lee asked Schwab to test this system and send him a check for whatever Schwab thought it was worth. Within a few weeks, Lee received a check for $25,000—a very considerable sum at the time! Now (for a more nominal sum), here is a variation on Lee's valuable counsel. Rank each item on your Daily List as a 1, 2, or 3 priority according to these criteria:

1 An *immediate or critical* "must-do," such as completing a budget analysis for tomorrow's board meeting.
A task requiring special *effort or concentration,* such as developing a new sales strategy.
A *stressful* task, such as criticizing a subordinate's work. If processing routine paperwork creates anxiety, it would be considered a priority-1 task.
2 Middle-range *basics,* such as a typical brief or report.
3 Low-priority tasks or *routine* busywork, such as reading a journal or reviewing standard contracts.

Avoiding ranking Daily List entries according to a more precise 1-to-10 scale forestalls the tendency to waste time obsessing over whether an item is a 5 or a 6. The 1-3 ranking will give you sufficient flexibility.

> **Action Step 3** Compile tomorrow's Daily List—ten tasks you can reasonably expect to complete in one day—from your calendar, the Master List, tasks that have evolved during the day. Rank each item either 1, 2, or 3, depending on urgency and the level of demand it makes on you.

Schedule no more than three or four 1's per day, with the remainder a mix of 2's and 3's. (See the garment manufacturer's Daily List.) One manager who tended to pack each day's list with six or more 1's soon abandoned the system in frustration after two hours' concentrated work netted him only the first three 1-level projects. It's simply not possible to muster the time or mental energy to accomplish more than a few

One Day's List
Garment Manufacturer

JOB	RANK
Phone calls: Pat re budget	3
Paul re lunch	
Conference center re date	
Smith, Lowry, Ryan callbacks	
Draft policy memo	1
Review sales figures for last year's fall line	2
Edit sales report	1
Compile figures for marketing paper	2
Letters: Brown re returns policy	2
Towers re shipping orders	
Gleason re contract	
Outline key points for next week's speech	1
Meet with partner to discuss staff raises (ranked 1 because of high stress)	1
Review Wilson contract	3
Read article in *WWD* on Milan shows	3

top priorities each day. So accept reasonable limitations and concentrate on achieving the best results on the two or three tasks that yield optimum benefit.

Some additional Daily List tips:

- Complete each task—or reach a natural stopping point—before moving on to the next one.
- Rewrite any incomplete projects onto the next day's list. *Do not* increase the Daily List to thirteen to accommodate

three "leftovers" from the day before. The Daily List is a road map, not a moral imperative.

- If a task reappears on several Daily Lists, consider dropping, delegating, or postponing it.

The Payoff/Priority Ratio

Acquire the habit of evaluating tasks in terms of payoff. Think of time as a return on investment. You wouldn't spend three hours to find a $30 bargain and then devote ten minutes to a $25,000 investment decision. Why, then, devote an hour to a task that affords little or no payoff in terms of your goals and responsibilities, meanwhile losing time from a project that might lead to a major business coup? To identify the payoff/priority ratio, subject your Daily List entries to a payoff analysis:

1 *High-payoff* tasks are those that promise to yield substantial or dramatic benefits: developing untapped markets, putting together a winning sales campaign, landing a major contract, dramatically increasing productivity.

   Typically, high-payoff projects are self-initiated, have a self-imposed deadline, involve considerable risk or uncertainty, and often take time to yield results. Because they may not be "must-do's" in the immediate sense, many managers fail to program time for these more creative, high-yield projects. However, it's important to try to enter at least one high-payoff task on the Daily List every day.

2 *Negative-payoff* tasks *are* must-do's—either a number 1 or 2 priority—because the consequences of ignoring or postponing them can be disastrous. Examples: processing paperwork, coping with emergencies, responding to the boss's requests.

3 *Medium-payoff* tasks are the basic, day-to-day substance of your job. Usually number 2 priorities, but occasionally number 1, they must be done, but you have considerable latitude as to when to do them. Examples: the preparation of a legal brief or a client's tax return.

4 *Low- (or nonexistent) payoff* tasks are those that offer little in the way of either positive or negative benefits. Examples: writing up minutes that are seldom reviewed, repetitive rechecking of orders, refining the content of a letter more than its importance would indicate. Such items should rarely appear on your Daily List, and certainly not as a number 1 or 2 priority. Consider which of these tasks you can prune, streamline, or delegate.

> **Action Step 4** Evaluate Daily List tasks in terms of their payoff: high, negative (unfortunate consequences if not done), medium, or low. Try to enter at least one high-payoff task on the Daily List every day, and cut down on low pay-offs.

When to Do It: Scheduling and Allocating Time

For Nancy Darcy, vice president of personnel, compiling a Daily List was easy enough; her problem was scheduling the time to execute it. Because her job required a lot of "people contact"—interviews, meetings, appointments—she frequently fell behind on less immediate demands. Most days, as she put it, "I'm lucky if I get through three items on my Daily List, to say nothing about paperwork, reading, or doing employee evaluations."

Your personal prime time is the pivot for planning the rest of your day. When do you feel most alert, most capable of

Evaluating Payoffs and Priorities

	CHARACTERISTICS	EXAMPLES	PRIORITY
High-payoff task	Promises significant benefits Often self-initiated Deadline often self-imposed Significant time gap between initiation and results is typical	Designing award-winning campaign Developing new accounting system to save the company money Opening new product markets	Typically, 1 Occasionally, 2
Negative-payoff task	Neglect or failure to act could be detrimental Imminent or arbitrary deadline Sometimes stressful or unpleasant Often involves troubleshooting	Sales report due tomorrow Emergency staff meeting to correct major error in client report Firing incompetent staffer Last-minute assignment from boss	Typically, 1 or 2 Occasionally, 3
Medium-payoff task	Usually involves basic aspects of your work Usually have some discretion as to when to handle Can often be delegated, in whole or in part	Routine meeting with client Accountant preparing tax returns Lawyer writing brief	Typically, 2 or 3 Occasionally, 1
Low-payoff task	Offers no significant payoffs, negative or positive	Busywork Rewriting an unimportant letter or memo Word-for-word reading of minor report or article	3, or unnecessary

Priority Key 1 = Urgent, demanding, stressful tasks; tasks requiring concentration
2 = Middle-range basics
3 = Lower-priority and routine tasks

clear, concentrated thought? First thing in the morning? Mid-morning? Late afternoon? Like the "sweet spot" on a tennis racket—the center point that gives your swing the most power and precision—your day also has a "sweet spot": a metaboli-cally determined "high" when you're full of energy and at your creative best. Scheduling priority-1 tasks during this peak time is the key to producing work of exceptional value. Take the case of a manager who routinely spent his early morn-ing peak clearing his in-box and returning phone calls. By 11:00 A.M., when he was ready to tackle demanding priority-1 tasks, his drive had dissipated. However, by reversing the time slots for "housekeeping" and creative activities, he began to forge ahead professionally.

To discover your own prime time, try working one-half of a crossword puzzle in the morning and the other half in late afternoon. During one or the other of those sessions, your ability to see connections will be significantly more acute. You might also draw up a rough chart noting your particular highs and lows. This pattern is fairly typical:

9:00 A.M. to noon	High-gear
Noon to 4:00 P.M.	Fairly alert
4:00 P.M. to 6:00 P.M.	Low-gear
6:00 P.M. to 10:00 P.M.	Fairly alert
After 10:00 P.M.	Resting

Experiment with time patterns. People who are most alert later in the day might plan to arrive at the office at 11:00 A.M. and work until 7:00 or 8:00 P.M. If this isn't feasible, the morn-ing "low" could be reserved for routine work, with priority-1 tasks scheduled for the afternoon and early evening hours.

Reserve *no more than* three or four hours a day (and often only one-and-a-half to two hours is realistic given other demands on your time) for priority-1 tasks. As your mental energy level drops, you won't be able to sustain concentration. This prime-time block and your daily paperwork/secretary session comprise the fixed points in your daily schedule. How you choose to arrange the rest of your day depends on your own personal temperament and the nature of your work.

Many managers prefer a flexible schedule for priority-2 and -3 tasks, handling these activities during nonpeak hours as circumstances permit. In any case, it's unwise to sidestep routine tasks. Putting a project that's on your mind on indefinite hold only creates anxiety. For organizer Mary Laurens, "backward scheduling" is the method of choice. She determines what time she must leave her office, then schedules what she has to do that day. "I schedule [tasks] into my day beginning with the time I want to finish. That forces me to set priorities."

This fluid approach works well for stockbrokers, those in advisory or counseling professions, people in the "creative" professions, sales representatives, and people in businesses that must respond to fast-breaking events. In contrast, administrators, planners, and many other managers prefer to program their time more precisely, preplanning by the hour and/or day. This is particularly important for managers whose administrative duties conflict with "people contact."

Designing a Time Program

When Nancy Darcy analyzed her day, it became clear that the problem was time fragmentation. She'd no sooner begin drafting an important report than an employee would drop in for an impromptu conference. Twenty minutes later she would return to the report, only to be interrupted by a phone call, and so the day went. For Darcy, the solution was a time program based on *consolidation:* scheduling similar activities—

appointments, paperwork, meetings, phone calls—into specific time blocks and factoring in some flexible time as well. (For Nancy Darcy's complete schedule, see Schedules Appendix.) You can establish such a personal program.

1 Divide your workday into "public" activities and "private" activities. A typical list might include:

PUBLIC ACTIVITIES	PRIVATE ACTIVITIES
Drop-in visitors and ad hoc meetings	Paperwork
Scheduled appointments and meetings	Research
Phone calls	Correspondence and reports
Unexpected events	Planning
	Reading

2 Select the most demanding activities and schedule them into your morning or afternoon *prime-time block*. For most people, these will be private activities like writing or planning. Other people a labor negotiator or sales rep, for example—will rank negotiations, phone calls, sales appointments, and other "public" activities as prime-time tasks.

3 Schedule less demanding tasks in *blocks during "lower" time*. Group meetings, appointments, and phone calls into a "public" block, either morning or afternoon. Spend half an hour reading during a 4:00 P.M. slump.

Or group activities into a weekly pattern: for example, reserve Monday and Tuesday for writing and planning, use the rest of the week for public contact. Consolidate regular staff meetings into one day, instead of distributing them throughout the week. Weekly scheduling is often practical for people whose work depends on the telephone. One securities analyst, for example, had to take most of his calls—his lifeline to information. At the same time, he needed quiet time for paperwork and thinking. So after he logged all incoming calls for two weeks and discovered that Thursday and Friday afternoons were fairly slow, those afternoons found him in a conference room working on evaluations and reports.

4 Put the program into motion by duplicating the blank scheduling form presented here and marking fixed points: the prime-time block, the weekly 4:00 P.M. staff meeting, tasks requiring equipment or people only available at certain times, your paperwork/secretary meeting. Around these fixed points, set times for the other blocks.

> **Action Step 5**   Determine your prime time. Slot into it priority-1 tasks from the Daily List and other high-demand activities. Either work lower-demand tasks into nonpeak time as events permit, or design a more precise time program by blocking "public" and "private" activities.

Summary: Five Action Steps to Increased Productivity

STEP 1   Record in a single notebook *every* idea, assignment, call, project, task, or errand—large or small, minor or important—as it arises. This is your Master List.

STEP 2   Review Master List daily. Divide large projects into manageable components. Eliminate and delegate the tasks you can, enter deferred tasks on calendar, im-

WEEKLY BASE SCHEDULE

	MONDAY	TUESDAY	WEDNESDAY	THURSDAY	FRIDAY
A.M.					
LUNCH					
P.M.					

mediate tasks on Daily List. Delete distributed tasks from Master List.

STEP 3　Compile tomorrow's Daily List—ten tasks you can reasonably expect to complete in one day—from calendar, Master List, and tasks evolved during the day. Rank each item either 1, 2, or 3, depending on priority and level of demand it makes on you.

STEP 4　Evaluate Daily List tasks in terms of their payoff: high, negative (unfortunate consequences if not done), medium, or low. Try to enter at least one high-payoff task on the Daily List every day, and cut down on low payoffs.

STEP 5　Determine prime time. Slot into it priority-1 tasks from the Daily List and other high-demand activities. Either work lower-demand tasks into nonpeak time as events permit, or design a more precise time program by blocking "public" and "private" activities.

6

Mastering the Timewasters

Do your best-laid plans often, or always, go awry? Allowing the insistent demands of office life—interruptions, meetings, travel—to run unchecked is the surest way to negate all your planning and scheduling efforts. The solution: Defend your plan by incorporating into your daily repertoire a number of simple techniques that will help you manage the timewasters that threaten to throw you off course. You *can* establish greater control—without being rude or shutting yourself off to others' needs.

Anti-Interruption Strategies: Your First Line of Defense

Reducing outside interruptions is a crucial aspect of any time-management program. Of course, each office has its own rhythm, a tempo not entirely subject to control. In some businesses that depend on telephone contact and meetings—sales, stockbroking, real estate—claiming private time during office hours is next to impossible. And all businesses have their inevitable "I must speak to you now" crises. So it simply isn't possible (or wise) for most people to block all interruptions or shut themselves away for an entire day. Indeed, a far-reaching network of contacts might be one of your most valuable resources. The individual who walls himself in too thoroughly risks being shielded from problems until they become crises. A more realistic approach, therefore, is to *limit* your control to specific parcels of time—prime time, occasional private work periods, scheduled appointments—and deal with the rest of the day more flexibly.

Barring real emergencies, ask your staff not to disturb you during designated interruption-free periods. If necessary, put your request in writing. One lawyer circulated this memo to his office:

> After considerable thought and a great many unproductive days, I have concluded it is vital to my work that I establish a "quiet period" during which I can get important jobs done without being interrupted by telephone calls, visitors, meetings, and other distractions. Consequently, I want to establish an interruption-free period of time from 9:00 to 10:30 A.M. to assist me in better and more productive use of my time. In this effort, I need all of the help that your skills, intelligence, and cooperation can provide. Thank you.

Closing some doors, however, means opening others. Let staff and colleagues know that you're available for questions, troubleshooting, and advice during the rest of the day. Nonetheless, guidelines must be established. How often do you take a call your secretary could have fielded, or meet with a client to discuss a routine matter that a more junior assistant could have handled? Your first line of defense, therefore, involves learning to eliminate avoidable distractions—and reduce the time spent on unavoidable ones.

Telephone Tactics

A ringing telephone is the insistent summons of modern life, and the decision not to take a call requires fortitude. The following techniques will help to establish firmer control over your telephone time.

SECRETARY INTERCEPT. Ask your secretary to shelter your interruption-free periods with all the diplomacy—and muscle—he or she can muster. Supply your secretary with a list of callers to whom you will always speak (boss, an important client), and those whose calls you will take only at specified times or under certain circumstances. Your secretary should elicit the reason for the call with a courteous: "May I tell Mr./ Ms. Jones what this call is in reference to?" Failure to give your secretary these instructions can result in "telephone tag." One magazine editor, for example, tried for four days to reach an economist who had just written an article for his magazine. When they finally spoke, it turned out that the editor simply needed the economist's social security number, which the latter's secretary could have easily provided—had the secretary known about the purpose of the call. Advance information also permits your secretary to gather up any necessary papers or information before you return a call. Often, your secretary will be able to field calls directly or refer them elsewhere. *Tip:* Your secretary should keep a log of all calls he or she does handle or refer, and report them to you during your daily meeting.

If you don't have a secretary, arrange an exchange with a colleague, taking each other's calls during designated periods.

VOICE MAIL. Be cautious about overusing voice mail, which is, so to speak, an office-wide answering machine. See the discussion of voice mail on pages 324–25.

APPOINT STAFFERS AS LIAISONS WITH REGULAR CALLERS OR CLIENTS. A staffer can serve as a "personal representative" for one or more frequent callers, handling all routine matters and referring callers to you only if a problem arises. Encourage clients to call their "personal rep" directly. The benefit for them is prompt attention.

KEEP CALLS BRIEF. Develop a roster of strategies for long-winded callers: "Let's make a telephone date. I have a break at 4:00 for ten minutes." One man who travels frequently returns calls from a phone booth at the airport. "When I tell people my flight leaves in five minutes, they tend to come to the point." Another manager has evolved this technique for dealing with the long-winded: "I keep a mental list of 'chatterers' and whenever possible I communicate with these people via memo or E-mail. I encourage them to do the same. It's saved me a lot of telephone time."

CONSOLIDATE CALL-BACKS. Return all calls at one time, beginning with priority calls. Shoot for a maximum two-day response time.

TIME YOUR RETURN CALLS. Call back when people are less inclined to chat: right before lunch or near the end of the day. Begin with a friendly but pointed: "Hi, Bob, I need a couple of quick answers if you've got a minute."

DEVELOP A UNIFORM SYSTEM FOR KEEPING TRACK OF CALL-BACKS. Says one manager: "I waste more time searching for messages and trying to remember who I have to call than I do on the phone itself." If you're prone to message slippage, try anchoring messages on an old-fashioned desk needle, or use a box. Avoid keeping them *under* anything, such as a paper-weight, where they can be buried. Some people list call-backs on their calendars, including expected return calls. When you have to keep track of numerous calls, both incoming and out-going, a formal phone log might be useful. Fashion your own (see sample below), or purchase forms that are available at stationery stores.

Dealing with Drop-in Visitors

A certain amount of interoffice visiting fosters a harmonious working environment. But when brief visits escalate into numerous and lengthy bull sessions, try one or several of these control methods:

"TAKE COVER." When possible, angle your secretary's desk so he or she can effectively intercept all visitors. A polite "John is busy now. Would you like me to interrupt him?" should deter all but the most nervy. Ask your secretary to

DATE	CALLER	TIME OF CALL	PURPOSE OF CALL	CALLER'S NUMBER

schedule an appointment with the visitor or suggest that the person come by at another, specified time.

If you don't have a secretary, or if your secretary's desk or office isn't near yours, keep your door closed during private work sessions. Even more effective: post a sign on your door or desk saying "Working privately between 9:00 and 10:30. Please come by later." One CEO took this idea a step further, installing a red panel light on her door—similar to those in broadcasting studios—which she turned on when she didn't want to be disturbed. If your desk is in the open, angle it so as not to catch the eye of passersby. Otherwise it's hard *not* to stop and chat.

Also try taking your work elsewhere. Work at home one or two mornings a week; decamp to a library or empty conference room; take colleagues to a hotel for long-range planning or brainstorming sessions.

CONSOLIDATE VISITORS. Schedule appointments and meetings into a specific block of time. The most practical method is to establish specific "open house" hours every day or several times a week, and encourage people to time their visits accordingly. If your secretary and staff are your most frequent visitors, set up regular meetings—daily, twice a week, or weekly as circumstances dictate—to cover all problems and questions at one time.

SET LIMITS. Limiting spur-of-the-moment sessions without seeming rude demands skill and tact. When someone pokes his head in the door saying, "Got a minute?" you might respond with "Could it wait until this afternoon? I'm really swamped right now." If you do decide to invite the visitor in, add that you "only have five minutes because. . . ." When the visitor is a subordinate, ask if the matter can keep until the next staff meeting. When the visitor is your boss, tactfully find out whether the matter is urgent since "I'm in the middle of a priority project." Most bosses will respect your attention to priorities.

One manager recommends use of a "time contract" for both scheduled and unscheduled appointments. "I begin these conversations with a polite but firm 'Let's try to wrap this up by such-and-such a time.' That sets both a goal and pace, and makes it easier for me to terminate the discussion at the appointed time."

CONFER IN COLLEAGUES' OFFICES. When colleagues ask to confer with you, try to meet in their offices rather than yours. It's much easier to excuse yourself than to ease someone out.

When an interruption is inevitable—whether phone call or visit—ease back into your work more smoothly with a *memory trigger*. Some people find it helpful to stop writing in mid-sentence; completing the thought later pulls them right back into the task. Others jot down a couple of key words to help them pick up the thread later.

You as Interrupter

How do you rate as an interrupter—of yourself and of others? Whenever you're tempted to drop in on someone else with a question or problem, ask: "What is the worst thing that could happen if I waited?" Check yourself out by logging your calls and spontaneous visits for one week, and evaluating whether their purposes really warranted the interruptions.

Beware another common—and disruptive—habit: keeping people waiting in your office while you do other things. Said a New Jersey coffee-machine supplier: "People lined up for their assignments in the morning, and I would let them wait endlessly while I talked on the phone. It didn't make for a happy working relationship." Focus on one person or issue at a time.

Fragmenting your own time is equally debilitating. One young sales manager who complained about frequent interruptions was himself the guilty party. He'd start the day by sorting no more than two or three letters before deciding he had to answer a memo from the warehouse manager. Halfway through the memo, he would get up to check his files and come across a note he had to discuss immediately with one of his colleagues. Then there were the frequent strolls to the coffee machine, the water cooler. . . . To keep yourself on track, finish each task before moving on to the next one. Jot any sudden ideas on your Master List for *later* action. And at least try not to involve others in your distraction.

Diagnosing Interruptions: Your Second Line of Defense

The techniques described above are based on the assumption that most visitors and callers *can* be postponed or channeled. Of course, there will always be some interruptions that must be dealt with immediately: for example, a buy decision on a materials shipment that must be made within the hour. However, when interruptions to which you *must* respond threaten to take over the day—when anti-interruption strategies have no effect—deeper issues may be involved. Like the sore throat that precedes a cold, a constant stream of interruptions suggests an underlying malady: A malfunction of the working system or a problem with your own management style. Finding the right cure begins with diagnosing the cause of the malady.

For at least one week, and preferably two, log every phone call and unexpected guest, noting the purpose of the call or visit and its duration. You can handle this informally, simply jotting each item on a piece of paper or, if you prefer a more systematic approach, making up an Interruption Log (see p. 150).

At the end of the logging period, cross out all *legitimate* interruptions: the genuine crises that could not have been predicted or prevented. Next, check off all calls and queries that your secretary or staffers could have handled (suppliers checking on due dates, clients requesting routine information, etc.). These are the *delegable* interruptions that should never have reached you in the first place. To eliminate these in the future, prepare guidelines for your secretary and staff about the kinds of calls that should be redirected.

Then, check off all routine or *garden-variety* interruptions—a staffer who dropped in with a question that could have waited until Friday's meeting, a client calling to chat, and so on. These are the calls and visits that can be postponed or fielded. If they continue to be a problem, review the tactics discussed earlier in the chapter for limiting, shortening, and rescheduling these distractions.

The remaining "problem" interruptions are symptomatic of a flaw in office procedures or management methods. They roughly divide into one of the three following categories:

Follow-ups on you: When calls begin "Where is the ⸺ you promised" or "I expected to hear from you last week," the problem isn't the telephone, but poor follow-up methods.

Solution: More attention to paperwork or task processing; more effective tickler systems. See Chapters 2, 5, and 8.

Staff inquiries: When subordinates continually seek you out for clarification of due dates, decisions, advice, support,

INTERRUPTION LOG

Week of ____

WHO	CALL?	VISIT?	LENGTH	PURPOSE	CATEGORY*

*Legitimate
Delegable
Garden-variety
Follow-up
Staff inquiry
Procedural

Leave "Category" blank until end of logging period.

or information, you can be pretty sure that you haven't fully explained the purpose and nature of an assignment or the range of their responsibility and authority.

Solution: Brief staffers fully about the why and how of every assignment. Make sure they understand how much authority they have. See Chapter 10.

Procedural/structural flaws: "Firefighting" calls or troubleshooting sessions are often the consequence of poor planning or awkward internal systems.

Solution: Identify the flaw and develop a method for circumventing it: perhaps better follow-up methods, regular planning sessions, or an office procedures manual. See Chapters 2 and 8. Examples:

The owner of a textiles firm was interrupted ten or fifteen times a day by his order clerks, who had no other source for the complex international trade information they needed. His solution: a chart for the clerks covering most queries. Similarly, a personnel department that was deluged with calls from job candidates cut the flow by two-thirds by sending each candidate an acknowledgment card stating, "We will let you know the status of your job bid within three weeks. We request that you do not call us in the meantime."

Now fill in the last column of the Interruption Log, categorizing each entry as either legitimate, delegable, garden-variety, follow-up, staff inquiry, or procedural. What percentage of total interruptions does the "legitimate" category make up? Fifteen percent? Fifty percent? Seventy percent? Unless your business *is* responding to late-breaking events, problem interruptions (that is, all the other categories combined) should take up no more than 20 percent or so of all unscheduled breaks in routine. A significant tilt toward problem interruptions suggests a need for review and implementation of the solutions described.

Streamlined Meetings

According to a study by the management consulting firm Booz, Allen & Hamilton, 299 managers spent half their time in meetings. And a sizable chunk of that time was absorbed by rambling discussions, political maneuvering, excessive socializing, and special-interest conflicts. Nor is time the only casualty. Five $70,000-a-year people spending ten useless hours a week in meetings can cost your firm well over $1,500 a week. Said the president of one small airline: "We were spending thousands of dollars at meetings to solve hundred-dollar problems. Now we don't call a meeting unless it promises to yield the company twice as much benefit as it costs us."

It isn't possible to arrive at an across-the-board determination of how much time to allocate for meetings because that figure will vary depending on your work. A senior management officer, for example, might spend 75 percent of his time in meetings, while for a technical expert 20 percent might be excessive. But you can determine if each meeting is necessary and, if so, whether it is doing its job.

Unnecessary meetings sometimes spring up because two people, trying to evade a thorny issue that just concerns them, call a general meeting. Said one manager of an engineering firm, "Turning an individual issue into a meeting is an industry problem." Can the question be handled by memo, telephone, an informal conference? For years, the four regional sales managers of a national manufacturing firm held monthly meetings in New York or Chicago, a practice that involved a great deal of preparation and travel time. Today, they meet only twice a year for longer planning sessions, and handle their monthly business via conference calls. Teleconferencing, or meetings via interactive television, is another option.

Some additional tips for cutting back on unnecessary meetings:

- *Establish a review process.* Often, committees set up to examine a particular issue outlive their usefulness. When possible, try to set a termination date at the outset, when a committee is formed. Or review its progress periodically, disbanding a committee that is no longer functional.
- *Consolidate.* The affirmative action director of a health-care corporation spent hours each month in individual meetings with divisional coordinators, covering basically the same information. Now she holds a monthly group meeting—which also helps the coordinators keep abreast of one another's activities and forges an *esprit de corps*.
- *Limit participation.* Since meetings tie up the time of some very high-priced talent, limit attendance to those directly involved. At the same time, make sure key people *are* present.

  Do you have to attend, or sit through the entire meeting? One analyst regularly enters meetings with the understanding that he will only stay for a short time unless the meeting is particularly pertinent to him.

When a meeting is to be held there is, presumably, a reason. Yet rarely are goals, issues, or purposes defined with any precision. Is the meeting doing its job? The first requisite for a productive meeting is an *action agenda:* a written list of specific questions or discussion topics. This agenda should be distributed at least a day in advance, and should include the desired objective of the meeting (decision, recommendation, update, etc.), papers or information that participants should bring, and any advance preparation (reading or studying certain documents) required. (See opposite page for a sample agenda from a law firm.) Major agenda items should be backed up with background materials, including a brief history, a list of proposed alternatives, and a recommendation as to which alternative to choose and why.

When feasible, have each participant prepare a brief presentation outlining a particular issue, possible solutions, and a proposed course of action. When planning an agenda for an extended conference or seminar, send a preliminary topic list to attendees for their comments, to ensure that you've covered all pertinent issues. For spur-of-the-moment meetings, state your objective immediately: "I'd like to get your reactions to the new ad campaign we're pitching. We're undecided between two approaches and I want your votes." In addition, employ these "productive meeting" tips:

- *Set limits.* To keep meetings on track, set a specific time limit and stick to it. Lunchtime or quitting time provides built-in limits. One publishing company, for example, begins its weekly editorial meeting at 4:00 P.M. and generally covers all business by 5:00 or 5:30. Another publisher opens the meeting at 3:00 P.M., and also finishes by 5:00. Try to cover all priority issues first and close the meeting at the appointed hour, holding pending matters until the next meeting.
- *Use lists.* For informal or impromptu staff meetings, as well as one-on-one appointments and phone conversations, make a list of all the issues you want to cover. Use your "meeting" or "referral" folders as a running agenda for ideas, questions, or matters to discuss.

AGENDA FOR THE WEEKLY MEETING OF THE PARTNERS
OF THE LAW FIRM OF SMITH, SMITH, HERTZ & SMITH

1 Should we increase our paralegal staff? Henry Bing-
ham has compiled statistics on the role, costs, and
benefits of paralegals based on the experience of
other firms. *Objective:* Decision, and if it is positive,
what steps to take next.

2 A very hefty percentage of our firm's resources is
directed toward servicing only three large corporate
clients. This leaves us highly vulnerable if even one
client should withdraw. Let's discuss this possibility, and what steps we might take to widen our base.
Objective: Discussion, and recommendations for
further action.

3 Farewell party for retiring partner. *Objective:* Decide who is going to be in charge of party arrangements, what gift we should get, etc.

The second requisite for productive meetings is a *follow-up
system.* Explains one manager: "Several months ago at an advertising meeting, the vice president closed with a vague 'let's
take a look into the portfolio of that hot new ad agency.' Well,
everyone there assumed someone else would handle the assignment. Of course, no one did, and two months later we learned
that the agency had accepted a competitor's account. Now we
follow up on *everything.*"

Try to reach a decision or hand-off point on each item, and
define steps and due dates to implement decisions, preferably
in writing. One effective device is to use a traditional steno pad
to differentiate general notes from tasks and assignments,

using one column for notes and the other for specifics. Have the assignments typed up and distributed that day or the next. When a meeting closes with a vague "Jill will look into that problem," request specific details—who is supposed to do what by when—so that the notes will be clear. To monitor recurring meetings, simply update the same basic agenda each week. In one corporate training department, the departmental secretary took complete notes at one meeting, which she typed up and E-mailed to participants. Thereafter, one of the participants simply handwrote new information on a copy of the previous week's agenda, and returned it to the secretary for updating and distribution. Some other practical tips:

- Begin each meeting by clarifying old business—checking on the status or results of previously assigned projects.
- Hold a meeting wrap-up five minutes before its close: restate decisions, and review assignments and deadlines.
- For impromptu meetings, record your own and others' assignments on your Master List. Then follow up with calendar, tickler, or referral folder.

Finally, productive meetings depend on *leadership*. Unstructured sessions are usually unproductive. Someone—either the ranking participant or resident expert—should act as moderator, ensuring that discussions adhere to the central issues.

To assess departmental or company meetings, you might keep an informal record for one or two weeks of all meetings attended—both impromptu and scheduled—and their duration. An evaluation of the following questions should help clarify the value of each meeting and identify any particular problems.

1 Were you a participant or essentially a spectator?
2 What specifically was accomplished at the meeting?
3 Was duration consistent with results?
4 Did certain individuals (perhaps including yourself) interrupt with side issues or special-interest topics?
5 Were all assignments, recommendations, and so forth clarified and followed up?

On the Road: Business Travel

Advance preparation is a must for frequent travelers. Many executives keep a prepacked toiletry and overnight kit at home, containing nightwear, robe, slippers, and such items as a radio, clock, or camera. This kit should be checked and replenished after each use so it's ready to go when you are. I also recommend preplanned packing lists—one for an overnight trip, one for a week's trip to one place, one for a week's trip to two or three cities. These lists can virtually automate packing and enable you to assemble everything in fifteen or twenty minutes.

Also useful is a ready-to-go travel briefcase, equipped with address book, pens and pencils, calculator, portable dictation equipment and cassettes, and prestamped mailers and envelopes. Check and restock after each trip. For a discussion of how to get the most out of traveling with a portable computer, see pages 319–20.

"You simply have to take the time to organize your work *before* you leave," says one manager, who systematically packs his briefcase to coincide with the different parts of his trip: work to be accomplished during flight "A" in the first compartment, work for flight "B" in the second compartment, and so on. List the papers you'll need on your calendar for the day before, and set up a "trip folder" to collect papers and materials as they turn up.

Prepare four copies of a written itinerary: one for yourself, one for your secretary, one for your spouse, and one for the hotel desk at your destination. Include hotels, appointments, and the names, office addresses, and office phone numbers (also, if possible, home numbers) of the people you'll be meeting. In addition, a travel checklist—a concise form listing all pertinent information—can be of great value. The sample on pages 160–61 was designed by Catherine Lee, a public relations vice president. Her secretary fills one out for each trip.

Here are additional practical tips for a well-planned trip:

- *"On location"*: Be sure to schedule enough commuting time between appointments, especially in a big city. New Yorkers particularly, who are used to picking up taxis within a limited midtown or downtown area, often find the "wide open spaces" of other cities unsettling. If feasible, you might wish to consider booking a limousine or taxi, rather than renting your own car. Pick up a taxi in the line at your hotel and keep the cab for the day. It's expensive but often worth the price in peace of mind.
- *Keeping up with paperwork:* To forestall a paperwork backlog, daily dispose of as many papers as possible with your secretary over the phone: dictate brief replies to letters; refer items to colleagues. Ask your secretary to process what routine mail he or she can, checking with you only on substantive matters, logging each item—noting sender, basic content, and action taken—to give you a rundown on your return. Appoint a backup person to whom your secretary can turn if something comes up that he or she can't handle during your absence. For your part, keep things moving along: E-mailing or taping letters,

transactions, and meetings summaries as you go, mailing cassettes back to the office in pre-prepared envelopes.

When Norma Fox, editor-in-chief of Insight Books, goes away for an extended trip, she asks her secretary to fax only the most urgent correspondence to her, and to stack the rest of the incoming mail into five piles: priority mail, ordinary mail, interoffice memos, manuscripts, and periodicals. Fox looks through the priority and interoffice stacks on her first day back, handling any pressing matters, and processes thereafter a fixed number of papers per day from each pile. She is always caught up within one to two weeks.

- *Expenses:* Many travelers prefer to keep receipts for all expenditures. Collecting receipts makes it easier to separate reimbursed expenses, personal deductible expenses, and personal nondeductibles. If feasible, use one credit card for all business expenses, and another for personal expenditures. Keep receipts in *one* place—preferably a compartment in your wallet or pocket calendar. One frequent traveler takes an expense account form with him, marking it up as he goes and giving it to his secretary for retyping on his return.

- *Planning your return:* Try to schedule your return for late afternoon or early evening, so that you're winding down at the end of a normal working day. Or return very early in the morning to start the day as you would any other. Returning in the middle of the day often makes it difficult to ease back into the office routine, especially if you're suffering from jet lag. To facilitate easy readjustment, you might leave an easy project on your desk, ready to be picked up smoothly on your return.

TRAVEL CHECKLIST

Catherine Lee
VP, Public Relations

FLIGHT INFO

Going   Return

_____ Reservations   _____
_____ Which airport?   _____
_____ Ground transportation   _____
_____ Seating   _____
_____   1st choice—bulkhead   _____
_____   2nd choice—aisle   _____
_____ Meal preference: _____
_____   1st choice—veg.   _____
_____   2nd choice—seafood   _____
_____ Tickets received   _____

AT DESTINATION

Hotel: _____

Single; queen-size bed   _____

Business discount rate?   _____

Confirmation received?   _____

Car booking (sedan)   _____

Rental company   _____

Rates $ _____

Directions to destination   _____
                                          _____
                                          _____

PERSONAL

Cash needed   _____

Cash arranged (traveler's checks)   _____

ITINERARY AND SCHEDULE CHECKLIST

Type up following information on sheet of paper that Ms. Lee will take with her:

Flight information	☐
Ground transportation	☐
Car rental information	☐
Hotel (address and phone)	☐
Hotel rate	☐
Name of hotel contact	☐
Reservation number	☐
Confirmation form stapled to itinerary?	☐
Schedule at destination (includes addresses, phone numbers, directions)	☐
Names, addresses, phone numbers, and fax numbers of people Ms. Lee wants to get in touch with	☐

MS. LEE'S "TAKE" KIT

Tickets	☐
Itinerary and schedule	☐
Cash	☐
Hotel brochure	☐
Company directory	☐
Travel briefcase (includes tape recorder, cassettes, papers, calculator, notebook computer, pads, pens, appointment book, business cards)	☐

Summary: Charting Timewasters and Solutions

First Line of Defense: Anti-Interruption Strategies

CALLS	VISITORS
Secretary intercept.	Secretary intercept.
Colleague exchange.	"Quiet hour" sign on door.
Appoint staffers as "personal reps" for regular callers.	Angle desk to avoid eye contact.
Roster of "getting off phone" techniques.	Take private work elsewhere.
Return calls at one time. Shoot for two-day response time.	Consolidate visitors into blocks of time.
Call before lunch or near end of day.	Set "time contracts."
	Confer in colleagues' offices rather than your own.

Second Line of Defense: Diagnosing "Problem" Interruptions

PROBLEM	SOLUTION
Routine calls or visits that are referrable	Give secretary/staff specific guidelines for redirecting and fielding calls and inquiries. Appoint staffers as "personal reps" for frequent callers and visitors.
People following up on you	Process paperwork and other tasks more promptly; use more effective tickler systems. See

PROBLEM	SOLUTION
	Chapters 2, 5, and 8. Keep associates abreast of progress.
Frequent staff inquiries	Brief staffers fully; clarify purpose of each assignment and range of staffer responsibility and authority. See Chapter 10, pages 237–65
Queries or confusion resulting from awkward office procedures or systems	Identify flaw and circumvent it; try better follow-up methods, regular planning sessions, an office procedures manual, employee training seminars. See Chapter 2 and Chapter 8.

Streamlining Meetings

Eliminate unnecessary meetings	Try an alternative: memo, telephone, conference call. Set review and termination dates for committees. Don't attend if your presence isn't mandatory, or stay only as long as discussion is relevant to you.
Action agenda	For formal meetings, distribute typed list of topics in advance; note papers/information participants should bring; define meeting objectives (decision, further study, update, actions, etc.). For informal meetings, convey same information orally. For periodic meetings, have someone update basic agenda.

Set time limits	Set a specific limit, and start on time. Five minutes before close, review decisions and assignments. Lunchtime and quitting time offer built-in limits.
Follow up	Clarify—in writing—all assignments and recommendations, and distribute to participants as soon as possible. Follow up at a subsequent meeting or during regular interactions with those people.
Take control	The meeting should be moderated, ensuring that discussion stays on track, either by ranking member or resident expert.

On the Road: Business Travel

Preplan	Keep prepacked overnight kit ready to go. For longer trips, automate packing with preplanned lists of clothing, accessories, etc.
Office preparations	Keep prepacked travel briefcase. Check and restock after each use. Prepare written itinerary and travel information. Note on your calendar for day before departure: all files and papers

	you'll need, and reminder to take "trip folder."
Process papers	Conduct daily paperwork session with your secretary via telephone. Dictate trip-related letters, assignments, etc., on the road and mail back to your secretary. Communicate by E-mail and fax if you use a portable computer. Keep receipts in *one* place.

7

Fight Procrastination by Finding Your Personal Work Profile

We have met the enemy and they is us.
—Pogo

Steve Williamson and Alan Drew own a small technical consulting firm. Both men put in a full eight- or nine-hour day, but when Drew leaves the office, it's usually with a full briefcase. He will often spend two hours "perfecting" a report that could have been completed in forty-five minutes. When it comes to time, he's his own worst enemy, a victim of the "But I've always done it that way" syndrome. Williamson, on the other hand, rarely brings work home. He accomplishes, during his eight hours in the office, tasks that might take Drew twice as long. The difference between the two men: Drew is effective—he gets his priority work done first—while Williamson is both effective and efficient.

Effectiveness, as defined by management consultant Peter Drucker, is doing the right job: knowing what to do and when to do it—investing your time for the greatest return. But effectiveness is seriously blunted without the second element of productive time use: efficiency, defined as *doing the right job in the right way*. Combining the two is the key to the time-management process.

How you use time often reflects long-ingrained habits. Like Alan Drew, many managers lose time not so much to externals like interruptions, but to their own brand of self-sabotage, be it procrastination, perfectionism, or an inefficient work style. They get caught up in a pattern because they've "always" done it that way. The solution involves rethinking your use of time: retraining yourself, unlearning counterproductive habits, developing a personal work style that's comfortable and functional, and finding the simplest, most economical way of doing things.

Procrastination: A Problem/Solution Approach

People procrastinate for all sorts of reasons: some because they dislike or feel overwhelmed by the task at hand, others because they don't know where to start or how to handle it. Still other people put things off because that final rush to meet a deadline is a kind of "high"; with adrenalin pumping and the mind racing, those last few hours can add excitement to an otherwise predictable routine.

But when procrastination begins to affect the quality of your work, it becomes a form of self-sabotage you can't indulge. You've hit bedrock when you delay a project to sharpen pencils by the gross; postpone a fifty-hour job until you have fifty hours; or plan to start a project "as soon as . . ." (fill in the blank!). Manufacturing artful excuses or busywork to justify avoiding a task only reinforces the habit. To establish a new, more productive set of habits, the first step is to identify the types of situations that ring the procrastination bell. The problems listed below cover most causes of procrastination. Choose the solutions that seem to work best for you. The point is to find a more comfortable and efficient way of handling all the jobs that usually get put off "till tomorrow"—a way that will release your energies for action.

Problem: A dull or unpleasant task.

Solution 1: Delegate. Whenever possible, let someone else do it: assign the project, or part of it, to a subordinate. Hire an outside service. Or swap tasks with a colleague. One magazine editor writes headlines for a colleague who takes on the proofreading she hates. Avoid the martyr's role by asking: "Is it more important that *I* do this job, or that it gets done?"

Solution 2: Reward. Create your own positive reinforcement. Promise yourself a specific treat when you've completed the job—anything from a new paperback to a day at the races. Have a favorite snack at arm's reach. Or keep music playing if it inspires you.

Problem: An overwhelming or complex project.

Solution 1: Divide the task into manageable components. When you're dragging your feet on a task that seems endless or insurmountable, break it down into simpler components and add one or two to each Daily List until the project is completed. To melt away long-term, repetitive projects, industrial psychologist Robert Tyson suggests making up daily "packages": reorganize three files a day; make four phone calls; answer five backed-up letters.

Try Alan Lakein's "swiss cheese" technique: punch holes into multifaceted jobs by executing "instant" tasks that can be done in five minutes or less. Start a major research paper with one phone call to get preliminary information; begin planning the annual sales conference by collecting hotel brochures. Taking these "baby steps" will often get you moving.

Solution 2: Divide large tasks according to time available. One entrepreneur produced documentation for a bank loan on alternate Sunday mornings between 6:00 and 8:00—her only "free" time. Health writer Jane Brody of *The New York Times* completed a 500-page book working from 5:00 to 6:30 A.M. on weekday mornings. Also try the variation suggested by negotiation specialist Gerard Nierenberg: choose tasks that will fill the time available. Tackle a bigger task during a free three-hour time slot, rather than several smaller jobs.

Solution 3: Handle a big job in "rounds." Build from the broad and general to the more refined. Sort a paper backlog into a few broad categories, as detailed in Chapter 2. Then decide how to handle each piece. Outline a report first, then draft it, then begin writing it.

Problem: No prospect of immediate results or benefits.

Solution: Build in "mini" completions. Motivating yourself to begin a project that won't come to fruition for weeks or months can be difficult. Provide yourself with that necessary sense of gratification by establishing interim completion points. Get feedback on the first draft of a policy paper. Publish a section of a long report in the company newsletter.

Problem: Being stymied. You don't know how to handle a project or where to start.

Solution 1: Identify action steps. Execution of any project must begin with one of seven specific actions: collecting information, writing a letter or memo, calling someone, seeing someone, giving an assignment, holding a meeting, or reading (reports, documents, etc.). In no special order, list as many specific tasks as come to you—two preliminary calls, library research, a proposal draft, and so on. Then establish an "action sequence"—organizing tasks in their order of performance. Finally, set deadlines, delegate what you can, enter personal-action tasks on your Master List and, when appropriate, transfer them to your Daily List, following up in the usual way.

Solution 2: Make an arbitrary start. If an "opening move" continues to elude you, make an arbitrary start. The big desk reorganization described in Chapter 2, for example, began with the stack of papers to your right, simply to establish a starting point. Or suppose you can't decide whether or not to break a report into two parts. *Make an assumption*—that the report will be a single document—and begin. If that approach isn't right, you'll soon realize it and can then make the necessary changes. Always be prepared to change a course of action if you seem to come to a dead end.

Solution 3: Prepare a task breakdown chart. Translate a broad but amorphous goal into concrete tasks by working from manifestations of the problem down to particulars by way of the task breakdown chart opposite.

Problem: A project requiring constant checking or monitoring.

Solution: Set up flagpoints. The prospect of riding herd on a project can be daunting enough to cause you to put it on indefinite hold. To minimize monitoring, establish checkpoints for all jobs that involve multiple processes or numerous materials. For example, group long lists of figures into

TASK BREAKDOWN CHART—AN EXAMPLE

Goal: Make unit more efficient without increasing office space or staff.

PROBLEM MANIFESTATIONS	WHAT TO DO	WAYS TO IMPLEMENT
Cash lag—billing or processing of receivables is too slow.	Open more space for accounts receivable equipment—only have space now for one computer, file bank, etc.	Call Beecher to recommend contractor. Call contractor to estimate cost of turning storage space into office space. Interview members of unit to define equipment and space needs (assign to Jim). Compare equipment capabilities, service, training, and cost (assign to Helen).
Project documents lost in files. Files expanding into cardboard boxes.	Improve information retrieval.	Reorganize files; call consultant. "File storage program." What do we keep, for how long? Defer till consultant's visit. Need new cabinets? Defer till consultant's visit. Investigate microfilm (assign to Helen)

. . . et cetera. As you begin to list specifics, more will quickly come to mind, breaking the log jam of inaction. Enter the items in the "Ways to Implement" column on your Master List, handling them in the usual way.

blocks of thirty or so and check each block individually. If a discrepancy occurs, at least the range of error will be confined to one block.

The following tips may also prove helpful in combating procrastination:

- *Plan an event.* Six months after moving to new quarters, the employees of one company were still surrounded by unpacked crates. So they sent out invitations to an office-warming party for the following month, thus forcing themselves to get the place in shape.
- *"Give in" to procrastination.* Do *nothing* for fifteen minutes. Then, according to time-management expert Alan Lakein, "you should become very uneasy . . . after ten minutes I'm off and running." Or try this variation suggested by a busy lawyer: stare at your papers, forbidding yourself to touch them for fifteen or twenty minutes. "By that time," he says, "you will be virtually on fire to get at them."
- *Apply the "well, as long as I . . ." technique.* "As long as I've got this file open, I'll organize it." "As long as this paper is in my hand, I'll process it."
- *Create a conducive physical environment.* Are the materials you need laid out conveniently? Although many people work effectively amidst (organized!) piles of paper, others find the visual clutter distracting. If you're one of the latter, clear everything off your desk except the task at hand, and work on nothing else for at least one hour.

  If your surroundings are depressing, your work may suffer. So brighten up whatever you can to create a pleasant and comfortable working environment.

When you can't pinpoint a specific cause for procrastination, deeper issues may be involved. Are you delaying a project because you question its value or the planned approach? Do you resist certain assignments because you feel you're not commanding the respect or salary you deserve? Is fear of failure holding you back from action? Are personal problems intruding on your concentration at work? A sense of the "why" of procrastination will give you a start in overcoming the problem.

The Search for Perfection

When he was asked to prepare a brief review of trade connections between the United States and Saudi Arabia, a financial analyst produced an exhaustive, meticulously researched study that not only won him no points, but brought him a reprimand from his superiors—because his time would have been more profitably employed elsewhere. A city planner spent hours drawing up a series of intricate and beautifully designed flowcharts, although his department's needs—and his own schedule—would have been better served by a more informal method. These are classic examples of perfectionism: a compulsive striving for an ideal of excellence or "organization" far beyond any actual utilitarian purpose.

Even more typical is the perfect job that never gets done. For years, one corporate training director talked about the manual he would write—when he had time. It would be a veritable standard for training manuals. Not surprisingly, since his expectation was so grandiose, he never found the time, and meanwhile his staff struggled along without written guidelines. An advertising executive who received a proposal from an artist friend planned to work up an impeccable presentation on it before passing it along to the creative director.

But she seemed never to have the time to do the kind of job she wanted. Weeks later, when she finally made her presentation, it was too late; the artist had received another commission and her company lost the services of a top-notch professional.

Consider whether you are putting (or thinking about putting) disproportionate effort into a task. Do the means suit the ends? Challenge yourself with these questions:

Does the payoff on this task warrant the effort put into it? Where is the point of diminishing returns?

Is there a simpler, less exacting way to accomplish it? What are the consequences, positive and negative, of using a less elaborate approach?

Will you be giving short shrift to other important projects because of the time you'll be spending on this one? Will your perfectionism result in a missed deadline or serious delay?

Another manifestation of perfectionism is the misplaced attempt to do *everything* perfectly, regardless of its relative importance. One newspaper assignments editor tried to deal so thoroughly with every idea that crossed her desk that she rarely met her deadlines. By allocating her time more realistically, she put minimum effort into less important tasks. She began categorizing each project as a *definite* interest, *probable* interest, *conceivable* interest, or *no* interest. Definites went into her action box; probables were sent out for other opinions and marked for follow-up within two weeks. Conceivables were acknowledged, shelved for several months, and then reviewed. "No's" were returned immediately with an appropriate form letter. The point is to gauge the minimum effort required to accomplish the desired result—to learn to recognize when enough is enough.

Finding Your Optimum Work Style

Fred Evans, who heads a branch office of a large manufacturing firm, has to prepare a monthly status report for the home office that includes employee evaluations and a production rundown. Because he dislikes doing the evaluations, which make up the first section of the report, he usually procrastinates on the report until the last minute. On the other hand, he enjoys the statistical analyses that comprise the second half of the report. Why, I asked him, didn't he begin with that section to provide the momentum to carry him into the evaluation section? He laughed. "Actually, I never thought of that. Since I was a kid I always heard 'first things first' and I guess the message really sank in. But for me, 'first things last' probably would be a better approach." The following month he made the simple switch. The upshot: the report was completed quickly and ahead of schedule.

The "how" of any project depends to a great extent on your personality and temperament. Like Fred Evans, you may find that "first things first" is not your style. Is your typical "method of attack" consistent with your temperament? Is pressure inspiring or crippling? Can you concentrate for long periods, or do you need frequent breaks? The point is to rethink your usual "shoulds" and "oughts" about handling projects. The only right way is the way that's natural and right for you. Working "against the grain" is a sure road to inefficiency—or procrastination. In contrast, true productivity is realized by identifying your work style and matching it to the task at hand.

What follows is a compilation of common work styles. Experiment with them for a week or so, then settle in with those that seem most comfortable.

Begin at the center of a task and work out. Start with the most profitable, difficult, or important parts of big projects. "Confront the demons all up front," suggests one publishing executive. "Otherwise, unpleasant or difficult tasks begin to loom larger and larger in the background. Sometimes it's painful, but in the long run it saves a lot of time." *Caution:* Beware of neglecting the easier tasks.

Begin at the outside and work in. Ease into tough assignments by warming up with simpler, routine, or more pleasurable aspects. One textbook writer, for example, always begins a new book by compiling an index card file of major research topics. This simple pre-preparation is usually enough to "psych" him for the complicated research and writing ahead. *Caution:* Overinvolvement with details may lead to neglect of major aspects. If you have a problem in getting to the heart of the matter, set a time limit on your ease-in tasks.

Follow a standard format. Establish a rhythm that carries you into the substance of a project. For example, I always begin client reports by writing a standard introduction— name, address, nature of consultation, and so on. Prepare simple outlines of all reports before writing them. Reread previous advertising copy before drafting new blurbs. Follow a well-established routine to ease into a difficult task.

Consider the deadline factor. Samuel Johnson pointed out that imminent execution "does concentrate the mind wonderfully." And for many people, putting a task off until the last minute is a positive inspiration. However, be sure you have the necessary information or preliminary documentation on hand before last-minute pressure builds. On the other hand, if you're immobilized by tight deadlines, factor in the extra time you'll need to maintain serenity.

Use "block" work patterns. Some people give over an entire afternoon or day to one major project, allocating other days for meetings or busywork. One manager maintains "project pockets," blocking out a minimum of three days a month for planning and writing policy manuals. *Caution:* Set reasonable limits. When you spend too much time on one project, you run the risk of obsessing over it, and losing all sense of perspective about the quality of your work. When your concentration and mental energy begin to flag—or when the sentence you've read three times makes no sense—quit.

Use "short burst" work patterns. For many people, variety is the spice of office life, and they prefer to break up their days, scheduling brief spells of concentrated work between appointments, paperwork, and so on. They often juggle two or three projects simultaneously, switching back and forth if attention flags. A New York editor who co-produces an independent cable TV production, doing all necessary work during her lunch hour, says, "If I had all day Sunday to work, nothing would get done, but with a limited, well-defined time like lunch, I become superorganized."

Caution: Breaking stride too often may lead to an array of unfinished projects. Try to work to a natural "pause" point on each task. If you can't point to substantial accomplishment over the course of a week, if everything is half-finished, you've slid over the line into distraction and need to refocus on one thing at a time.

So far we've concentrated on creating a working climate that will permit you to take advantage of basic efficiency techniques. The remainder of the chapter will help you to build that integral combination of effectiveness *and* efficiency.

Realizing True Efficiency

Certain actions are profoundly efficient—as direct, simple, and graceful as the beautiful arc of connection between quarterback and receiver on a good pass, or the elegant motion of a mason laying bricks. True efficiency is, simply, economy of means, and is unrelated to the popular notions of robotic rigidity or frantic activity. I once refused a commission from a young, hyperenergetic investment banker who wanted every minute of his day "packed" with activities in his quest for "increased productivity." His pseudoefficiency threatened his health, peace of mind, and, in the end, the productivity he so urgently sought. He failed to realize that the simplest, least wasteful system is the key to realizing both efficiency and greater productivity.

For lawyer Ralph Anderson, realizing efficiency began with a stroll back to his days as a junior entrepreneur. "When I was ten," Anderson recalls, "I had a morning paper route. Damned if I didn't manage to fold, pack, and deliver all those papers, pick up groceries for my mother, and eat breakfast— all before school started. But somewhere along the way I lost those ten-year-old smarts. Now so many of the things I do— from preparing briefs to researching a case—seem to take longer than they should. What am I doing wrong?"

Actually, it's less a case of what he's doing wrong than what he's not doing: utilizing the six key efficiency techniques that came so naturally when he was younger—standardizing, consolidating, redistributing, anticipating, fitting means to ends, and using time so as to get the most productive return on his time dollar.

STANDARDIZE. Find a routine way to handle repetitive tasks. Every morning Ralph followed the same procedure: dividing the papers into three piles, which he and his "assistants" (his mother and sister) folded; adding them to a nearby burlap sack; and following a delivery route plotted out so that he only covered the same territory once.

Identifying tasks that are susceptible to standardization releases time and mental energy for tasks that are not. For example: Develop a basic format for the weekly inventory-control report and simply add new figures each week. Formulate a consistent protocol for the weekly staff meeting and follow it religiously. Many of the techniques proposed in this book, from sorting papers to scheduling, are standardized procedures. See Chapter 3 for more information about standardizing paperwork.

CONSOLIDATE. Combine separate actions. A luncheonette waitress is a time-and-motion expert's delight. She delivers an order to the next table, brings set-ups to yours, wipes your table, collects your order and other orders, and picks up stacks of dirty dishes as she returns to the kitchen. She is a splendid example of consolidation.

Group your actions in similar fashion. When you're off to pick up your restitched briefcase at lunchtime, check your Master List for other errands, and try to take care of as many as possible. Similarly, return all phone calls at once; dictate all letters at one time; pull all files you'll need for the day.

Consolidate the activities of other people as well. Distribute assignments to secretary and executive assistant at the same time. Cover a number of items in one informal session with several staff members. If possible, meet with several prospective clients or customers at the same time. Doctors usually "run" several patients simultaneously: one undergoing preliminaries with a nurse, a second being examined, a third waiting in the doctor's office for a post-examination conference. Does your work lend itself to a similar approach: Can you schedule parallel meetings with several clients, and can certain aspects of your job be handled by a subordinate?

REDISTRIBUTE. Ralph managed to press his mother and sister into service. Follow his tactic and solicit the help of your secretary, assistants, and colleagues whenever possible. Use the services of consultants and professionals. Have a travel agent handle all the arrangements for the Caribbean sales conference. Hire a photo researcher to find the artwork for the new brochure. It can't be said too often: delegate.

Save time on personal errands as well. Use merchants—druggists, dry cleaners, grocers—that offer pick-up and delivery services. Hire a messenger service to deliver packages. One working mother employed a taxi company to chauffeur her children to their various appointments. See Chapter 10 for more information on delegation and consulting services.

DEVELOP AN OPTIMUM PHYSICAL LAYOUT. Arrange your office to facilitate simple, spare movement patterns. Can you reach your computer, files, calculator, and so forth with a swivel of your chair? Do you have all the equipment you'll need for a new project easily accessible?

ANTICIPATE/PREPLAN. Identify aspects of a task that are susceptible to advance preparation. Ralph put his sack and bike into position the night before.

An engineer who has not yet received final specifications for a stress analysis can calculate certain stress points in advance. Lawyers can research the plaintiffs' backgrounds before receiving all the particulars of the case.

Preplan the basics for the day to come: check your calendar

and make up tomorrow's Daily List before leaving for the day. Decide on clothing and breakfast fixings the night before, and have everything ready that you'll need to take to the office: notes for the next day's meeting, the evening's theater tickets, whatever.

Fɪᴛ Mᴇᴀɴs ᴛᴏ Eɴᴅs. Avoid putting disproportionate effort into any project. This is no recommendation for less than full investment in your work, but for execution that fully meets the demands of the task and stops there. Before beginning a complex or involved project, evaluate whether it could be simplified—reduced in frequency, scope, or detail. Whenever a project seems to be taking longer than it should, or when you're setting up a new project, consult the Task Efficiency Audit on the opposite page to help improve your performance and keep yourself on track.

Getting the Most from Five Minutes

- *Use small parcels of time.* Handle small projects while you are waiting for appointments, standing in lines, or stalled in traffic. Tuck a small stack of articles or reports in your briefcase or handbag. Carry a pocket recorder for "in transit" dictation.
  What you can do in five minutes:
    Make an appointment.
    Prepare a meeting attendance list.
    Dictate a short letter or write a note.
    Boot up your computer.
  What you can do in ten minutes:
    Make a brief phone call or two.
    Organize a small pile of papers on your desk.
    Proofread a short report.

TASK EFFICIENCY AUDIT

1 Is your "method of attack" consistent with your temperament? Do you respond well to pressure, or does it cripple you? Can you concentrate for long periods of time, or do you need frequent breaks? — *Find your best work style*

2 Can you utilize a format from a previous similar project, or incorporate pertinent aspects of it? — *Standardize*

3 Do project components fall into natural groupings? — *Consolidate*

4 Can subtasks be delegated? Can you use an outside service to save time? — *Redistribute*

5 Is the equipment you'll need easily accessible? Can you prepare certain aspects in advance? Collect certain information? — *Anticipate*

6 Are you overchecking results, or being more precise than is warranted? Can you simplify the task? — *Fit means to ends*

Jot notes for next week's meeting agenda.
Order tickets for a concert or ball game.
What you can do in thirty minutes or less:
    Outline a report.
    Skim a report, marking sections for later study.
    Skim journals, magazines, newspapers.
    File a week's worth of papers in desk-side files.
    Organize a stack of papers.

- *Double up on tasks.* Many tasks that don't require your full concentration can be handled simultaneously. Listen to taped reports while driving to work, or dictate letters while stuck in traffic. Learn a foreign language or take a course—on tape. Sort and sign routine papers while returning routine phone calls; flip through trade magazines or your junk mail folder when you're on the phone with a long-winded caller.
- *Make good use of nonpeak hours.* Eat lunch before or after the rush, or order in. Try to time trips to the bank and other busy places to avoid lunch hour or rush hour. Avoid banks altogether on Fridays, when many people cash paychecks. Can you change your schedule to avoid rush hour travel?
- *Plan ahead.* If you do commute, have your change ready before moving on to a toll road. Or hang a cabbie's change dispenser from the dashboard. Check your calendar before leaving the office for an appointment or errands to see if you have coordinated as many activities as possible.
- *Plot direct movements.* Make your rounds in one part of town at one time. Plot your course to move in the most direct way. The magazine *Execu-time* posed this question: "Should your dry cleaner, auto repair shop, and shoe man *really* be in your home neighborhood, or would you be better off dealing with someone near work? Try to find services on your commuting route for the least lost time of all."
- *Think "quick and easy."* Consider alternatives: is the expressway really the only way to get to work? Would a less-traveled secondary road provide a faster, more hassle-free commute?
- *Use public transportation*—train, bus, subway, taxi—when feasible. Leave the driving to them and tackle some of your work, read, or rest. Or consider a car pool.

SUMMARY: WHAT IS YOUR PERSONAL WORK PROFILE?

Procrastination Primer

PROBLEM	SOLUTION
You dislike the task.	Delegate if possible. Create motivation by planning a reward upon completion.
The project is overwhelming in its complexity.	Break into simpler steps and tackle one or two each day. Choose tasks to fill the time available. Handle projects in rounds.
Payoff—and gratification—are not immediate.	Build in "mini" completion points that will provide some immediate gratification.
You don't know how to handle a task.	Identify action steps, then formulate their sequence.
You don't know where to start.	Make an arbitrary start. Make an assumption and follow through. If it's the wrong approach, try another until one works out.
The task requires extensive supervision.	Set up checkpoints that will allow you to monitor less often. Check parts, sections, or blocks of the work.
Perfectionism.	Evaluate whether the payoff warrants the effort you're giving the task. Gauge the point of diminishing returns. Consider whether there's a simpler, less

PROBLEM	SOLUTION
	exacting way to accomplish the task, and whether your existing habits will mean serious delays.

Work Style Audit

STYLE	DESCRIPTION
Begin at the center of a task and work out.	Start with the most profitable, difficult, or important parts of big projects.
Begin at the outside and work in.	Ease into tough assignments by warming up with simpler or routine aspects.
Follow a standard format.	Establish a rhythm that carries you into the substance of a project.
Consider the deadline factor.	If last-minute pressure is challenging, fine, but be sure you have all the necessary materials on hand. If pressure is immobilizing for you, factor in plenty of extra time.
Use "block" work patterns.	Schedule an entire day, or days, for one major project, allocating other days for meetings or busywork.
Use "short burst" work patterns.	Break up your day, scheduling brief spells of concentrated work between appointments, paperwork, and so on.

Efficiency/Effectiveness Audit

TECHNIQUE	DESCRIPTION
Standardize	Utilize a format from a previous similar project, or incorporate pertinent parts.
Consolidate	Group related tasks or components, and handle them at one time.
Redistribute	Delegate tasks to secretary, assistants, colleagues. Use outside services or consultants whenever feasible.
Develop optimum physical layout	Arrange your office to facilitate simple, spare movements.
Anticipate	Collect materials for a project in advance. Identify aspects of a task that are susceptible to advance preparation.
Fit means to end	Simplify your procedures; do only what's necessary to accomplish your goal and no more.

8

Project Management

Make everything as simple as possible, but not more so.
—ALBERT EINSTEIN

Frank Harvey, vice president of marketing at a large food service company, runs an in-house project-management seminar for managers. He initiated the seminar because when he was a young manager, a missed deadline almost cost him his career. He recalls:

> I'd had almost no training in project design and control, but I was ambitious and convinced my boss to let me handle a major project: setting up a market research study on new food trends that included forecasting the results of potential changes in our product lines. I managed to get the various steps in motion, but I was hopeless at tracking all the details. And because there were so many problems with the field study, I was way behind deadline on the report. My boss, who was getting flack from above, probably would have fired me except for the fact that bringing someone else in would have meant even more delays. What ultimately saved my

neck was that the report was damned good—when I finally finished it.

Which is why I started the seminar. Because I know what inexperience can mean, I think it's critical for young managers to learn how to organize and monitor a complex project. And not-so-young ones too. In fact, a number of senior managers are taking the course.

A project is any highly complex task that involves numerous subtasks, intricate scheduling, and complicated monitoring techniques. It can range from conducting a study or producing a film to planning the annual sales conference or masterminding a corporate acquisition.

Although many important jobs can be handled informally through the Master List, others require the kind of formal organization to which Frank Harvey refers. Project design and management includes seven steps, regardless of the task. While the steps themselves remain constant, execution varies depending on the sophistication and complexity of the task. Therefore, after a brief definition of the procedure, this chapter will follow three projects—"graded" by complexity—through the project-management process.

Project Design and Control: Overview

1. *Set a goal.* What is your purpose? To develop a new product? Reposition an established one? Recommend a course of action? Always set a concrete objective: not just "increase sales," but increase sales for what product or division, in what region or territory, by what percentage.

2. *Set a final deadline.* Has the project deadline been established? If not, set your own.

3. *Break the project down into subtasks.* Define the steps required to meet your goal.

4. *Organize subtasks into appropriate order of performance.* Where will you start? What comes next? Progression depends on both the nature of the subtask and the appropriate time sequence. Some projects have a *sequential line of development*—meaning tasks are handled one at a time, with each one completed before you move on to the next. Others have a *parallel line of development*—meaning several tasks are handled simultaneously.

5. *Set target dates and benchmarks.* Set a deadline for each subtask. Always try to factor in some extra time to cover delays or problems. It is often useful to set milestone points as well—specific review dates for evaluating overall progress and modifying your course when necessary.

6. *Assign subtasks to self and others.* Delegate all possible subtasks to subordinates and, when feasible, outside consultants or professionals. Check that everyone knows his or her responsibilities and deadline dates. Add the tasks you'll be personally handling to your Master List, transferring them to Daily Lists as appropriate.

7. *Monitor progress until completion.* Set up a project sheet: a list of all tasks, to whom delegated, and due dates. Keep these sheets on your computer and/or in a special folder in your action box for a daily check. Make sure that you are feeding your own jobs onto your Daily List, and following up with others as necessary. Cross off completed tasks in heavy ink, thus visually highlighting any items that are lagging behind schedule.

These general principles apply across the board, even to extremely complex projects. In fact, PERT/CPM (Program Evaluation and Review Technique/Critical Path Method), a highly sophisticated system originally developed by the navy to monitor the Polaris Project, is based on these same rules of project management.

Project Design and Control: Execution

To illustrate the differences in execution for projects of lesser and greater complexity, this section covers three "typical" tasks, beginning with:

Grade 1

Your boss asks for a report analyzing the reasons for a 7 percent drop in sales in your division, and what you plan to do about it.

GOAL. Investigate downturn and arrive at recommendations for the future.

DEADLINE. Two weeks.

SUBTASKS AND SEQUENCE. To arrive at an initial subtask list, mentally "walk through" the project, listing tasks in no particular order. Then organize them into *working blocks*—groups of related activities—as illustrated opposite.

Once subtasks are grouped into blocks, determine the order of progression. This project is a classic example of a *sequential line of development,* in which each block of tasks is dependent on completion of a previous block. In other words, initial research must be compiled before making your trip. What you learn from the trip will, in turn, determine how you approach planning-block tasks. And finally, these must be completed before you can begin actual writing. So action is clear and straightforward: research, travel, planning, and writing.

TARGET DATES AND BENCHMARKS.   Plan one week for research and travel, and reserve the second week for planning and writing the report.

ASSIGNMENTS.   You decide to send your second-in-command to Portland and to visit the Dallas office yourself. Have another staffer collect data on new technologies, and ask your secretary to make travel arrangements and gather up research reports and documents. Since you'll have to devote a lot of time to this task during the next two weeks, arrange to delegate or postpone other items on the agenda.

MONITOR.   Monitor progress via calendar, tickler file, or referral folders.

Grade 2

Find a way to reduce overhead.

GOAL.   When assigned a task this vague, set a concrete goal: "reduce overhead by 10 percent." Choose a figure at random if necessary. You can always increase or scale it down at a later point.

DEADLINE.   Six months.

SUBTASKS/WORKING BLOCKS.   The key difference between Grade 1 and Grade 2 projects is in level of sophistication. The subtasks in a Grade 1 job are generally clear and obvious—compiling research, analyzing data, writing a memo, and so on.

Subtask List (Grade 1)

INITIAL TASK LIST	WORKING BLOCKS
Compare monthly sales figures for all branch offices	
Check effect of previous policies on the problem	Research block
Collect relevant data: new technologies that might affect sales, effect of competition, internal personnel problems, poor advertising	
Plan field trips to Dallas office (where decrease is most marked) and Portland office (where sales have increased)	
List calls to be made, letters to be written	Travel block
Set up appointments in Dallas/Portland	
Make travel arrangements	
Compile all facts	
Outline presentation	Planning block
Firm up recommendations	
Draft report	
Edit report	
Make final revisions	Writing block
Prepare distribution copy	

In contrast, Grade 2 projects require an initial conceptual analysis *before* subtask breakdown is possible. A research study, for example, could be handled in one of several different ways, depending on the theory you're trying to prove. So you must first pinpoint issues or problems before you can delineate specific subtasks. In this particular case, an overhead rise could be caused by one of several factors. Those factors, in turn, will determine your subtasks and blocks. Your first step, therefore, is to *analyze possible areas of investigation and then translate them into practical subtasks and working blocks,* as illustrated on page 194.

In addition to these tasks, you intend to come up with a *recommendations block,* which will include planning long-range solutions and writing a report. Finally, there will be an *implementation block*—the tasks necessary to translate your recommendations into action. However, the specific nature of the tasks involved in these latter blocks will depend on the results of your research.

SEQUENCE AND PROGRESSION. Unlike the Grade 1 task, with its simpler sequential development, this project involves a parallel line of development, meaning that several subtasks from each block have to be handled simultaneously. To simplify this juggling act, select as your starting point, *no more than two or three tasks from each block, either the most central or the first-stage jobs.* In this case, you decide to begin with two "labor" *research block* tasks (checking and comparing past and present salaries) and two "supplies" *research block* tasks (getting supply costs; checking size and frequency of orders).

TARGET DATES AND BENCHMARKS. Set a deadline date for each subtask. In addition, set three or four "milestone" points

CONCEPTUAL ANALYSIS (GRADE 2)

CONCEPTUAL BLOCKS	SUBTASK LIST	WORKING BLOCKS
Salaries	Check current salaries	
	Check industry guidelines	
	Compare past and present salaries	"Labor" research block
	Determine whether salary increases correlate with production gains	
	Interview employees	
	Meet with boss	"Labor" action block
	Make cutbacks	
Supplies and materials	Get supply costs	
	Compare past and present costs	
	Find out size and frequency of orders	"Supplies" research block
	Check whether pilfering is a problem	
	Institute an inventory control system	
	Have employees check out supplies with department manager in writing	"Supplies" action block
	Print and distribute supply-control forms to monitor usage	

throughout the six-month period to evaluate overall progress. Aim, for example, for a 5 percent decline at the end of the first three months.

ASSIGNMENTS. The wide range of tasks involved in this project will probably mean bringing in a diverse group of assistants, including staff, secretary, and perhaps outside consultants. Delegate as many jobs as possible, reserving for yourself only those that call upon your particular expertise or experience.

MONITORING. Since this project will require more extensive follow-up than calendar or tickler can provide, use a project sheet. A simple method is to draw up a "General Assignments Sheet" similar to the one on page 257. For backup control, enter all subtasks—from all blocks—onto a wall calendar according to due date. Again, cross off completed tasks with a very dark line, to make uncompleted tasks stand out.

Grade 3

Plan annual sales conference.

GOAL. Arrange a four-day sales conference to be held in December at a Florida hotel. Plan an agenda that stresses development of new markets.

DEADLINE. Eight months.

SUBTASKS AND SEQUENCE. What distinguishes a Grade 3 project from Grades 1 and 2 is its sheer magnitude. It probably incorporates many Grade 1 and 2 tasks. Since the sales conference project is so large, encompassing perhaps hundreds of specific tasks, organizing them into clear and easily monitored relationships is crucial to the success of the meeting.

Organize this project in a two-step chart process. Head a sheet of paper with the two or three primary project blocks. For the sales conference, the two primary blocks are *logistics* and *content*. List under each column as many subtasks as come to mind at this early stage. Keep adding jobs as they come up. Your first-stage task breakdown might look something like this:

LOGISTICS	CONTENT
Make travel arrangements	Plan agenda
Find out who's coming	Book speakers
Book hotel	Organize meeting format
Plan meals	
Plan recreation	

Next, for each block, organize the subtasks into logical sequence with a tasks-by-levels chart (see "logistics" sample on p. 198), which divides subtasks into three levels:

Level 1: Basic preliminaries and first-stage tasks that can be carried out without reference to any others. For example: planning the agenda, gathering names of probable attendees, collecting hotel brochures, listing possible speakers.

Level 2: Tasks that hinge upon completion of one or more Level 1 jobs. Composing announcements, for instance, must wait upon a definite agenda.

Level 3: Tasks that hinge upon completion of one or more Level 2 jobs. Final confirmation of hotel reservations would have to wait until announcements were sent out and a definite attendees list was set.

This method is particularly useful for control over numerous subtasks, many of which "run" simultaneously. Some subtasks, such as preparing a printed brochure, might be so complicated as to warrant a tasks-by-levels analysis in their own right.

TARGET DATES AND BENCHMARKS. Set deadlines for early-stage tasks. Be very generous with time estimates according to Murphy's well-known law: if something can go wrong, it will. Hold off on detailed deadlines for later-stage tasks until you're closer to the time to begin them. However, do set "block" deadlines. Plan, for example, to complete certain basic *logistics* tasks—booking a hotel, arranging for meeting rooms—in three months. Within four or five months, aim for completion of more detailed tasks: arranging meals, planning a "golf day," and so on. Set similar milestones for *content* tasks: plan to book all speakers and set a firm agenda by the end of three months.

ASSIGNMENTS. Since so many tasks are involved, delegate sub-blocks: have one staffer handle all travel arrangements; charge another with booking hotel rooms and meeting facilities, and arranging for meals and entertainment. Or, hire a travel agent to free up staff time for other obligations.

MONITORING. Use your tasks-by-levels chart to monitor progress. As each task is completed, cross it off heavily in dark ink to highlight lagging areas. In addition, arrange regular biweekly meetings with project lieutenants to update the status of all tasks and deal with any problems.

Logistics Tasks-by-Levels Chart

	Level 1			Level 2			Level 3	
ASSIGNED/DUE	TO	TASK	ASSIGNED/DUE	TO	TASK	ASSIGNED/DUE	TO	TASK
4/2–4/7	SMS	Collect hotel brochures	–5/31		Book hotel	–9/30		Confirm hotel
4/3–4/9	LT	Estimate no. attendees	–6/15		Send notices to attendees	–11/3		Plan meals
5/1–5/30	TFP	[Book speakers]*	–10/1		Arrange for audiovisual equipment	–11/3	RJH	Make up equipment installation checklist
4/2–4/11	SMS	Contact travel agent	–10/1	SMS	Make travel arrangements	–12/1	RJH	Supervise equipment installation
			–10/15 (Liaison NJF)	Hotel	Plan golf day			

*A bracket indicates that a task is a "feeder task" from the "content" Tasks-by-Levels Chart, which would have to have been completed in order for the logistics to go forward.

Specialty Tickler Systems

Follow-up is the bridge between plans and results. For most tasks, calendar notations, tickler files, referral folders, project sheets, and a tasks-by-levels chart (used singly or in combination) are quite sufficient for follow-up. However, recurring tasks—projects handled on a regular basis, whether daily, weekly, or monthly—and certain specialty situations require special methods. What follows is a compilation of practical techniques.

For Recurring Tasks

Simple status report: Design a standard form listing every step and subtask associated with a recurring project. Leave space for changes and modifications. Update daily or weekly as needed. The creative director of a cosmetics company designed a "Department-Store-Giveaway Status Report" to track the myriad details involved in producing such items as the totes available for $12.95 if you buy $50 worth of cosmetics. Every Monday she reviewed the report with her assistant, giving new instructions and following up as necessary. An updated report was on her desk the following morning, which she used as a guide for the rest of the week.

MONTHLY CHART. The International Closing Schedule chart on page 201 was prepared by a specialist in international sales who was responsible for at least one daily report and sometimes as many as seven or eight. He duplicated multiple copies of the schedule, crossed off each day's tasks when completed, and tossed the chart at the end of the month to begin the next cycle with a fresh copy. This kind of chart can be adapted to many uses—activities, reports, meetings, and so forth.

THE SHE SYSTEM.   This imaginative method for monitoring numerous recurring tasks is based on a progressive card-file system designed by Peggy Jones and Pam Young, authors of *Sidetracked Home Executives*. To set it up, you'll need a small index-card box; three sets of index cards—white, yellow, and green; and three sets of dividers (two Monday–Friday sets and one 1–31 set). Here's how it works:

1 Jot each daily task on a white card. Write weekly tasks on yellow cards, monthly tasks on green cards. Put the two Monday–Friday divider sets in the front of the box, followed by the 1–31 dividers.

2 Start the system on a Monday. Put all daily (white) task cards behind the first Monday divider. Also include weekly and monthly tasks (yellow and green) scheduled for Monday. Distribute the remaining weekly cards into "Tuesday," "Wednesday," and so on, and put monthly cards behind their date in the 1–31 divider. So, for example, Wednesday's sales report card is filed under "Wednesday," and the marketing report always due on the fifteenth goes behind "15."

3 Work through the Monday cards. As you complete each task, transfer the card to its next category: a daily task to Tuesday, a weekly task to next Monday (that is, into the second Monday–Friday set), and a monthly task to its date.

4 To avoid neglecting monthly tasks, check these cards every night, pull the next day's cards, and add to the

INTERNATIONAL CLOSING SCHEDULE

1st week / month	1. MOPS Report 2. Tideout sales 3. Verify G/L codes 4. Book Std. Costs—MOPS 5. Book loss on returns 6. Book Non-Std. Cost Allocation 7. D.E. & A.D. commission accrual 8. Report Export Sales—MTD—to Gen. Acctg. +1	1. EOM Report 2. Tieout sales 3. Book sales—EOM 4. Prepare/Dist. Daily Sales Report (Mo. End) 5. Insurance Accrual/Charge 6. Caribbean D.D. and Cable Cost Transfer 7. Review entries +2	1. Prepare miscellaneous entries 2. J.E. Cutoff—3:30 P.M. for input to First Ledger +3	1. First Ledger, Pegs, Comparisons entries 2. Verify Intnl. entries 3. Check Ledger/Budgets 4. Preliminary Income Statement 5. Misc. adjust. entries 6. Prepare Sales/Request Comments +4	1. J.E. Cutoff—3:30 P.M. for input to Second Ledger 2. Prepare Sales WKI 3. Receive wks. invoices from Customer Service +5
2nd week / month	1. Second Ledger, Pegs, Comparisons 2. Verify Intnl. entries 3. Check Ledger/Budgets 4. Check Suspense file/J.E.'s hitting Second Ledger 5. Prepare Income Statement, Sales Expense Comments 6. Prepare/Dist. Daily Sales Report 7. Report Export Sales—MTD—to Gen. Acctg. +6	1. Review Income Statement 2. Financial Review 3. Finalize Income Statement 4. Prepare monthly credit memo report for Cost Accounting +7	1. Final Ledger, Pegs, Comparisons 2. Prepare Export Trade Sales by Product 3. Prepare complete monthly income package +8	1. Compile paid invoices for Mid-East & A.D. using historical T.B. 2. Collate commission folders +9	1. Distribute income package/budgets 2. Verify open invoices in D.E. folder to T.B. 3. Prepare worksheets on paid invoices 4. Collate commission folders 5. Receive wks. invoices from Customer Service +10
3rd week / month	1. Prepare/Dist. Daily Sales Report 2. Report Export Sales—MTD—to Gen. Acctg. 3. Continue commission folder verification and collate +11	1. Continue commission folder verification and collate +12	1. Forward commission check request to Supervisor, Intnl. Finance for approval +13	1. Prepare/Dist. Daily Sales Report 2. Forward commission check request to Mgr., Credit for approval +14	1. Prepare/Dist. Daily Sales Report 2. Forward commission check request to V.P. Intnl. for approval 3. Receive wks. invoices from Customer Service +15
4th week / month	1. Prepare/Dist. Daily Sales Report 2. Report Export Sales—MTD—to Gen. Acctg. 3. Prepare A.D. wire transfers. Forward to Supervisor, Intnl. Finance for approval +16	1. Prepare/Dist. Daily Sales Report 2. Forward A.D. wire transfer to Mgr., Intnl. Finance for approval 3. Process D.E. commission check request +17	1. Prepare/Dist. Daily Sales Report 2. Forward A.D. wire transfer to V.P. Intnl. Finance for approval +18	1. Prepare/Dist. Daily Sales Report +19	1. Prepare/Dist. Daily Sales Report 2. Verify commission check request and mail 3. Receive wks. invoices from Customer Service +20

"daily" section for handling tomorrow. So, on Thursday the 14th, pull all cards behind "15" and put them in the "Friday" section.

When the week is over, the first Monday–Friday set will be empty, and the second set becomes the first set. And 'round it goes.

FLOWCHART. A flowchart is a method of translating task programs into visual form. It can be used to track recurring tasks, or to monitor a one-time project. The simple flowchart opposite is used by a cosmetics company to trace product design and production. The process starts with "prototype confirmation" on the left, and concludes with "fill available" on the right. The "prototype confirmation" circle has three branches: "formula" (the product itself), "package," and "copy." Each branch follows its own line of development, and the branches are not rejoined until "assembly," the next-to-final circle. The advantage of such a comprehensive visual plan is to ensure that the three lines march along in sync, and to pick up any snafus or delays immediately.

TAB CARDS. Tab cards—a card with months and days preprinted across the top—are a useful device for monitoring dates. You can have them made up by a printer to your specifications. A literary agent, in order to keep track of semiannual royalty payments from publishers, made up a tab card for each book. A brightly colored plastic tab picked out the due date for the next payment. When a publisher's payment schedule was, say, February and August, the tab for the book in question covered February and then, when the check arrived, it was shifted to August. If, at the end of February, any February tabs remained, the agent began making inquiries.

PROGRAM EXECUTION

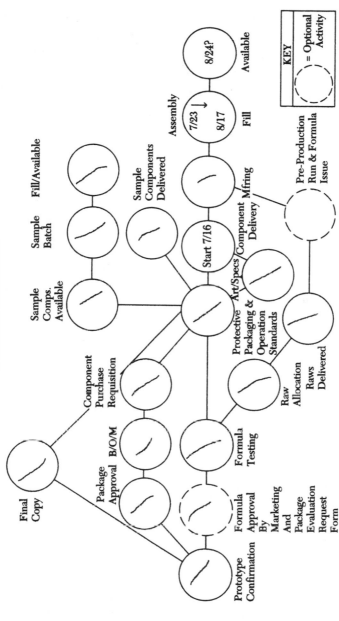

Cosmetics company standard program flowchart. The circles are blank to begin with. A diagonal line, indicating that the procedure has started, will become an "X" when it has been completed.

In another application, a recording company used tab cards to keep track of production dates for records and album covers. For precision's sake, two tabs were used: one to pick out the month, and one to pick out the day.

Tab cards are also useful to record general information as well as tracking due dates.

A variant tracking strategy for royalty payments was established by another literary agent. This agent used ordinary index cards for each book, and organized the cards in a box by month. The card for a February and August book was filed first under February and then, when payment was received, it was moved to the August section. If any cards remained in February at month's end, that was the agent's cue to start calling.

For Specialty Situations

SPECIALTY TICKLERS.   The basic daily/monthly tickler system for tracking paperwork can be adapted to numerous situations. The editorial department of one magazine kept a set of monthly folders for all incoming articles. So, for example, when the editors had planned the August issue, a list of commissioned articles went into the "August" folder, as did the articles themselves as they arrived. A month before deadline, the editor checked the articles against the list and immediately began riding herd on lagging writers.

A "box" tickler was the solution for a small printing outfit with order-fulfillment problems. Management installed two sets of wall boxes: a "daily" set labeled 1 through 31, and twelve "monthly" boxes. As each print order went into work, it was assigned a follow-up date one week before fulfillment. A copy of the order was placed in the appropriate daily box (or monthly box, if further ahead). Each day, the person who monitored the print orders went through the contents of that day's box, following up with the production department to confirm that the schedule could be met. If it could not, there was enough time to take appropriate remedial measures.

A notebook tickler was the method of choice for one salesman who wanted to follow up on customers and leads at regular intervals. He organized a looseleaf binder by month, assigned each lead a sheet, and "moved" sheets through the notebook. So, for instance, if he called on a contact on February 15, the sheet was moved to April to remind him to schedule another call. He also used the sheets for notes and comments, which gave him a running record of all his contacts.

Law Firm Calendar Controls. According to one source,* 30 to 40 percent of the malpractice claims filed against lawyers are a direct result of failure to meet legal and jurisdictional due dates, meaning claims may be lost by default. Establishing a fail-safe "docket control system" is, therefore, an essential for any law firm. Try one of the following reliable methods:

Double diary. Your secretary enters response dates on his or her calendar *and* your calendar. Your secretary reminds you of due dates during your daily meeting and, for backup, also provides you with a typed list of responses due.

File notations. You enter due dates or response dates on a sheet clipped to the front of a client's file. Your secretary picks them up from the file, enters them on his or her calendar, and reminds you on the appropriate day.

Card file system. This method is appropriate if your office produces a high volume of reminders. Use index-card file

*Robert Wilkins, "Is Your Calendar Choking You?" (film).

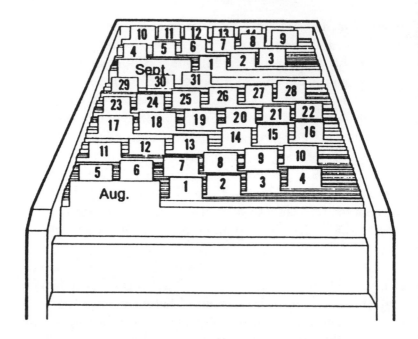

boxes organized by month and day, using monthly dividers followed by thirty-one daily dividers. (See illustration above.) Make up three index cards—white, green, and blue—for each client or case. File the white card, *the trigger*, on the date when preparation of papers should begin; file the green card, *the prompter*, one week before deadline; file the blue card, *the control*, on the deadline date. Remember, though, that by the time you reach the green card, you're bumping up against your time limits, and may have to red-flag that task. To keep pressure at a minimum, check tomorrow's file before you leave every night, and enter white-card tasks onto your Daily List.

Backup control system (optional). Assign each case a page in a looseleaf notebook listing tasks to be performed, deadline dates, statute of limitations if relevant, who is in charge, any court actions, and whether index cards are in place. Whenever an index card turns up, make a notation in the notebook ("white card, 11/15, filed papers"), thus putting a history of the case at your fingertips.

These manual systems should be backed up by computerized "ticklers," but I recommend not relying on the computer alone.

Summary: The Seven Stages of Project Management

STEP 1 Set a *specific* goal.

STEP 2 Set a final deadline.

STEP 3 Break project into subtasks, and group related subtasks into *working blocks*. When a project is unusually broad or abstract, first identify the underlying issues or problems, then translate these issues into practical subtasks and blocks.

STEP 4 Organize subtasks into an appropriate progression, either a *sequential line of development* (tasks handled one at a time, with each completed before moving on to the next) or a *parallel line of development* (tasks handled simultaneously). For the latter, begin the project by selecting two or three core tasks from each block.

STEP 5 Set subdeadlines for individual tasks and steps. Establish periodic benchmarks for the evaluation of overall progress.

STEP 6 Delegate specific tasks or groups of tasks to subordinates and/or outside consultants. Add your own tasks to your Master List, feeding them into your Daily List as appropriate.

STEP 7   Monitor less complex tasks with calendar, tickler
         files, and referral folders. For more intricate projects,
         use a task sheet or tasks-by-levels analysis, heavily
         deleting completed tasks so as to visually highlight
         any that are behind schedule. To keep track of recur-
         ring tasks, make up a status report, monthly chart, or
         progressive card file. If follow-ups are numerous, or
         require a special system, set up a box, looseleaf,
         or card-file tickler, and/or enter on your computer.

9

Time Evaluation: From Objective to Reality

*The strongest principle of growth
lies in human choice.*

—George Eliot

Getting organized is not an end in itself; it is simply a means of getting from where you are to where you want to be. Ultimately, the productive use of time is a personal judgment; by your actions through the day, month, year, do you meet the priorities and goals you've set for yourself? Time spent *not* getting where you want to go, no matter how efficiently you might not be getting there, is time wasted. This chapter, therefore, focuses on the broader issue of the "why" of time—what you are making time for—through three different time-analysis exercises:

Day-to-day analysis: This exercise tests your mastery of the paperwork/time/interruption techniques described in this book, and shows how to pinpoint—and solve—any remaining trouble spots.

Professional analysis: This exercise enables you to design your own management-by-objectives (MBO) profile: to identify specific goals, zero in on your strengths and weaknesses, and direct your time in a way that will further your professional life.

Long-range analysis: This appraisal will help you to assess long-range aspirations and refocus your time if you're on the wrong track. Where do you want to be in five or ten years?

These exercises can be used independently or together. Whether you employ one, two, or all three depends on your needs and your sense of current dislocations. One senior manager with a firm handle on her professional goals bypassed the MBO profile, but found value in the day-to-day and long-range examinations. Another executive, who managed daily activities efficiently, focused on career development with the MBO exercise.

Measuring Day-to-Day Mastery: An Eight-Step Process

In order to get where you want to be, you need to take a look at where you are right now. The tool for this analysis is the Time Log, which, like a large-scale topographical map, brings all features of the landscape into sharp relief.*

The Time Log is a daily diary that tracks your activities in fifteen-minute intervals. A blank form is provided here. You are invited to enlarge and reproduce this form, or design your own. (For a look at a completed log, see p. 219.) Every fifteen

---

*This analysis is intended for use *after* basic systems are in place and functioning relatively smoothly. If time management and paperwork are still chaotic, the log will simply confirm the state of chaos.

ate: _____

TIME LOG

	TASK	IN REGARD TO	WITH	PRIORITY	P/I*	COMPONENT**
9:00						
15						
30						
45						
0:00						
15						
30						
45						
1:00						
15						
30						
45						
2:00						
15						
30						
45						
1:00						
15						
30						
45						
2:00						
15						
30						
45						
3:00						
15						
30						
45						
4:00						

*P = planned. I = interruption.
**This column is used for MBO analysis. Leave blank for day-to-day exercise.

minutes, write down what you're doing; what the task involves or refers to; and other people involved if the task is a call, meeting, or appointment. Also assign a priority to the task: 1 for urgent or demanding tasks, 2 for middle-range basics, and 3 for low-priority activities. Then note whether the activity was planned (P) or involved an interruption (I).

Keep the log for at least one week, entering each day's activities from the moment you arrive at the office until you depart.

Include coffee breaks, interoffice visiting, lunch, and any other activities. Use a timer or computer alarm to keep tabs on what you're doing at each interval. At the end of the week, schedule an hour or so of private time, equip yourself with six different-colored transparent highlighter markers, and analyze your logs* as follows:

STEP 1   *Telephone calls.* With one marker, highlight all telephone calls, and add up calls made or received during the week. How many were "legitimate"; how many qualified as "firefighting" intrusions or unwelcome interruptions? If there are more of the latter than you'd like, review Chapter 6, and reduce firefighting calls to the 15 or 20 percent mark.

      Also calculate average time per day spent on the phone, and total telephone time for the week. Are the calculations in proportion to your job? Obviously, a heavy liaison/contact job will involve more telephone time than a job where constant interaction is less necessary.

STEP 2   *Scheduled appointments.* Highlight all scheduled appointments with another marker. Are you seeing people with whom staffers could meet instead?

STEP 3   *Drop-in/ad hoc appointments.* Mark drop-ins and other ad hoc appointments with a third marker. If ad hoc get-togethers outside your designated "open house" hours total more than 15 or 20 percent of all appointments, review the techniques in Chapter 6.

STEP 4   *Meetings.* Score meetings in a fourth color, and note the percentage of your daily/weekly time spent in

---

*Duplicate several copies of your logs before marking them up, because the same log is used for the MBO exercise.

meetings. Is this percentage appropriate to your job? Review the tactics in Chapter 6.

STEP 5 *Paperwork, projects, writing, planning.* Tally up the amount of time spent on private work of this kind, and score these activities with another marker. Rarely is the problem too much time spent. Most managers should plan a solid 25 to 30 percent of time for paperwork and projects, although that figure will vary depending on your work. A manuscript editor might use close to 75 percent of the day for private work, while 10 percent might be sufficient for a person in sales. A substantial private-time tally can, however, be misleading if it is dissipated on remedial activities like catching up on backed-up letters, searching for lost files, and reworking routine reports. If considerable paperwork seems to be of the "finger in the dike" variety, review Chapters 2, 3, and 4, and the section in Chapter 7 on perfectionism.

STEP 6 *Calculation of priority/payoff ratio.* How many activities qualify as number 1 priorities? As 2's, 3's? Averaging more than three or four 1's per day means poor planning or inaccurate rating. One manager rated 75 percent of his log entries as 1's, but in fact, he had failed to differentiate between genuine and lesser priorities.

How do your priorities stack up? Review the priority/payoff chart on page 134, then consider these questions:

- Do *any* number 1 or 2 priorities qualify as high payoffs? If not, resolve to *enter at least one high-payoff task on every Daily List.* Try to devote a solid 20 percent of your time to these tasks.

- How many 1's and 2's qualify as negative pay-offs? Were any the result of poor planning or earlier neglect? If firefighting and catch-up activities consume too much time, review Chapters 2, 5, and 8.
- How many 2's and 3's are medium-payoff tasks? Although they should and will occupy the bulk of your time, can you delegate some medium-payoff tasks that you don't find especially interesting, challenging, or enjoyable? Most medium-payoff tasks should show up as number 2 priorities if you're planning and delegating effectively.
- Are *any* 1's or 2's low payoffs? There should be no such thing as a 1 or 2 low-payoff task. Challenge suspect entries by asking: "Is this the best use of my time right now?" Review low-payoff 3's and assess the consequences of eliminating or delegating them.

    Finally, evaluate your priorities against time investment: on average, 1's should take up one-and-a-half to two hours a day; 2's (which usually include meetings and appointments) should take up about four hours; 3's, the rest of the day.

STEP 7   *Consolidation vs. fragmentation.* With the last marker, draw a line through all remaining log entries. Does your log now resemble a rainbow—with broad bands of color? If so, you're successfully consolidating your activities. However, if your log resembles a Jackson Pollock painting, you are fragmenting your time. Review the control tactics described in Chapter

6, and study the blocking techniques and work styles outlined in Chapter 7.

STEP 8   *Efficiency wrap-up.* Now review all tasks listed in your log and ask yourself:

- Am I complicating tasks, putting more time into them than warranted?
- Am I simplifying and streamlining, using efficiency techniques whenever possible?
- Am I taking on inappropriate work? Doing too much for others? Failing to delegate?

Designing a Personal MBO Profile

In recent years, the concept of management by objectives has been virtually deified by a business community eager to increase productivity in an uncertain economy. But management by objectives is simply another way of stating the most basic principles of organizing: *identify your objectives; define the steps necessary to reach those objectives;* and *assess progress on a periodic basis.* Following through on these objectives in a timely way is, by definition, productivity. But sometimes there's a catch: the objectives stated aren't always the right ones.

When goals are specific—to increase sales by 10 percent or bring in X amount of new business—productivity can easily be quantified. But how can you measure the work of a marketing manager? Write more reports? Ludicrous though it sounds, many managers are getting the message that their abilities are being measured by tasks that amount to make-work. An MBO chart will often list vague objectives such as "Be more open in communication," or redundant tasks like "Develop new accounts receivable system" when the present system will do. This poorly thought-out approach to objectives is inimical to real productivity. With so many managers inventing busywork for themselves and their staffs because job objectives are so vague, important work is being neglected at all levels.

This section is designed to enable you to work up your own practical MBO profile: to help you pinpoint specific, professional objectives; analyze how well your present use of time squares with these objectives; and guide you in making time for the work that's important to you professionally and personally.

What Are You Paid to Do?

For Martin Aldrich, partner in a telecommunications firm, work had become frustrating and tedious. "When I started this business, I loved the work, the challenge. Now, I feel like I'm on a treadmill. I'm so busy with details that I have literally no time for what I really want to do. I need to get back on course, but I don't know where to begin."

As we discussed his problem, Aldrich mentioned some very cogent advice once given to him by a tennis pro: "Focus on three fundamental things only: stand sideways to the net, stand still, and watch the ball until it hits the racket. The rest is basically icing." Aldrich was seeking a similar focus in his work. He needed to pinpoint and concentrate on the basics. What he was articulating is a fundamental principle of productivity:

I   Establish two or three clear-cut objectives.

What *are* you paid to do? Oversee new product development? Manage the company's finances? Negotiate contracts?

Formal job description aside, start to devise your own "hard" job objectives by working up a one-sentence concrete job description. That is, if you come up with locutions like "aid in impacting implementation of . . ." or "interface with . . . ," try again. Or try this exercise: how would you describe your work to your spouse or a very close friend in a moment of stark candor? Write down the description. That's reality—the point from which you can begin to formulate authentic and practical objectives. With your description in mind, follow this two-step process:

1 Break your job into six or seven *major components*—your chief areas of responsibility. Typical components could include sales, new business, financial management, making deals, negotiating contracts, public relations, customer service, increasing revenues, planning, managing staff, administration, research, technical work, statistical analysis, and marketing.

For Martin Aldrich, the components list included planning, increasing client revenues (selling and marketing), research (new technologies), administration, and staff management.

2 Next, nominate two or three of these components as *core components*—the functions that you see as the heart of your job. These should be functions that you handle well, that you enjoy, and that provide the highest payoff in terms of your contribution to the company and your own career aspirations. Sniff the air: Is there a whiff of increased competition? Are economic clouds or new technologies on the horizon that can affect your business? This wind-sniffing will help you to discern where your company or department should be tomorrow, and your role in helping it get there.

When Aldrich analyzed his list, he zeroed in on increasing client revenues and planning for taking the company public.

These core components are your objectives—the focal points around which to structure your time. Which brings us to the second principle of productive time management:

| Evaluate the amount of time you devote to your objectives.

Take a fresh copy of your Time Log and fill in the final column, noting which major component, if any, each task relates to. Then check or star those that qualify as core components. Now look at each of the four task categories—phone calls, appointments, meetings, and paperwork/projects. What percentage of these activities relate to your major components? Your core components? Is a high proportion of your time going to nonessentials, or do most activities reflect major and/ or core components?

When Martin Aldrich looked over his completed log (p. 219), the discrepancy between his objectives and his present use of time was glaring. Hours devoted to unnecessary phone calls and drop-ins left virtually no time for the selling and planning he'd deemed his core responsibilities. Moreover, the substantial amount of time theoretically devoted to paperwork/planning was misleading because few paperwork log entries were high-payoff planning or selling tasks. In fact, when we divided the contents of Aldrich's in-box and action box into three categories, "planning" accounted for one item of paper, "marketing" about five, and "other" (staff memos, client letters, research reports) spilled over the two boxes. As a result, Aldrich learned some rather painful home truths.

TIME LOG (MARTIN ALDRICH)

	TASK	IN REGARD TO	WITH	PRIORITY	P/I	COMPONENT
9:00	Coffee/Chat	Company picnic	Bill (partner)		I	Administration
15						
30	Call	New prices	Ralph Stevens	3	I	Administration
45	Call	Service question	Ann Patrick	3	I	Administration
10:00	Mail Processing			2	P	Administration
15						
30						
45						
11:00	Meet w/ secy.	Plan day		1	P	Selling
15	Call	Schedule appt.	Jim Mead	1	P	Selling
30	Call	New product	Stan Rivers	3	I	Research
45						
12:00	Dictation	Letters to Chambers, Crane, Hart, re problems with accts.		2	P	Administration
15						
30						
45						
1:00	Lunch					
15						
30						
45						
2:00	Appointment	Stock offering	Ted Jones	1	P	Planning
15						
30						
45	Call	Service question	Bob Dane	3	I	Administration
3:00	Call	Service question	Carol Hanes	3	I	Administration
15	Appointment	Hart problem	Ed	3	I	Staff mgmt.
30	Appointment	Brown acct.	Pat	3	I	Staff mgmt.
45	Appointment	Farkas acct.	John	3	I	Staff mgmt.
4:00	Staff meeting	Presentation for new client	Pat/Steve/Bill/ Ed	2	P	Planning

Unfortunately, he wasn't a great manager of people. His "other" stack of papers was so large primarily because clients were bypassing the staffers assigned to their accounts and applying directly to him. He often second-guessed or countermanded staff decisions, creating time-consuming pseudo-emergencies, not to mention confusion and general ill will. To ease the immediate problem, Aldrich was given a crash course in delegation and follow-up techniques. For the longer term, given his temperament, he was advised to divorce himself from the staff-management role, either by switching off that function with one of his partners, or by hiring a supervisor. Which brings us to the third principle of productive time use:

> Identify time-intensive components that don't match your area of expertise, your goals, or your personality, and find a way to eliminate, delegate, or reduce them.

To analyze your own situation, look over your log and zero in on problem areas.

1. *Which components are ill-suited to your talents, interests, or temperament?* Is there any aspect of your work that you spontaneously organize? Your phone listings, sales calls, a particular type of project? How you assert yourself is very revealing of priorities, interests, and weak spots. Do you prefer analyzing a balance sheet to settling a disagreement between employees? Does research give you a headache? Does it take you three hours to write ad copy that someone else could toss off in twenty minutes? Do you prefer working with others to private work?

SOLUTION. *Reallocate "weak" components and focus on your strengths.* Can you hire someone? Delegate to subordinates? Exchange certain functions with a colleague? Bring in a partner? Hire an office manager or administrative supervisor? Use an outside service or consultant?

Case 1 Two real estate partners who each did a little bit of everything found themselves covering similar ground and often second-guessing each other. When a procedural snafu lost them a major property, they decided a modification was in order and began by listing their individual strengths and weaknesses. One knew the technical end of the business backwards and forwards; the other enjoyed the thrust and parry of deal-making. So they successfully divided responsibilities into an "inside" area (scouting the market, research, technical expertise, administration) and an "outside" area (selling, negotiating, community contact).

Case 2 Ellen Cady, an independent clothing designer/manufacturer, was also trying to do everything—but without the help of a partner. Her initial list of major components included clothing design, fabric selection, overseeing production, marketing/selling, and business planning. The quality of her designs was being affected by the time she was giving to other functions. Since design and fabric selection were her core functions, she decided to reallocate selling, keeping a few favorite customers for herself and turning the rest over to independent sales representatives. Her reps also developed new outlets for her wares, an area she'd been forced to neglect in the past. As for business planning, since she couldn't afford to hire a business manager, she began seeking a partner whose business acumen would complement her design skills.

2. *Which components offer little or no payoff in terms of your overall goals and objectives?* Are any components no

longer appropriate to your level or position in the firm? Are you hanging on to certain projects or responsibilities out of habit or a misguided desire to prove you can still "do it all"? Are these functions cutting into time that would be more profitably spent elsewhere?

SOLUTION. *Eliminate, delegate, reduce.* Eliminate what you can. For the rest, delegate at least a portion of these functions, and reduce the time given to those you must handle personally.

Case 1 For Patrick Hickok, a senior investment banker who headed the international division of his firm, a heavy travel schedule left little time for his core, high-payoff activities: planning and developing new business. One week out of every two months was spent in Japan, and every three months he spent a week or more in Latin America. He'd received these travel assignments many years ago, and had continued making the trips because it simply didn't occur to him not to. To free time for functions more commensurate with his current position, he assigned these trips to a subordinate, making only one trip every four months for overall review.

Case 2 When Stuart Baker, training director for a large corporation, took his job several years ago, the department was small and he personally ran many training courses. But as the department grew, he realized that in order to gain time for planning and development—his core activities—he needed to step back from teaching to reviewing the work of trainers.

Before accomplishing the shift, Baker had to establish training criteria and procedures. So he made time to write a manual outlining the information and guidelines that the trainers needed, as well as course-effectiveness assessment techniques. Sometimes, reallocating a significant job component requires careful preplanning—a very high-payoff task.

A useful tool for checking out your activities vis-à-vis your objectives is to make out a regular *activities report.* Once a month or so, list all your major meetings, tasks, and projects; the rationale for each; what component it reflects; your short-term and long-term goals; short- and long-term projected results; and how the results relate to short- and long-term goals. Use the form provided as a guide. This monthly update will make it easier for you to weed out suspect activities more quickly and save wasted time that is presently going to unimportant or inappropriate projects.

3. *Are the core components that have most appeal to you consistent with the actual nature of your job?* Is there a significant discrepancy between what you'd like to be doing and what you're supposed to be doing?

SOLUTION. *Identify your real interests and find a way to increase involvement with them.* Do you have to stay with your present job? Would you be happier doing something else? Could you shift responsibilities and give more time to the functions you find most congenial? Could you make a lateral move within the company to a department or division better suited to your interests? If analysis indicates that you're a square peg in a round hole, zero in on appropriate goals and methods for realizing them with the long-term goal discussion that begins on page 227.

ACTIVITIES REPORT

TASK/RATIONALE	WHAT COMPONENT DOES IT SATISFY?	GOALS SHORT-TERM/LONG-TERM	RESULTS SHORT-TERM/LONG-TERM

Case 1 A sales manager complained bitterly that constant interruptions from staff and customers left him little time for proposal writing or planning. But when we analyzed his time to see what could be delegated, it became clear that being available to his sales reps and customers *was* his job. In his case, a new position that matched his more reflective temperament proved to be the best solution.

4. *Do all components seem equally important, interesting, and enjoyable?* Do you find it impossible to choose one or two components as core functions? Is the prospect of eliminating or delegating any functions even more unappealing than the frenetic schedule required to handle them all?

SOLUTION. *Take components in sequence.* The key to this dilemma is to establish an appropriate sequence by translating some short-term goals into long-term goals.

Case 1 Furniture accessory designer Paul Litkin had established a formidable set of objectives: market screens, market upholstery products and services, and also design fabrics. And he didn't wish to turn over any of these areas to someone else. So, "sequencing" for Litkin meant marketing screens first, since he had already gained some visibility in this area, *then* branching into upholstery, and *finally* developing fabrics.

Exercise 1 How much time would you like to devote to each core component in the best of all possible worlds? How much time do you think you can devote to each in "real world" terms? Your goal lies somewhere between the two. Set a date for reaching this goal, and mark it on your calendar. For example: "Within six months I intend to spend 30 percent of my time on planning activities." Translate these percentages into a "days per month" figure, and draw up a small chart illustrating your proposed time shifts. The owner of a financial consulting firm, for example, who decided to step up his sales/marketing activities and reduce the time he was presently devoting to product development, blocked out his chart as follows:

ACTIVITY	PRESENT	GOAL
Consulting	5–10 days per mo.	OK as is
Sales/Marketing	3 d.p.m.	Expand to avg. 6 d.p.m.
Research	3 d.p.m.	OK as is
Product development	5–10 d.p.m.	Reduce substantially

Relog your activities for one day approximately every two months until you've reached your goal.

Exercise 2   Two or three times a week, look over your appointment calendar and Daily List and ask: "What did I actually do today?" "Did my activities match my priorities and objectives?" "Have I spent time on high-payoff tasks and core components?"

Exercise 3   Every month, rank each task on your Daily List by payoff. Is there at least one high-payoff activity? Are low payoffs negligible or nonexistent? Do medium payoffs reflect core components? Are negative payoffs real necessities as opposed to crises manufactured by poor planning or procrastination?

What Do You Want to Do with Your Life?

Graphics designer Milton Glaser challenged his students at the School of Visual Arts to define future goals with this provocative assignment: design a perfect day for yourself five years from now. Not a fantasy day, but a real day that is completely satisfying in terms of work, relationships with family and friends, and physical environment.

Is this perfect day an extension of your present life or a complete turnabout? Does your career reflect what you want from life, or are you doing what you're "supposed" to do and hating it? Do you have time for the organizations, projects, and interests that are most important to you? Are you using your time to achieve the kind of life you want for yourself and your family? Although the pressures of daily life tend to obscure the outlines of long-range plans, if you feel your present course is not leading you toward your future vision, here is an approach to shaping your life to conform to your real priorities.

With your perfect day in mind, start by listing specific goals. Which position in your company do you aspire to—a flagship position like president or executive vice president? Or would you prefer to develop technical expertise? Perhaps there is a specific goal to strive for on behalf of your organization: increasing its size, increasing sales, developing a commanding market position. Or do you dream of setting up shop on your own? Does another profession beckon: law, medicine, journalism? Do you see yourself in Congress? Would you like to make a film? Focus your efforts on behalf of society?

If specific career goals aren't forthcoming, devise your own aptitude test by matching your capabilities against various types of tasks, as discussed in Chapter 10.

The other side of the equation is lifestyle: what kind of life do you want, in what environment? Would you prefer to be based at home, or does frequent travel appeal? Do you enjoy spending time with colleagues, family, and friends, or are you happier in relatively solitary pursuits? Are you exhilarated by the pace of urban life, or more content in suburbs or country?

In a special, private notebook, list as many goals as imagination can conceive, and star the four or five goals that you would choose to concentrate on if you only had six months in which to accomplish them. Then begin to translate one of these goals—choose the first starred one if there's no clear favorite—into reality by breaking it down into concrete tasks.

To foster career advancement, consider taking advanced certificate courses, or initiating projects visible to higher management. Does big money beckon? Read money-making "how-to" books and biographies of entrepreneurs. Sign up for how-to-run-a-business and business-promotion courses. Register for a real estate broker's licensing course. Do you have political ambitions? Add "join a political club" to your list. Volunteer for a campaign. If you dream of living in France, check out the qualifications for, and availability of, positions in international business, diplomacy, law, or travel. The point is to move in the direction that matches your skills and desires by translating *every* goal, no matter how vague or general, into specific tasks.

Transferring these tasks one by one to your Daily List is the key to turning these fantasies into reality. To overcome anxiety about the prospect of change, start on a small scale. You might register for a course on one day. On another day, drop into the library to check out some reference books. At least two or three times a week thereafter, add a concrete, goal-related item to your Daily List. Balance these additions by cutting down on activities that don't match your long-term goals. A goal that is right for you can lead to a new life. One publishing professional who loved fishing now supports himself by writing books about his hobby.

In general, however, don't expect to make a direct leap. For example, to move from marketing associate toward marketing director, an initial short-term goal might be to prepare a paper—perhaps recommending new techniques for analyzing consumer trends—to draw the attention of higher management. Even better: Plan to submit your paper to professional journals in your field. Make that paper a reality by entering "Outline consumer-trends analysis" onto your Daily List, and continue feeding bite-size portions of the analysis onto the Daily List as you would any other complex task. Set interim stages for each major goal, and monitor progress with specific checkpoints. Organize tasks, for example, into six-month blocks, and enter the six-month checkpoints on your calendar.

As time goes on, if goals seem unrealistic or incompatible with your chosen lifestyle, they can be set aside or revised. Testing goals and discarding inappropriate ones will free you to focus on what's really important to you.

Summary: Three Analyses of Productive Time

DAY-TO-DAY ANALYSIS. For one week, log each day's activities at fifteen-minute intervals, listing each task, other people involved, priority, and whether planned or interruption. Then evaluate entries according to the effectiveness guidelines outlined below, and refer to appropriate chapters to solve any remaining trouble spots.

CATEGORY	EFFECTIVENESS GUIDELINES	REFER TO
Telephone calls	"Interruption type" should average no more than 15–20% of all calls.	Chap. 6 Phone interrupt. Pages 143–45
	Is total appropriate to your job? *Criterion:* Many liaison/contact duties = heavy phone load. In less "interactive" post, numerous calls indicative of problem.	Chaps. 2, 8 Follow-up. Pages 52–58, 199–207 Chap. 10: Delegation. Pages 239–65
Appointments	*Scheduled:* Could some be diverted?	Chap. 6 Drop-ins. Pages 145–47
	Unscheduled: No more than 15–20% of appointment time.	Chaps. 2, 8 Follow-up. Pages 52–58, 199–207
	Is total appropriate to your job? Use same criteria as above.	Chap. 10 Delegation. Pages 239–65

CATEGORY	EFFECTIVENESS GUIDELINES	REFER TO
Meetings	*Quantity:* Total time appropriate to your job?	Chap. 6 Meetings. Pages 152–57
	Quality: Meetings productive, on track?	
Paperwork/projects/ planning	*Quantity:* Reserve 25–35% for these tasks (most mgrs).	Chap. 2 Paperwork. Pages 37–62
	Quality: Is time spent on work itself, or on remedial catch-up, nonessentials, details, etc.?	Chap. 3 Streamlining. Pages 65–85
		Chap. 4 Filing. Pages 86–114
		Chap. 7 Perfectionism. Pages 175–77
Priority/payoff ratio	*Time frame:* 1's–1½ to 2 hours per day; 2's–4 hours (includes meetings and appointments); 3's, rest of day.	Chap. 5 Time management. Pages 121–33
	Try to devote 20% of priority-1 and priority-2 time to high-payoff activities.	

CATEGORY	EFFECTIVENESS GUIDELINES	REFER TO
Consolidation/ fragmentation	Score activities in different colors. *Desirable:* "Rainbow" effect with broad bands of color. Indicates successful consolidation. *Undesirable:* Random distribution of colors. Indicates activities are fragmented.	Chap. 5 Scheduling. Pages 133–38 Chap. 6 Interruptions. Pages 141–52 Chap. 7 Work styles. Pages 175–77
Efficiency wrap-up	*Task analysis:* Are tasks too complicated, time-consuming, inappropriate, delegable? Is there a problem with perfectionism or procrastination?	Chap. 5 Master/Daily Lists. Pages 121–33 Chap. 7 Work styles/efficiency. Pages 167–83 Chap. 8 Project management. Pages 187–98 Chap. 10 Delegation. Pages 239–65

Special note on use of time logs for professional billing: Attorneys and other professionals who bill for their time often find it difficult to keep a strict accounting and sometimes end up with a reconstruction of the day's events that has more to do with imagination than reality. Attorney Martin Morrissey solved this problem by setting a beeper to go off automatically every half hour. Another lawyer keeps track of his day in six-minute intervals, by setting an automatic beeper on his wristwatch. Peter Einhorn keeps a small pad on his desk and notes whatever he's doing (phone call, letter, appointment)—and the time—whenever he starts a new task. He puts the accumulated slips into a special basket on his desk; at the end of the day his secretary collects them and enters them on a time sheet. He follows the same procedure when he's out of the office, making notes on a small pocket pad.

A Midwestern accountant records "start" and "stop" time for her activities on a small dictation machine. Her secretary types these notes up every week and computes the billable time for each client.

You might also wish to ask your secretary to keep a list of all phone calls and appointments, noting the duration of each.

PROFESSIONAL ANALYSIS. Work up your own MBO profile by defining two or three clear-cut career objectives. First, break your job into its major components—your chief areas of responsibility. Next, choose two or three as core components: those functions that you handle best, that you find most congenial, and that offer the greatest payoff to you and your company. Then, evaluate how well your present use of time squares with these objectives. Specifically, what percentage of the calls, appointments, meetings, and paperwork tasks in your log qualify as major components and as core components? If you're giving too much time to nonessential or less important components, pinpoint the "weak" functions: those that don't reflect your objectives, skills, interests, or temperament. Can some be eliminated altogether? Could others be delegated to a subordinate or outside service? Can you reduce the amount of time you're now spending on these functions? Can some be postponed for a time, or handled in a different sequence?

LONG-RANGE ANALYSIS. To begin to meet some long-range goals, first envision a perfect day for yourself, and then translate this vision into concrete objectives. List specific tasks in a long-range planning notebook and begin to add these tasks, organized in six-month blocks, one at a time, to your Daily List.

PART III

THE ART OF BEING A BOSS

10

Managing Staff

Although we have so far focused on personal organization—your papers, workload, and time—these procedures are part and parcel of a larger system that depends as much on the contributions of your staff as on your own talents. Which leads us to a key question: What *are* your staff members contributing? Do they use their time to best advantage for the firm, for themselves, for you? Are they wasting their time and talents on the menial or mundane, or do they stretch themselves to the limit of their capabilities? Do their responsibilities allow them to broaden their strengths, buttress one another's weaknesses, and generally complement each other? Orchestrating the skills and time of everyone who works for you so as to produce results is a key test of your input and direction as a manager.

Some years ago, when Michael Ryan took over as head of new product development for a small manufacturer, he inherited a staff that his predecessor had described as "impossible." Says Ryan:

My predecessor blamed all the department's problems on the staff, and that was true so far as it went. Deadlines were missed regularly; paperwork piled up. But when I talked to everyone, it became clear that the real culprit was my predecessor's rather laissez-faire management style. Other than giving out assignments, he had little contact or communication with his staff, so they had no idea what his priorities were or what he expected from them. Also, he never made the effort to find out where their talents lay or what they were capable of doing.

His philosophy was "what you see is what you get." Obviously, he saw very little and got even less. My feeling is "what you give is what you get." And just last month, this "impossible" staff won the highest productivity rating in the company.

What Ryan was describing is the communication and reciprocity that underlie effective manager/subordinate relationships. When your staff members understand how their individual contributions affect the entire group, and are willing to pull together for the mutual benefit of all, the whole becomes greater than the sum of its parts. Learning how to develop and channel this "human power" into a productive and efficient unit is the focus of this chapter.

When human power is not being channeled to best advantage, there will be static on the line. Regular occurrence of two or more of the indicators below points to a need for more effective staff management:

- Frequent staff interruptions and requests for guidance, instruction, or clarification
- A perennially jammed action box
- A crammed briefcase taken home on many evenings, on weekends, and on vacations
- Assumption of many tasks because you do them better than anyone else

- Tendency to second-guess staffers, "go over their heads"
- Too much reverse delegation; staff refers tasks to you
- A frequent need to redo staff assignments because they are unsatisfactory
- Staff deadlines frequently missed or postponed; last-minute bursts of activity often necessary
- Tendency to interrupt staff "to see how things are going," especially in area of former specialty
- Strict monitoring of the appearance of staff members' desks and other details
- Problems over "perks" and status
- Strained atmosphere, low morale, high turnover, displays of temperament by you or others

The How-To of Effective Delegation

For Ron Kramer, senior vice president at an engineering firm, a crash course in personal organization seemed essential. His in-box resembled the Leaning Tower of Pisa. His time was fragmented by constant staff interruptions. And to keep up with his workload he often worked evenings and weekends, toting home a bulging briefcase almost every night. Even more troublesome was his department's spiraling turnover rate. In the last year alone, Ron had lost five of his best people.

Although he failed to see the connection among these symptoms, his problem wasn't so much personal disorganization as faulty staff management—or, more specifically, fear of delegating. He shared a reluctance common among managers to relinquish control of his fiefdom. Most papers in his in-box should have been referred elsewhere. And his late nights and weekends had less to do with drive and ambition than with his inability to let go of many projects. When he did delegate, his directions were so vague that staffers frequently had to request further instructions. Which led many of them to look elsewhere for more challenging and creative work.

Without delving too deeply into the psychology of reluctance to delegate, it is useful to recognize some of the factors involved. Perhaps most common is the "I'll do it myself, no one can do it better" syndrome. Probably you *can* handle much of the work more efficiently than anyone else. But is that the best use of your time? There's bound to be someone else who can do it well enough, or can be trained to do it as well or better. Second cousin to this syndrome is the widespread belief that personal value is measured by sweat rather than results. Free yourself from the martyr role by asking: "Is it more important that I do the job myself, or that it get done?"

Another factor is the tendency to equate delegating with abdicating responsibility. Yet with effective follow-up methods, you can in fact maintain overall control and accountability. Nor will delegation lead to a staff "power coup." Although many managers feel threatened by employees who are powerful and effective, staffers whose talents and imaginations are fully engaged in challenging work rarely have the time or inclination for power games. In fact, such games are likely to arise more readily in an atmosphere of frustration. Finally, there is the sense—a legacy from our Puritan forefathers—that "palming things off" on others is vaguely un-American.

On the contrary, an effective manager is one who *actively seeks* to develop his subordinates' skills. And generous delegation of challenging work is the key to developing good manager/staff relationships. Not only does this release you to concentrate on your short- and long-term goals, but it can make the difference between keeping and losing competent staffers. According to several studies, compensation is *not* the main reason why people become committed to a job. Rather, it is the opportunity to learn, to hone skills, and to tackle work that is personally rewarding. Moreover, unless you delegate, the total operation you control is restricted by the limits of what you, personally, can accomplish. Delegation is not simply a means of increasing productivity, but a means of actually *multiplying* it—by one-third or more.

What to Delegate

Although the precise nature of referrable tasks will vary according to your job and responsibilities, here's a useful rule of thumb from one successful entrepreneur cited in *Boardroom Reports:* "I can get twenty percent more work done by sticking to what I do best. I rate each new item in my [Master List and action box] from one to ten, according to how well it matches my strong points. Then I work only on items that rate over a seven. The rest I delegate, or find an outside expert who can handle them better than I can."

There are three ways to handle delegation—by task, by function, or by goal. *Task* delegation is the most immediate method. Specific tasks or subtasks are assigned to subordinates: rewriting a report, researching a project, designing a new sales brochure. A *function* involves a group of tasks related to one particular activity, such as sales, research, or personnel. For example, Carlton D. Burtt, formerly an executive vice president at Equitable Life, divided his responsibilities into several functional areas and delegated each area to a vice president. Each month, the vice presidents submitted a "telegraph-style" memo updating their activities, to which Burtt responded only if there was a problem. Weekly staff meetings were then reserved for substantive discussion and long-range planning.

A *goal* refers to the various tasks necessary to fulfill a particular objective: increasing sales by 10 percent, developing new markets, improving productivity. The Keene Corporation, a New York-based conglomerate, developed an interesting method for goal-directed delegation. Senior people and subordinates assemble to hammer out specific goals—for example, opening a West Coast sales office, or developing contacts at a new engineering firm. Each goal is assigned a certain number of points, and points are worth money. Goals are then delegated to appropriate staffers who are responsible for the entire operation and who may, in turn, delegate subtasks. At designated times, the entire group reviews the goals and makes any necessary modifications.

Knowing what to delegate, however, won't do you much good if you fail to follow through on your intentions to let go. Admittedly, this may be difficult at first. As one manager said, "After years of doing everything myself, delegating doesn't come naturally." However, retraining yourself toward the delegation habit carries an extremely high payoff.

An interesting and effective way to enlarge your perception of delegation options is through a "delegation audit" of your Master List. Write every outstanding task on your Master List (including subtasks of larger jobs) in one of three columns: tasks that can be wholly reassigned, tasks that can be shared or reassigned in part, and tasks that only you can do. Then review each column, starting with "self," as in the sample comments on pages 244–45.

Go through this Master List exercise once a month until delegating becomes habitual. Another useful what-to-delegate exercise is to imagine you're going out of town for two weeks. To whom would you assign the projects and paperwork in your action box? Select appropriate delegates, and then actually make those assignments.

To Whom Should You Delegate?

The cardinal rule of delegation is this:

> Assign tasks to the most junior person who has the skills and rank necessary to complete the assignment successfully. If no one meets these criteria, find or train someone.

This rule is based on simple economics: if someone at a lower salary level can handle a task, why tie up the time and energy of higher-priced talent? At the same time, the abilities and talents of your employees will be challenged. For your part, this involves learning how to match skills and tasks—choosing the right person for the right job. Five basic "pointers" follow:

1. *Learn to recognize the conceptual skills that underlie various functions.* For example: A gregarious, outgoing individual is likely to make an effective salesperson. Someone who is patient and who can simplify abstract concepts might be a good candidate for a training position. A staffer able to see the "big picture"—who is analytical by nature—would probably make an effective planner. An exceptionally well-organized person would be the logical candidate for an operations assignment.

2. *Know your staff's strengths and weaknesses—and your own.* Find out what each person can do. Be prepared—without penalty or dismay—to transfer a task from one person to another once the first individual has exercised his or her particular skill. An example: The owner of a consulting firm drafted a sales brochure, which she turned over for revision to the PR director. This professional did a fine restructuring job, but the text remained wordy and dense. So a professional copywriter

Delegation Audit

SELF TASKS

In general, the tasks you do yourself should reflect your skills, priorities, payoffs, and enjoyments. Challenge each item in the "self" column against these negative indicators:

- "I'll do it myself because no one does it better." *Comment:* Your people's skills are your capital. Whom could you find or train to do it well enough—or better?

- Allure of past history. Example: carrying out as sales manager the habitual tasks of a salesman. *Comment:* By transferring "used-to-be" responsibilities to staffers, you give them more scope to grow, as you grow yourself.

- Insignificant tasks. *Comment:* Dictating replies to routine queries is probably something your secretary should handle.

COLLABORATIVE TASKS

Parts of a task can often be reassigned or shared:

- *Draft* Dictate key ideas to someone else who will draft the report.

- *Edit/revise* Sketch out rough report, memo, or brochure for another to edit, revise, or polish.

- *Screen* Ask subordinates to select materials for your attention. Example: A bank training director asked trainers to select the most interesting student credit papers, from which he selected three to send to the credit department.

- *Segment* Structure a project in overall form, then assign different portions to staff.

- *Summarize* Summarize long reports, and flag materials for your attention. Ask staff to submit

REASSIGNED TASKS

Show cause for every task you feel *cannot* be reassigned. The following should be reassigned:

- Tasks not related to your personal strengths.

- Tasks no longer commensurate with your present level.

- Tasks that do not correspond to your high-payoff or core components.

- Tasks that a more junior person can do, or can be trained to do.

- Tasks that fit into another's specialty, whether in-house person or outside consultant.

Tip Identify repetitive tasks (requests for materials, information, prices, etc.) that can be permanently assigned elsewhere.

- Tasks left undone over time. *Comment:* The first hedge against procrastination is to find someone else to do it. Don't be the martyr.

"option" papers, listing factors and outlining alternatives, worded for a "yes" or "no" response.

- *Recommend* Staffers present proposals and problems to you with their solutions and recommendations. Return problems presented by subordinates without solutions with notation "**Recommend** a course of action and let's discuss," or "Please handle."

- *Research/background information* Gather back-up data, such as statistics, documentation, history. Example: A lawyer reviving an old case asked paralegals to list previously filed materials so he could pinpoint what he needed without going through the files himself.

was hired to translate the concepts into crisp, "selling" copy. This was no failure on the part of the PR director. She had gone as far as she could, and then turned the job over to another expert. For a computer department head who was spending two hours a day—usually after work—updating a complex staff assignments chart, help was closer at hand. In the next office there was a retired military man to whom such charting was child's play. Testing your subordinates with various kinds of projects, at varying levels of complexity, is the only way to discover their capabilities. This knowledge also offers you what John Neuman, formerly a principal of the consulting firm McKinsey & Company, calls a ready-made "skills bank" that you can tap for special projects.

Sometimes matching skills with tasks means *not* delegating. The skills that make an excellent salesperson are not necessarily those that make the best sales manager. "Often," points out R. Alec Mackenzie, "we lose our best salesmen this way and achieve our poorest sales managers."

3. *Coordinate everyone's skills, including your own, so that staffers can complement and buttress each other.* Creating that complementary whole discussed earlier is rather like assembling a jigsaw puzzle: your sense of everyone's strengths and weaknesses determines the "fit." The top-drawer analyst who designs superior planning charts might need a partner whose "people" skills enable him to motivate staff to meet chart deadlines. The more extroverted partner in a real estate firm could take the "outside" role of selling and doing deals, while the more reserved partner is responsible for research, planning, and administration.

4. *Consider potential delegatees other than your staff.* When you've exhausted your own resources, look to colleagues elsewhere. Seek their special expertise on a project, and offer

your own services in return. When appropriate, delegate to your boss.

If you tend to rely heavily on a particular subordinate, assigning especially demanding tasks to that person, there may come a point where you have in effect delegated him or her into an upgraded job. A young colleague, for example, proves so adept at shepherding large projects to completion that he becomes *de facto* project manager. Though fine in principle, job challenge can become a problem when title and compensation no longer match what has become a more responsible position. To avoid tension, if you can't actually promote an individual who has advanced, try, in addition to supporting his or her interests with *your* superiors, to find some method of compensation through perks or recognition. If this is not feasible, restrict delegable tasks within certain limits to avoid creating a significant discrepancy between position and responsibility.

5. *Consider outside services* when no one in-house is right for the job. A consultant can serve when you need to fill in staff gaps. To solve a specific problem. For independent evaluations or audits. To save time, money, frustration, and errors. To expand options. To plan for the future.

Ask around; satisfied clients are your best sources. Check with professional associations. Review journals in the field to find out who is writing articles.

For a large job, interview three or four firms or consultants. Request specific details on previous work they've done. Get references *and check them*. Be specific about your needs and expectations. In turn, the consultant should interview you to define the scope of your operation and what you hope to accomplish from the consultation. Beware of the consultant who knows the solution before he begins the job. Ask serious contenders for a written proposal. Look for the following in the proposal:

MISSION.   There should be a statement of purpose: to increase sales, improve productivity, or whatever. The scope of the study should be clearly defined—analysis plus recommendations, implementation, and so on.

STRUCTURE.   Sizable tasks should be broken into stages or "interim deliverables." The proposal should include a work program for each stage: specific tasks and procedures, number of days involved, names and ranks of senior people. Trainees, if any, should be identified as such (and paid for as such). If your staff will be needed for backup or assistance, that should be stipulated in the proposal.

Note: Once work begins, the consultant will move on to the next stage when you have signed off on the preceding one. Generally, however, unless option-to-continue is explicitly defined in the agreement, such approval is pro forma and the consultant will move directly to the next stage unless the preceding work has been unsatisfactory or there is some other difficulty. You should be reviewing progress with the consultant on a regular basis to forestall hitches or surprises.

FEES.   Consulting fees are usually time-based. Within broad guidelines, each field or locale has its own norms. Some projects are charged on a per-job basis, but expect these to come fairly high.

Each time-based stage should be assigned a minimum fee and a maximum estimated fee. To protect yourself against overrides caused by delays or inadequate time estimates, make sure the proposal stipulates that the consultant notify you of problems in advance, so you have enough time to modify the job if you wish to stay within budget. An increased fee rarely means that you're being cheated. Although an experienced consultant will incorporate the most likely snags into his original costing, there are too many variables for every problem to be anticipated. The best way to deal with such an override is to remain flexible *as long as* (1) you are informed of the revised estimates as early as possible, and (2) you have the option of modifying the job or proceeding.

IMPLEMENTATION AND FOLLOW-UP. Libraries are full of painstakingly prepared studies that were never implemented. Therefore, I strongly recommend that some kind of implementation-and-review procedure be incorporated into your initial agreement. Otherwise, what's the point? Some clients keep consultants on retainer for a period of time following implementation of accepted recommendations to handle any problems that arise, or for periodic review.

CONSULTANT/STAFF RELATIONSHIP. Enlist the full cooperation of every staff member who will be working with the consultant. Explain exactly what you hope to accomplish from the study and when you can honestly do so, neutralize staff fears about possible reorganization (firing, demoting, reallocating responsibilities, etc.). Let staffers know what kinds of questions they'll be expected to answer, how much time they'll have to give to the consultant, what his or her range of authority is, and to whom to apply if a problem arises. One client sent the following memo to his staff:

On Thursday, May 24, Expert Consultants Corp. will be in the office from 10:00 A.M. to 6:00 P.M. They have been retained to advise me on use of space and office equipment in preparation for our upcoming move to new offices. Because I'd like to cover all possible problems, would each of you please begin keeping track of any specific difficulties or issues as they come up, and have your list on my desk by 5:00 P.M. on May 23.

Assign one manager as a liaison with the consultant on a daily basis. This person should also deal with any staff problems. In addition, arrange to meet with the consultant weekly for progress reports. Ask all managers affected by the study to evaluate the final report. Finally, set a "sign-off" due date for implementation of accepted recommendations, and another, later date for resolution of any contested or unacceptable recommendations.

How to Delegate: The Assignment Loop

Telling someone what to do is a subtle art. An uncertain or tentative tone, or an overbearing one, can lead to lack of direction on the one hand, or to friction and resentment on the other. Says time-management expert Edwin Bliss, "The key to delegation is the word *entrust*. When you delegate, you entrust the entire matter to the other person, along with sufficient authority to make necessary decisions. This is quite a different thing from saying, 'Just do what I tell you to do.' "*

This element of trust, which underlies all effective delegation, implies mutual commitment. For your staff members, it means a commitment to meet your expectations to the best of their abilities. For you, it means a commitment to give staff your full cooperation, backing, and recognition. A specific four-point procedure follows:

---

*Edwin Bliss, *Getting Things Done: The ABC's of Time Management*, revised ed. (New York: Macmillan, 1991).

1. *Define the project: its purpose, importance, deadlines, and the scope of the delegatee's responsibility.* A political candidate asked his assistant to "research" several of the towns on his upcoming campaign tour. She spent hours writing up detailed histories, only to find out later that he'd simply wanted a few facts to customize his speeches. Was it her mistake? Certainly she should have clarified the time investment warranted, but her hesitancy in speaking up is quite common. Fear of seeming stupid—or wasting the boss's time with too many questions—keeps many employees silent, so the responsibility for clarification is yours. If your people seem regularly to overstep, understep, or misstep with regard to their assignments, they probably don't know what they are supposed to do. What, precisely, do you want? Why do you want it? How and when do you want it? What *don't* you want? Be as specific as possible in clarifying the purpose, deadline, format, and limitations of a task so your staffer can decide how to organize his or her own time and priorities. If the project is ambiguous or complex, ask your subordinate to restate the assignment, and back up verbal instructions with a written assignment memo.

Whenever feasible, ask staffers to set their own deadlines. Self-imposed time limits are perceived as equitable, and are more likely to be met on time. When you're reassigning a task delegated to you, set the staffer's deadline a few days before your own. Another good idea, particularly with more junior staff, is to request a quick look at first-stage efforts. One lawyer has his staff "just spit out written work in a first draft so I can see that they're going in the right direction." This sampling procedure will protect you from the unpleasant surprise of an unwanted finished product.

Will the staffer have responsibility for the entire project, or just one or two components? As a general rule, try to delegate according to the "whole job" model rather than the "assembly line" model. In the latter, as its name implies, several people are assigned to various parts of one project, each person giving the bolt a twist before passing responsibility over to the next person in line. The "whole job" model, in contrast, involves giving one delegatee responsibility for an entire process—up to the limit of his authority—until a result is achieved. In one theatrical agency, for example, the head of the firm has bookers negotiate all contract clauses within the standard range, bringing to his attention only special or problem clauses. The staff assistant to a hospital administrator has as his bailiwick the division chief's meeting, which includes moderating the meeting, having the minutes made up, following up on assignments, and reviewing results with his boss before the next meeting.

One large sales firm conducted an interesting experiment that illustrates the benefits of the "whole job" approach. Half of the sales force worked as an assembly line, with each person responsible for one limited task: taking orders, fulfilling orders, installing the equipment, and so forth. The members of the other group were each given total responsibility for servicing several specific accounts. Both groups started out at parity, but within a short time, the whole-job group pulled ahead in terms of number of sales and degree of customer satisfaction. Apparently, the assembly-line group wasted considerable time and energy untangling the numerous communications snafus that came about through frequent turnovers of responsibility from one person to another. Even more critical was the motivation factor. The assembly-line group felt little incentive to do more than the absolute minimum required. Responsibility for an entire process, however, fostered for the whole-job group a greater sense of commitment and a maximum investment of time and effort.

2. *Provide the necessary authority, resources, and support.*
Having assigned a task, does your subordinate have the authority to make decisions, to delegate to others—to do whatever is necessary to complete the task? Peter Drucker suggests that the effective executive ask superiors, colleagues, and subordinates: "What contribution from me do you require to make your contribution to the organization? When do you need this, how do you need this, and in what form?"*

Sue Jaffrey, executive assistant to a trade magazine publisher, was asked to put together a presentation for the upcoming national trade show. She, in turn, asked several of the production and design people to provide certain materials, a request they ignored because it didn't come from the top. They refused to acknowledge her right to give them orders, and they remained uncooperative—until the publisher stepped in and clarified Jaffrey's status as his surrogate.

This sort of tangle is quite common in the business hierarchy. And again, it's up to you to take the initiative and define—for the delegatee and anyone else involved—his or her degree of authority and autonomy. Among the possibilities:

- Subordinate has full authority to make a decision without consulting boss.
- Subordinate makes decision, but informs boss and anyone else involved, to prevent any surprises or unexpected problems.
- Subordinate recommends a final decision, which boss must approve.
- Subordinate presents alternative solutions to boss, who makes the decision.
- Subordinate presents relevant information from which

*Peter Drucker, *The Effective Executive* (New York: HarperCollins, 1985).

boss narrows down feasible alternatives. Boss then makes final decision after consulting with subordinate.

Here are two ways to give out the same assignment:

Minimum authority: "We need new copiers for the department. Ask everyone how many copies they make per day. Get prices from five companies. Also get their service and repair contracts. Then bring this analysis to me and we'll go over it."

Maximum authority: "Get the best deal you can on new copiers for the department" (perhaps within a certain budget). *Tip:* Request that every memo submitted about a problem include specific recommendations and/or possible solutions. This encourages assumption of creative responsibility by staffers.

In addition to identifying the delegatee's range of authority, there are other factors to consider. Have you allocated enough budget and sufficient "people power" in terms of additional help that the delegatees may need? Do they have the necessary materials and physical resources at their disposal? Are you giving them enough time, or have you made other, equally pressing demands on their time? And perhaps most important: Do they have the necessary training or expertise? If not, are you prepared to provide it? Executives who are reluctant to make the "capital investment" of time required to train their people often pay for it later—wasting even more time redoing substandard work and solving problems. Don't overlook the time-honored method of apprenticeship. An advertising executive said, "Each new person we add to the creative staff works under one of our most talented people to start."

HOW TO GET READY TO INSTRUCT

Have a Time Table—
How much skill you expect him to have, by what date.

Break Down the Job—
List important steps.
Pick out the key points. (Safety is always a key point)

Have Everything Ready—
The right equipment, materials and supplies.

Have the Workplace Properly Arranged -
Just as the worker will be expected to keep it.

Supervisional Training Dept.
THE GOODYEAR TIRE & RUBBER COMPANY
Akron, Ohio

KEEP THIS CARD HANDY

HOW TO INSTRUCT

Step 1—Prepare the Worker
Put him at ease.
State the job and find out what he already knows about it.
Get him interested in learning job.
Place in correct position.

Step 2—Present the Operation
Tell, show and illustrate one IMPORTANT STEP at a time.
Stress each KEY POINT.
Instruct clearly, completely and patiently, but no more than he can master.

Step 3—Try Out Performance
Have him do the job—correct errors.
Have him explain each KEY POINT to you as he does the job again.
Make sure he understands
Continue until YOU know HE knows.

Step 4—Follow Up
Put him on his own. Designate to whom he goes for help.
Check frequently. Encourage questions.
Taper off extra coaching and close follow-up.

If Worker Hasn't Learned, the Instructor Hasn't Taught.

This old card designed by The Goodyear Tire & Rubber Company to instruct supervisors on how to train workers is as charming and succinct a précis of the art of delegation as one might wish.

3. *Delegate for results.* The key is accountability: setting firm standards and letting staffers know they're responsible for meeting those standards. One bank vice president frequently rewrote inadequate proposals submitted by his staff. Better tactic: returning them with comments and demanding better work. Really *react* to your staff members' output and give them enough feedback so they know where they stand. At the same time, let your staff people handle projects in their own way. In other words, don't confuse tactics and goals; set a standard for results, not methods. Said a steel company execu-

tive, "You don't even try to control how people do their jobs. There's no way to do that—furthermore, no purpose. Everyone does the job a different way, and they all want to show how well they can do it their way. The function of a supervisor is to analyze results, rather than try to control how the job is done."

Let subordinates find their own way to the solution. On the other hand, offer plenty of "easy access" periods for problem-solving and troubleshooting. When a problem does arise, don't—except in an emergency—second-guess your staffer by making a decision "over his head." Use the opportunity to show him or her how to handle it.

4. *Review progress and follow up.* Setting deadlines and enforcing them establish a company beat or "tempo," ensuring that decisions are made promptly and tasks are handled with dispatch. For ordinary purposes, follow up with calendar, tickler file, and/or referral folders. But when assignments are particularly numerous or complex, more elaborate monitoring may be necessary. Try one of the following:

> *Assignment control log.* One senior investment banker devised the general assignments sheet (opposite page), which was used to record *all* department projects, including his own and those of his secretary. He checked the log daily, crossing off completed tasks and, when necessary, calling staffers in for a status update. A variation, appropriate when staffers are juggling numerous projects, is to keep a separate log for each individual. (*Tip:* if you receive many projects, you may find it helpful to keep your own log.)
>
> Such a log also provides a ready source of data for performance evaluations, and ensures that staffers receive credit for their work.
>
> *"Job forms."* This method, based on a checklist concept, is appropriate for any project involving standardized subtasks

GENERAL ASSIGNMENTS SHEET

DATE	ASSIGNMENT	TO WHOM	DUE	DELAY*	COMPLETED BY

*This refers to legitimate delays or postponements, which should be noted so as not to penalize the subordinate unfairly.

that are distributed among several different people. The form lists each subtask, the name of the delegatee, and the due date. It is clipped to project materials, and each individual signs off as he or she completes the task. The graphics department of a large corporation used a job form for each of the brochures it produced. At the end of the day, the department head reviewed each form, made a list of outstanding tasks, and outlined the next day's priorities accordingly.

Wall calendars. For one marketing director, a monthly wall calendar was the method of choice for keeping track of the twenty reports her staff produced each month. As each report was assigned, her secretary added it to the calendar under its due date, using a different-colored marker for each delegatee. For information on other complex project controls, see Chapter 8.

Staff meetings. When the direct reporting staff is a small group (no more than seven or eight people), you may wish to cover most assignments—from assignment to progress reviews to follow-up—at daily or weekly staff meetings. Says one senior accounting executive: "My office has forty-five people and hundreds of detailed projects. I had no time to stay informed. Then I started holding short daily planning meetings in my office [with my key people]. People come in to report on key projects, and we arrange priorities. The system gives me much better control." For a theatrical booking agency, the solution was two weekly staff meetings: one for brainstorming and planning, the other for a more structured review and follow-up.

There are a number of advantages to this method: each person learns what everyone else is doing, and drop-in interruptions are likely to be less frequent since staffers can hold questions or problems until the meeting. For details on structuring meetings, see Chapter 6 (pages 152–57).

Encouraging Employee Contributions and Commitment

A very important aspect of effective delegation is encouraging subordinates to think creatively about their work and exercise initiative.

Martin Edelston, publisher of *Boardroom Reports* and *Bottom Line Personal,* has developed an extremely effective system that encourages employee ideas and commitment, which he calls "I-Power."

It's a simple system in which all employees are asked to come up with at least four improvement ideas per month. The ideas range from a secretary's suggestion to move the file cabinets closer to her desk to save her fifteen minutes of walking time per day (almost eight working days per year!) to a suggested change in mailing processes that saved the company more than $100,000.

Edelston found that the occasional "big" idea, though gratifying, is not the key, but rather that the torrent month after month of an accumulation of "small" ideas, with everyone thinking about improvements all the time, has made a tremendous difference in how his employees think and work.

Taking Aboard New Staff: A Cost/Benefit Formula

Do you need additional staff to help deal with increased responsibilities or expanding business? Perhaps. But you really can't make that decision until your department is running as smoothly as possible. First, take a moment to consider these questions: Is your present staff working at optimum efficiency?

Are you delegating effectively? Are departmental systems well-organized? Are you and your staff well-organized individually? An overwhelming workload does not necessarily indicate a staff shortage. Just as likely, the culprit is internal disorganization. If, however, you can give a definite "yes" to the above questions and the workload still seems to be more than you and your staff can handle, a new person might be the solution. To resolve the question, use the following seven-step cost/benefit formula:

1 Collect two to three weeks' worth of your Daily Lists. Check off all potentially delegable tasks—that is, tasks you could delegate to someone else if you had someone to delegate to—and roughly estimate how much time was given to each.

2 Divide these tasks into two categories: managerial-level tasks and clerical-level tasks.

3 Group the managerial tasks into blocks. The owner of a textiles firm, for example, came up with four blocks—pricing, office management, supplier liaison, and trouble-shooting—that he could turn over to a staff assistant. Tally up time spent on each block.

4 Group delegable clerical-level tasks into blocks: routine correspondence, screening, intraoffice liaison, and so on. Tally up time spent on each block.

5 Can any task blocks be reassigned to existing personnel given (a) their knowledge and skills, (b) their potential to be trained, and/or (c) the existing demands on their time? If not, proceed to the next step.

6 *Costing stage.* Multiply your own hourly salary by the number of hours you spent on potentially delegable tasks (Steps 3 and 4). Then divide by the number of weeks covered, to reach a weekly average. If that figure is higher

than the estimated salary of a new employee, or in the same general range, there is a solid economic basis for considering a new staffer.

An example: An $85,000-per-year manager spends thirty hours in a three-week period on tasks that could be handled by a more junior staffer. Multiplying that time by his salary of $41 per hour—$1,226—then dividing by three (the time period involved), he arrives at a weekly average of $408. Which means that approximately $21,000 per year ($408 × 52 weeks) of his time is spent on lower-level managerial tasks. This is a substantial figure that might incline one to seriously consider hiring new staff.

7 *Benefit stage.* A salary analysis is not necessarily conclusive. What is the benefit? To what use would you put that released time to make good—or better than good—the additional salary? A partner in a small record company found that turning over most of his administrative duties to a new staff assistant meant more time for his primary objective—selling. Even if his success rate was only modest, the additional income would more than cover the new assistant's salary.

To justify benefits when a direct dollar comparison isn't possible, determine what your fundamental skills are—what the company is paying you to do. An example: A compensation manager's chief asset was his analytical skills, exercised through planning, policy development, long-range forecasting, and the design of custom compensation packages for senior executives. However, nearly one-third of his time was taken up with job evaluations and other routine tasks that someone with less experience could easily handle. So he submitted a proposal for a professional-level subordinate, explaining how he planned to use the extra time he would gain and how the company would benefit.

Managing Your Boss

Let's suppose that yesterday your boss handed you a list of priority projects. Today, a new—and contradictory—list sits in your box. What can you do? Below are some ways to work around a boss who's an inconsistent delegator.

• *Clarify via memo.* When you perceive a conflict between assignments, press for clarification as diplomatically as possible. The project-estimate specialist at a real estate firm frequently sends his boss notes like this:

> In order to pull the Maxwell estimate figures together by next Tuesday as you requested, I'll have to postpone evaluating the office building plans you gave me yesterday. Unless I hear otherwise by the end of the day, I'll assume you want me to go with the Maxwell project.

Similarly, when instructions are ambiguous, send a memo clarifying your understanding of the assignment—and your role—and close with the following phrase: "Please don't take the trouble to respond to this unless you wish to modify your instructions."

• *Clarify priorities.* Here's an interesting suggestion from time-management specialist Bob Preziosi: list each major priority on a Post-It, arrange them in rank order as you understand it, and ask your boss if he or she agrees. This can be an illuminating exercise.

- *Propose an alternative.* Sam Miller, a deputy creative director at a large advertising agency, frequently received substantive assignments from his boss without the authority or resources to make them happen. Problems had occurred several times in the past because of this gap between assignments and authority. So Sam decided to turn this seeming liability into an asset, and use these assignments to expand his authority and range of responsibilities. Each time a relevant project came along, he wrote up a presentation, citing causes of difficulty, consequences, and recommendations for change. Here's how to structure such a presentation:

1 Analyze time wasted and/or confusion generated by handling the project as presently planned.
2 Propose one or more specific alternatives.
3 Define other, more productive ways you could be using your time if the suggested changes were implemented.
4 Analyze the time your boss is wasting on activities you could be handling—if you had the authority. If relevant, also define the more productive ways your boss could be using his or her time if changes are implemented.
5 Point out any additional benefits of the changes: increasing departmental productivity, creating a better departmental image, and so forth.

When you're satisfied that you've achieved the right tone—dispassionate, professional, amiable, with no hint of grievance—submit the memo, make an appointment to discuss it in more detail, and keep following up until the matter is resolved. The same approach is equally useful when you want to "sell" your boss on your own initiatives or goals.

Some additional tips:

- Request a due date on all assignments. Make sure you can realistically meet it.
- On a long or complex project, if you're not assigned benchmark dates, assign them to yourself.
- If a deadline must be changed midway, inform your boss immediately—not on the day the task should have been turned in.
- Press for the support or information you need to complete a task: "Here's what I've done. Here's what I need from you to finish this project."

Summary: Delegation Checklist

Symptoms of ineffective delegation	Frequent interruptions and inquiries from staffers.
	Reverse delegation: staffers send projects up to you.
	Frequent need to redo substandard assignments.
	An overflowing action box.
	Frequent need to work late to catch up.
What to delegate	*Tasks:* Projects on your Master List. Elements of complex tasks. Routine and repetitive tasks.
	First-stage drafting, screening, or summarizing tasks. Tasks on which you're procrastinating.
	Functions: A particular activity, such as sales, research, personnel.
	Goals: A specific objective: increase sales by 10 percent, set up new branch office, etc.

Delegatees	Staff (professional, secretarial, clerical). Consultants and outside services. Peers (tradeoffs). Boss (occasionally).
	Match skills and tasks: understand the broad skills underlying important functions; know your staff's strengths and weaknesses; coordinate skills to create a complementary whole.
How to delegate (the assignment loop)	*Defining:* Define task and scope of responsibility.
	Priority: Set purpose and priority.
	Backup: Provide necessary authority, support, and resources.
	Accountability: Delegate for results and accountability.
	Monitoring: Set deadlines and follow up.

11

On Secretaries:
The "Team of Two"

Secretaries are rarely considered part of "the team." As a result, many managers tend to underutilize the time and talents of the one person who could become their most valuable associate. This chapter proposes a rethinking of this narrow vision, and outlines a practical method for helping your secretary become part of a genuine "team of two." The benefits of such a relationship—for both of you—are many. As one top executive pointed out: "The best thing that ever happened to me was having a secretary who wanted to work for a president. I was not the president, so she set out to help me make it. She had a tremendous impact on my effectiveness, and yes, I made it."*

*Coleman Hogan, of the McCord Corporation. Quoted by R. Alec Mackenzie in *The Time Trap: How to Get More Done in Less Time.*

The Executive Secretary

Are you underutilizing your secretary's skills? Does she spend the bulk of her time on routine clerical tasks like filing, transcribing dictation tapes, or typing reports and memos? Is this the best use of her time? Could she be taking over some of the more complex tasks you're currently handling? Are you limiting her effectiveness—and yours—by holding to a narrow definition of a secretary's job?

(Note: Elsewhere in this book I usually refer to a secretary as "he or she," in recognition of the fact that these days male secretaries have established a definite presence in the business world. This form of reference would be very cumbersome in this chapter, however, because it refers to the secretary constantly. Therefore here I use only the female pronoun. In most businesses, career secretaries are still preponderantly female.)

Secretarial duties fall into five "core" categories and five "superogatory" categories, which can be broken down as follows:

CORE	SUPEROGATORY
Typing and transcription	Meetings
Telephone	Reading
Screening	Office supervision
Calendar work (appointments, follow-ups)	"Boss management"
Filing	Independent projects

Within each category, the range of specific tasks can vary from a very basic Grade 1 level to a sophisticated Grade 3 level.

What distinguishes these grades is the degree to which a secretary acts autonomously, exercising independent judgment. While a Grade 1 secretary might confine her filing activities to the physical act of placing papers in file folders, a Grade 3 secretary might set up an entire system. More specifically:

Grade 1 encompasses the most fundamental secretarial functions: typing letters, answering phones, taking dictation, filing, and so on. Generally, a Grade 1 secretary will act entirely on your instructions, taking little or no independent action.

Grade 2 involves more substantive duties that presuppose some independent judgment. Grade 2 tasks might include: prescreening the mail, assessing junk mail and handling standard inquiries; fielding phone calls; making appointments for you; tracking the progress of assignments given out at meetings.

Grade 3 is a "senior secretary" level that entails responsibilities requiring a high level of initiative. Some examples: composing letters for your signature; managing your calendar and generally scheduling your day; summarizing reports and articles for you; supervising less senior clerical personnel.

The key to building an effective partnership is to help your secretary expand "core" functions to the Grade 3 level, and take over as many of the superogatory functions as you and she, together, deem feasible and useful. Where do you begin this developmental process? By identifying your secretary's current duties and comparing them against the checklist on pages 270–72, which rates each task as a Grade 1, 2, or 3. When you've completed the checklist, you should have an accurate picture of your secretary's duties and basic "grade level." Now analyze your results as follows:

1 Is your secretary currently handling most or all Grade 1 functions to your satisfaction? If not, where does the problem originate? Have you perhaps neglected to give her specific instructions or feedback? It's not uncommon to find bosses accepting a poorly typed letter instead of making it clear that such work is unacceptable and asking their secretaries to redo it. Remedy the situation by giving her guidelines for each task.

   If the problem originates with her, try to find out her reasons. One manager, for instance, discovered that his secretary was neglecting certain basics because she was bored. When he balanced these tasks with more challenging work, her attitude changed dramatically. Another manager learned that *he* was the problem: his habit of interrupting his secretary with frequent "must-do" tasks made it impossible for her to get through her clerical work on time. Better planning on his part solved that problem.

   Occasionally, this analysis reveals a square peg in a round hole. For one advertising executive, it confirmed a growing suspicion that her assistant wasn't secretarial material. The young woman wrote terrific blurbs, but was, in the executive's words, "out to lunch" when it came to straightforward typing or filing. The solution in this case was an amicable separation: the assistant was transferred to a slot where she could develop her writing talents, and the executive hired a new secretary.

2 How many of the tasks you checked off qualify as Grade 2 or 3 functions? Two, five, ten? Are you satisfied with the mix between Grade 1 core duties and more substantive

THE SECRETARY PROFILE

TASK	DOES SHE DO THIS?	IF NOT, YOUR CHOICE OR HERS?	TASK GRADE
Mail and Paperwork			
Opens and sorts incoming mail.	_____	_____	1
Collects files pertaining to new correspondence.	_____	_____	1
Discards junk mail.	_____	_____	2
Can use a dictating machine.	_____	_____	1
Returns typed letters for signature within a day.	_____	_____	1
Handles routine inquiries.	_____	_____	2
Brings to your attention papers requiring action.	_____	_____	2
Drafts replies for your approval.	_____	_____	3
Handles much correspondence on her own, reporting back to you.	_____	_____	3
Composes letters from your key ideas.	_____	_____	3
Telephone			
Asks all callers for their name and the nature of their business.	_____	_____	1
Collects information you'll need for call-backs.	_____	_____	2
Makes sure you've returned all calls.	_____	_____	2
Handles many calls on her own, or refers callers elsewhere, reporting back to you on her actions.	_____	_____	3
Makes many calls on your behalf.	_____	_____	3

(Continued)

Screening

Screens drop-in visitors, directing them elsewhere or setting up definite appointments for them. _____ _____ 1

Protects your private time from interruption. _____ _____ 2

Deals with many drop-in visitors on her own, reporting back to you. _____ _____ 3

Puts files or relevant documents on your desk before scheduled appointments. _____ _____ 2

Greets visitors; escorts them to your office. _____ _____ 1

Calls to remind you of "another task" if guests stay past time. _____ _____ 2

Calendar Work

Compares your calendar with hers daily. _____ _____ 1

Knows where to reach you at all times. _____ _____ 1

Makes tentative appointments for you. _____ _____ 2

Makes definite appointments for you and coordinates your schedule. _____ _____ 3

Maintains tickler file. _____ _____ 2

Filing

Files at least once a week. _____ _____ 1

Maintains records-retention plan. _____ _____ 2

(Continued)

Reading

Marks articles and relevant sections of long reports for your attention.	_____	_____	2
Summarizes main points of articles and reports.	_____	_____	3

Meetings

Sits in to take notes.	_____	_____	1
Tracks your assignments and, when you're the leader, makes sure others fulfill their assignments.	_____	_____	2
Attends meetings as your representative.	_____	_____	3

Office Supervision

Keeps track of, and orders, office supplies.	_____	_____	1
Arranges servicing for equipment.	_____	_____	2
Funnels clerical work to less senior personnel or temps.	_____	_____	3

Other Services

Makes travel arrangements.	_____	_____	2
Organizes office functions: conferences, luncheons, etc.	_____	_____	⅔
Monitors your time; i.e., makes sure you follow through on daily tasks.	_____	_____	2
Takes on independent projects.	_____	_____	3

tasks? Do the high-level functions tend to fall into one particular category, such as paperwork, meetings, or office supervision? This analysis may offer you some valuable clues to your secretary's interests and talents. If so, you should also consider whether her talents match your needs. Laura White, a sales manager, realized that her secretary was terrific at "people" functions—supervising other clericals, attending meetings, fielding phone calls. But White needed someone who could do research and take over some of the reports she had to get out each month.

Once you know what you want from this partnership and where your secretary's strengths lie, compile a list of the tasks you would like to add to her duties or see upgraded. Use the "secretary profile" checklist as a guide in selecting tasks. One busy manager responsible for numerous monthly reports realized he could gain more quiet time for planning and writing if his secretary took over all routine correspondence and attended certain less important meetings in his stead. Perhaps you'd like your secretary to take on several specific independent projects, or reduce your reading load by reading articles or reports and summarizing or highlighting key sections.

Ask your secretary to look over the checklist as well, and to draw up her own list of tasks she'd like to handle. Then sit down together and compare lists. Is she willing and able to take over certain duties on your list? Are there any significant discrepancies between your list and hers?

This is the time to clarify expectations and make any necessary compromises. One manager, for instance, asked his secretary to attend certain meetings for him, a request to which she acceded reluctantly. And it soon became apparent that she wasn't temperamentally suited to the task. Because she felt rather intimidated in the meetings and was passive by nature, she neglected to speak up and ask certain key questions. So her reports to her boss were less than complete. The point is to be realistic about your needs and hers. An assertive, outgoing secretary might reach Grade 3 levels on screening or meeting functions, while remaining at Grade 1 when it comes to paperwork. Another secretary, although reliable, might simply be unable to muster the personal initiative necessary for Grade 3 duties. Then, too, you may not wish to give your secretary the authority implicit in Grade 3 activities. In which case, while your relationship may not become the ideal "team of two," it will—more importantly—be a realistic and functional partnership on Grade 1 or 2 levels. Whether or not your secretary reaches Grade 3 in every (or any) category is less important than whether she develops her skills in those areas you deem significant to your mutual productivity.

When you come to terms about her expanded scope of duties, write out a job "contract" that outlines her new functions and specifies both your expectations and hers. Then select one or two tasks as a starting point. Will she need any special training first? If so, schedule instruction sessions. Once she's learned the ropes, review her progress at weekly "developmental" meetings, and encourage her to discuss any problems. Try to hold these weekly meetings until you're satisfied that she's mastered the task—or until it becomes clear that it's not going to work out.

While this type of partnership is based on shared goals and needs, it also involves mutual obligations. For your part, this means actively supporting your secretary's efforts to develop her craft. Some useful tips follow:

• *Make your daily meeting with your secretary the keystone of your day.* In Chapter 2, this meeting was discussed only in terms of processing paper efficiently. It is, however, an equally important means for organizing the whole day for you both. Instead of interrupting each other at will throughout the day with questions or instructions, use this time to outline the day's assignments and priorities, both yours and hers; to discuss any problems; to clarify tasks; to answer questions; and to update previously assigned projects. Then try to avoid giving her additional assignments or switching priorities midstream.

If possible, arrange for someone else to take phone calls during this session. Otherwise, your secretary should inform all callers that you're in a meeting and take brief messages.

At the end of the day, schedule another five- or ten-minute wrap-up session to cover any questions that arose during the day and begin planning for the next day. *Note:* When you're rarely in the office, and a daily meeting isn't feasible, schedule a definite session at least once or twice a week.

• *Shelter her time.* A secretary handling several Grade 3 functions is going to need some interruption-free, private time. For at least an hour a day, arrange to have a receptionist or another clerical staffer take the telephone—or, if necessary, take calls yourself.

When routine typing and filing pile up, consider bringing in a temp, freeing your secretary for more substantive work. One manager, in fact, has made this a weekly habit. Every Friday a temp comes in to clean up the week's typing, duplicating, collating, and filing. She also covers the phone, giving his secretary almost an entire quiet day to work on priority projects.

• *Let others know your secretary is your surrogate.* Some clients and colleagues may resent having to deal directly with your secretary, perceiving it as a slight. So it's a good idea to try to anticipate and neutralize such reactions. Let your associates know that you have complete trust in your secretary's abilities—that, moreover, they're likely to get a faster response by working directly with her on routine matters. Make a point of introducing her by her full name to all visitors:

"This is Jane Marshall," not "This is Janie." This basic courtesy is likely to make them more willing to work through her in the future.

Whether you or your secretary arranges your appointments isn't important. What is critical, however, is consistency. However you choose to handle appointments, be sure to coordinate your desk and pocket calendars with your secretary's. Make calendar coordination a fixed feature of your daily meeting.

If your secretary makes all appointments, she should try to find out the precise nature of the visitor's business to facilitate advance preparation. She should also place all relevant files or data on your desk before guests arrive. If you prefer to screen appointments, ask your secretary to make them tentative and call people back before the end of the day to confirm those you have approved. Try to allow at least ten or fifteen minutes between appointments and, if possible, try to group appointments—rather than spreading them out throughout the day—to consolidate free time.

At the end of the day, your secretary should give you a typewritten copy of the next day's agenda, including addresses and phone numbers of outside appointments and reminders about deadlines, errands, and so on. One busy physician who is rarely in the office at the end of the day has her secretary fax the next day's schedule to her home fax. Another secretary telephones the next day's program into her manager's home answering machine.

If you are frequently out of the office, try to keep your staff abreast of your whereabouts. Senior executive Winston Reynolds leaves his appointment calendar open on his secretary's desk for the four or five people who might need him.

• *Keep her informed.* There is one unbreakable "information" rule: *always tell your secretary where you're going and when you'll return to the office.* Beyond that, try to keep her fully informed about your plans, goals, and projects. The more she knows about your work, the more she'll be able to handle on her own. Use her as a sounding board. Secretaries often know more about what's going on than do their bosses. And if she's hooked into the office grapevine, her advice and information might prove invaluable.

• *Keep yourself informed.* The old saw about no news being good news should not be your modus operandi when it comes to your secretary. One executive assumed that all was well because her secretary never said otherwise. But the secretary's resentment was filtering out in other ways: messages conveniently "forgotten," letters that sat in her in-box for days. Since many secretaries are afraid to challenge a boss directly, passive resistance becomes the only available outlet. The solution is to let your secretary know that you're always available to discuss problems or grievances, and that you're willing, within reasonable limits, to work out an agreeable compromise or solution. If necessary, try to make a point of asking her how she feels about new tasks or assignments and whether she's encountering any special problems.

Herewith, some common grievances—and solutions:

• *Personal errands.* In the words of one secretary: "I really resent the 'servant' tasks: picking up theater tickets for my boss and his wife, buying birthday cards for his relatives. I wouldn't mind if it were an occasional favor, but it's become a regular routine." *Solutions:* One executive hired a college student for several hours a week to run personal errands. You can also hire personal shoppers.

• *Interruptions.* A tendency to interrupt secretaries at will is a major source of irritation. If you suspect that you're fragmenting your secretary's time with frequent questions or emergency projects, try a variation of the "interruption log" described in Chapter 6 (see p. 150). Ask your secretary to log each time you interrupt her for one week, then go over the list together. If a high proportion of "break-ins" indicates poor planning on your part, review Chapters 2 and 5 on paper and task management. One manager, for example, discovered that he interrupted his secretary at least ten times a day to request papers or ask the whereabouts of certain files. Planning what he needed at the beginning of the day solved the problem and also gave him a greater sense of control.

• *The 4:45 P.M. "must do."* Unnecessarily assigning work at the end of the day is particularly irritating to many secretaries. Try to give your secretary most letters and assignments by 3:00 P.M., so she can schedule her own time accordingly.

The Executive Secretary: An Endangered Species?

It wasn't so very long ago that one way of distinguishing a manager or professional from a secretary was that the manager didn't type. In fact, a consultant tells the story of being quite embarrassed some years ago when, during a consulting assignment, her client saw her typing up her report and said pleasantly but firmly, "I'm paying you too much money for you to let me see you typing." And so it was.

But with the personal computer having become not only ubiquitous but invested with a kind of allure, that line, though certainly not disappeared, has blurred considerably. People who wouldn't have been caught dead typing ten years ago today enthusiastically swap pointers about their favorite word-processing programs.

This widespread shift, which is very apparent on the middle-manager level, and in smaller companies and in some companies perceived as cutting-edge on senior levels as well, has forced a reevaluation of the role of the executive—that is, private—secretary. If so many people are doing their own typing, then shouldn't secretaries, in their traditional one-on-one role of personal assistant to a single individual, be on the way out?

What seems to be developing is a mix in favor of a word-processing pool, on the one hand, to type longer pieces, and administrative assistants (AAs) to assist in a kind of "new space" between the traditional manager and secretary. Said one executive, "The personal computer, in combination with voice mail on our telephone system, has greatly reduced the need for the traditional secretary. Now, the members of our organization that previously did secretarial work are doing administrative tasks."

My own take on the situation, which diverges somewhat from prevailing trends, is this: Managers whose secretaries spend the bulk of their time on straight dictation/typing tasks can probably make an easy transition to a WP/AA arrangement. In contrast, for a manager whose secretary consistently spends a high percentage of time on screening and substantive tasks, the switch would probably have adverse consequences. A private secretary's chief asset is her ability to make judgment calls *on behalf of one individual,* an expertise that cannot, by nature, be pooled.

In fact, the nature of a good executive secretary's services are so substantial that I think a new method of compensation should be tried. The problem now is high productivity for marginal pay.

What I propose may sound somewhat radical. It seems to me that there should be an independent secretarial career line that parallels management advancement, whereby secretaries *are promoted as secretaries,* not changed into managers.

Secretary grades would be established by a combination of

skill level (which could be determined by a review of the kind described in this chapter) and the rank of her manager. Thus, a Grade 3 secretary to a middle manager could earn a higher salary than a Grade 1 secretary to a senior manager. I also propose that a Grade 3 salary be approximately in the middle-manager ballpark, and that lower grades be established proportionately.

Although to my knowledge this method of compensation remains untried, I believe it would generate a level of enthusiasm and initiative, and a tapping of genuine talent, that would yield a dramatic gain in productivity. Payment that acknowledges the very real "multiplier" contribution of a highly skilled secretary will, I suspect, unleash a powerful business resource.

Sharing a Secretary

Alice Baker, a systems analyst for a data processing firm, shares a secretary with three other analysts. In the last two years, the four analysts have had six different secretaries. With one exception, they all quit within four months, overwhelmed by the burden of playing private secretary to four bosses, each of whom felt his or her work had top priority.

A secretary who works for more than one boss—and some secretaries support up to seven—simply doesn't have the time for many (if any) of the superogatory functions discussed earlier. Still less is it her job to run personal errands. Nor can she mediate between the conflicting demands of her various bosses. If sharing is to work out for all parties, the managers involved must be willing to cooperate with each other, and coordinate their workloads and assignments equitably and realistically. Some practical tips follow:

- *Allocation of work.* Set up a "work center" on your secretary's desk: a stack of boxes, each labeled with a manager's name. You and your colleagues put her assignments into your individual boxes, marking date, time of submission, and desired return date. Add a big red check mark or star to priority projects. Also try to set deadlines that are realistic. Your secretary then works through the priorities first, and processes the remaining tasks in strict order of submission. If an urgent task comes up, the manager concerned should first clear the break in routine with his colleagues before giving the secretary the green light.
- *Color coding.* Assign a color to each boss, and use that color everywhere, on materials ranging from files to phone messages.
- *Instructions.* For projects requiring special instructions or background information, save your time and hers by using a ready-made form. Fill in the necessary details and attach the form to the assignment. A sample form appears on page 282.
- *The telephone.* Another set of labeled compartments on your secretary's desk can function as a "message center" from which you and your colleagues are responsible for picking up your own messages. Also try to arrange a telephone hour during which you and the other managers take all calls, giving your secretary some quiet time for priority tasks.

The Paraprofessional

Fifteen or twenty years ago, the semi-managerial position of paraprofessional barely existed. Today, many businesses are employing paraprofessionals, particularly law, consulting, and

ASSIGNMENT

Date: _____

Time: _____

Please return by: _____

From: _____

Assignment: _____

_____

☐ Report ☐ Draft   ☐ Single-space   Duplicates to:

_____

☐ Letter ☐ Finished ☐ Double-space   _____

copy   _____

☐ Memo   _____

Special instructions: _____

_____

_____

☐ Red check if assignment has very high priority.

architectural firms. The paralegal remains the paradigm for this type of job. However, the definition of a paralegal varies widely from law firm to law firm. In some, paralegals are college-educated and specially trained. Their assignments, largely conceptual in nature, may include research, summarizing of data, first-draft briefs, preliminary interviews with clients, and other "client servicing" work. A group of "professional paralegals" typically will share secretarial support. Usually, a "professional paralegal" system of this kind runs smoothly because hierarchical lines are clear, with the paralegals firmly established as semi-managers.

More problematic is a system utilizing paralegals drawn from the secretarial ranks. Their lawyer bosses often continue to perceive them as secretaries—with many still doing clerical tasks—while their erstwhile secretarial colleagues may resent their new status and occasionally sabotage them. Remedying this caste problem requires some formal acknowledgment of the change in status. Among the possibilities:

- Distinguish the upgraded paralegal by sending her to a training course for a week or two, whether or not she needs it.
- Compensate paralegals for extra effort as you would any other professional—with bonuses rather than overtime.
- A paralegal should not type unless she's clearly drafting her own project. If possible, paralegals should have some clerical help.
- Select a neutral and well-respected "monitor" to funnel work from paralegals to secretaries. Providing a buffer is extremely important in defusing any resentment a secretary may feel about taking orders from a former peer.

Without a Secretary: For Freelancers and Independent Professionals

If you're an entrepreneur or freelancer without secretarial support, processing paper will be more of a burden. Although the

TRAF procedure described in Chapter 2 applies to you too, your "refer" box will not get much use, while your "action" box will swell proportionately. To keep up with the accumulation, four tactics may be helpful:

1 Allocate enough paper-processing time. Begin with an hour each day and increase or decrease as quantity and experience dictate. If, on the other hand, you're frequently out of the office, you may prefer to reserve a weekly "administrative" day or half-day for paperwork.

2 Take advantage of every possible standardization procedure and efficiency method. See Chapters 3, 7, 12, and 13.

3 Consider purchasing or leasing a small copier. Several companies make reasonably priced small models suitable for an entrepreneur's needs. If you do a fair amount of copying, your own machine will not only enhance efficiency, but save you numerous trips to the local copy store.

4 Hire whatever part-time or irregular help your resources will allow. The key here is to isolate a *type* of activity you don't need or want to do yourself. For example, one freelance journalist maintained, in her words, "a stable of elves" ("little people who run around a lot"). These were high school students, paid the going baby-sitter's rate, who ran errands after school and on Saturdays, checked sources, made phone calls, and typed preliminary drafts of articles. Another entrepreneur hired a graduate student for half a day a week just to compose letters. More typically, part-time helpers are assigned straight typing, tape transcription, and/or stenographic tasks. Outside services are also available for these latter duties.

Summary: A Guide to Boss/Secretary Teamwork

With an Executive Secretary

1 Encourage her to expand "core" duties (typing, telephone, screening, calendar, filing) to Grade 2 and 3 levels—exercising greater independent judgment and initiative—and to take over as many substantive extras as you and she deem mutually useful. When you come to terms on tasks to be upgraded or added, draw up an informal contract outlining these responsibilities and clarifying both your expectations and hers.

2 Make your daily meeting with her the keystone of your day. Use this time to discuss assignments and priorities, solve problems, clarify tasks, and so on. When a daily meeting isn't feasible, schedule a longer, weekly session.

3 Shelter her time by arranging phone coverage for an hour or two a day to give her quiet time for priority work. When routine tasks pile up, bring in a temp.

4 Keep her informed about your whereabouts, plans, goals, and so on.

5 Keep yourself informed. If she has any problems or grievances, encourage her to discuss them with you. Try to avoid interrupting her with frequent questions or "must-do's," sending her on personal errands, or assigning work at the end of the day.

With a Shared Secretary

1 Set up a "work center" on her desk: a set of labeled boxes (one per boss) into which all assignments are placed,

marked with date, time of submission, and deadline. Use another set of labeled compartments for a telephone "message center."

2 Clear any switch in priorities with your colleagues first before giving her the go-ahead. Otherwise, she should handle all priority work first, then tackle everything else in strict order of submission. Mark priorities with a red check mark.

For the Freelancer

1 Allocate "administrative" time for processing paper.
2 Take advantage of all possible standardization and efficiency techniques and equipment.
3 Employ all the part-time and irregular help your resources will allow.

HIRING AND FIRING GUIDELINES

HIRING

Preliminary Considerations

- According to a report by the Bureau of Labor Statistics, secretarial schools graduate only two-thirds of the secretaries needed to fill the 305,000 yearly job openings. So widen your "selection pool" by considering hiring two part-timers to share one full-time secretarial job. Since part-timers usually aren't interested in moving up, they're more likely to stay on. Parents with small children and aspiring actors and artists are your best candidates for this kind of job-sharing. Or hire a retiree. Mature secretaries receive high marks for reliability and loyalty.

Interview Tactics

- Before the interview, write out a comprehensive and accurate job description, including all basic functions (paper processing, the daily meeting, telephone work, screening, dictation, making appointments, filing, etc.) as well as more substantive duties (supervising clericals, attending meetings, arranging for travel, ordering supplies, bill-paying or bookkeeping functions, etc.).
- Ask each candidate how she might handle various situations: a persistent caller, a frequent drop-in visitor you don't wish to see, an angry client. Ask her to describe herself, so as to judge how articulate she is.

(Continued)

Is she willing to learn new skills, such as using a new word processing or other computer program or a dictation machine? Find out what she'd like to see the job develop into. Find out what tasks, if any, she would prefer not to handle.

- In addition to the standard typing and dictation tests, ask candidates to retype a letter marked up with handwritten changes and requiring simple grammatical and spelling corrections.

- If "extras" will be involved in the job, like making coffee or picking up your lunch, contract for them in advance. Be clear about special circumstances: Will she often be alone in the office? Will she have to work late fairly often or put in much overtime?

The Transition Period

- Ask your current secretary to prepare a manual of office procedures and an up-to-date file index. The manual should include a list of your chief business associates, an explanation of the filing system, and general information about routine office procedures (location of various forms, etc.). If possible, have your new secretary start a week before your current secretary departs.

FIRING

Boss/secretary relationships don't always work out, and it is sometimes necessary to institute separation procedures:

(Continued)

- To forestall the possibility of lawsuits or union intervention, begin compiling a "show cause" record of assignments undone, done incorrectly, completed late, and so on. Send your secretary all assignments in writing and make a duplicate of those assignments for your own records. Put her on warning twice, two weeks apart. Then, if things don't improve, fire her.
- Firing is an unpleasant task at best, but the sudden departure of a secretary can create havoc in the office if you've allowed yourself to become too dependent on her. It's a good idea, therefore, to familiarize yourself with the office set-up: how the files are arranged, where various documents are kept, and so on. Otherwise, even if your secretary is just out sick or on vacation—or quits unexpectedly—you may find yourself at a loss. The procedures manual and file index mentioned above are valuable tools to have on hand at all times, for just such circumstances.

PART IV

GETTING

ORGANIZED

THE

ELECTRONIC

WAY

12

Using Your Computer to Get Organized

In the computer age, the process of getting organized is the same as it's always been. It is a mental process, a process of decision-making. The intent of this chapter is to describe how computers—ranging from full-sized desktop models to pocket-size electronic organizers—can be used as organizing and time management tools. However, the ubiquitousness of computers, and of computer chat, has obscured the fact that these tools are still quite mysterious to a lot of people.

The computer's ability to sort and regroup textual elements into many configurations and to transfer text with simple keystrokes from one document to another within one's own computer and/or to another computer across the corridor, or across the world, vastly extends the reach of organizing.

But conversely, the very vastness and comprehensiveness of the computer's abilities is much more than some people either want or need. For some, to use a computer to get organized is like shooting a fly with a bazooka—there's just too much firepower for the need. It's surprising how many computer-literate people, including computer company executives whom you might expect to have computerized their personal systems, continue to employ the same tried and true manual techniques for personal organization and time management because they simply work best for them.

A third path lying between wholesale adoption and complete abstinence is to employ computerized functions selectively, to fit certain situations or needs. One executive, for example, conducts weekly electronic mail meetings with his far-flung staff group, while handling his personal organization and time management with traditional calendar and yellow-pad "to do" lists.

So it is not the intent of this chapter to influence you toward jettisoning your calendar and pad in favor of a computer, or the other way around, but rather to lay out a menu of some of the ways computers can assist you in your organizing effort. You can then choose which techniques make sense in view of your own computer comfort level or willingness to learn and your organizational requirements.

Three caveats. First, if you are really not temperamentally suited to the very precise and somewhat hypnotic interaction with a computer, you might do better to leave the actual use of computers to your secretary and assistants. Second, don't get so caught up in the allure of computing as to lose sight of common sense. One executive found that an assistant, asked to monitor the progress of a group of job candidates, had spent hours searching for the correct software tracking program, when a simple index-card setup was perfectly adequate to the task. And third, be wary of getting to the point where you and your colleagues are exchanging so much information by computer that ordinary human contact is substantially diminished.

The ebb and flow of opinion, "body language," intuitive cues, and weaving affiliations are as fundamental to doing business as is exchanging information.

Organizing, as mentioned before, is essentially a conceptual, decision-making process that stays constant regardless of the tools used for its execution. Two important things to remember are that equipment itself can't organize you, and that an organizing/time management program will not totally replace your existing manual methods.

This chapter recapitulates key organizing concepts developed elsewhere in *The Organized Executive*, including the TRAF paperwork system, the Master List/Daily List time-management system, scheduling and calendar management, communicating and handling interruptions, staff and project management, handling meetings, and efficient travel, and shows how they can be translated into an electronic approach. It defines, for example, what it means to "TRAF" on a computer, the special features of a computerized Master List, and the like.

To start, this chapter undertakes to provide a basic overview of what a computer is and to point out basic features. Readers knowledgeable about computers might prefer to turn directly to page 302 for the discussion of how to use computers and organizers in organization and time management. For more information on basic computer terms, turn to the glossary on page 333.

Computers, Networks, and Electronic Mail

Desktop Computers

A desktop computer is the full-size "basic" computer that comes to mind most often when people think of a personal computer, or PC. It is composed of a central processing unit or CPU (the boxy casing containing the innards of the machine), one or more floppy disk drives (visible as slots in the CPU), a keyboard, and a monitor. A printer is a separate machine (a "peripheral") connected by cable to the computer, which on command inks out on paper what has been entered on the screen.

Most PCs fall into one of two main categories: the IBM group, consisting of IBM PCs and the IBM-compatible brands, such as Compaq and Dell; and the Macintosh, manufactured by Apple Computer. An "IBM-compatible" is a computer that runs on the same MS-DOS operating system as the IBM, and that can run software designed for the IBM.

Portable Computers

Most portable computers are single units, as contrasted with the several components of a desktop. That is, screen, keyboard, CPU, and hard disk drive are all in one compact package with a carrying handle. It is almost like a portable typewriter fitted with a screen that flips or pulls up from the unit for use. Peripherals such as floppy disk drives and modems may be internal or external to the unit, depending on the capacity of the model.

You can copy any or all of your computer files and programs

DESKTOP COMPUTER FEATURES

Most desktop computers today have the following minimum specifications:

- Internal hard disk (Storage capacity of 80 megabytes or more is recommended.)
- One or more floppy disk drives (3.5" and/or 5.25")
- RAM ("random access memory," or working memory) of at least 2 megabytes
- A monitor, color or monochrome, capable of displaying graphics as well as text and numbers
- Internal modem or fax modem
- Extra slots into which various devices can be plugged to expand capacity or provide special capabilities

SERVICE FEATURES

Service is a major factor in choosing a computer. Look for the following:

- Length of warranty. Three years is considered "top of the line."
- Is there a period of on-site service during warranty? Make sure your service contract specifies a definite response time—for example, eight to twenty-four hours.
- Round-the-clock telephone support for the life of the computer.

from your office desktop to your portable and back again, which means your office can go with you wherever you go.

Certainly light weight, high speed, a crisp display, and a comfortable keyboard will top your portable wish list. But for portability you give up something, perhaps in keyboard design, or ease of entering numeric information. You must choose your portable carefully to balance deficits against advantages.

Portables come in a range of sizes: the lunchbox, the laptop, the notebook, and the subnotebook, whose keyboards are intended for typing, and the hand-held palmtop computer, which is too small to permit ten-finger typing. Finally, there is the hand-held organizer, or "personal information manager."

LUNCHBOX OR LUGGABLE. This is really a portable desktop computer. It is about the size and weight of a portable sewing machine. It has a screen like those of other portables, but otherwise it can have virtually the same capability and feel as a desktop computer. A luggable is too heavy and bulky for use on the move, and in any case usually requires an AC outlet.

LAPTOP. Any portable computer that can be used on the lap can be considered a laptop, but specifically the term means a fairly large unit—about the size of a briefcase—that weighs eight pounds or more. Even though the smaller and lighter notebook portable has gained tremendously in capacity and has therefore overtaken the laptop in the marketplace, the heavier laptop still has its fans, because the closer to full-size a portable is, the more apt the keyboard is to approximate that of a desktop computer. Some laptops are so substantial that people use them as their "first" computer, in lieu of a desktop. Laptop manufacturers include NEC, Compaq, Sharp, IBM, and Toshiba.

NOTEBOOK.   Notebook computers are about the size of an 8½-by-11-inch paper notebook and weigh less than eight pounds—some as little as four pounds. The handy size and weight are counterbalanced by more compromises in design. However, with dramatic improvements in notebook design and engineering, most portable users find that notebooks fully meet their needs; some notebooks are available with color screens. The crowded notebook marketplace includes Compaq, Dell, GateWay 2000 (IBM), Macintosh PowerBook (Apple), NEC, and Toshiba.

SUBNOTEBOOK.   This category of portable computers is characterized by even lighter weight—two to four pounds. Contenders in this portion of the portable computer market include Apple, Atari, Dell, and Zeos.

PALMTOP.   The palmtop is the first computer-in-your-pocket, weighing in at about eleven ounces and literally fitting into the palm of your hand. The dominant model is the Hewlett-Packard 95LX. Palmtops are real computers, not glorified organizers. The HP95LX is IBM-compatible, and comes with a modified version of the spreadsheet program Lotus 1-2-3 installed. Its tiny keyboard does not permit ten-finger typing, but is fine for shorter memos and notes.

ELECTRONIC HAND-HELD ORGANIZERS.   These computerized "personal information managers," which measure roughly three by five inches and weigh under eight ounces, are among the handiest tools for on-the-go organization. You can type information on the mini-keyboard, and then, using any word in the entry, call the whole entry up onto the small screen. They also include a calendar and schedule, calculator, and phone and address directory. Some organizer models also offer extra "cards" for functions such as expenses and language learning.

Because organizers are a hand-held dumping ground for anything that might pop into your head, they can be particularly useful for people who don't consider themselves organized. Entries never get lost; they can always be retrieved.

These organizers are self-contained systems. If, however, you also use a PC, select an organizer with a linking device that permits you to transfer data between your organizer and the PC. Cables that permit you to exchange data directly between one organizer and another are also available.

The Sharp Wizard and the Casio B.O.S.S. are well-known organizers.

PEN-BASED COMPUTERS. And now for something completely different. Pen-based computers are an entirely new type of portable PC on which you write with a stylus—a special pen—upon a pad. The pad is a computer. To date, not all the bugs have been worked out. For example, pen-based computers recognize only printing, not cursive handwriting. So far they are used primarily by people who collect information in the field, such as insurance adjusters and salespersons. The information they write on the pad can be transmitted instantly by modem to the home office. The IBM ThinkPad, the Apple Newton, and models from NCR and Grid are current products in this field.

For a closer look at features and accessories available for portable computers, see the Appendix on page 336.

Networks

In many companies, the company's computers are hooked up to a common hard disk (called a file server) that allows individuals to exchange documents and share printers, modems, and other peripherals. Networks are enormously efficient in that they allow many people, such as everyone in a project group, to view, edit, and refer shared work-in-progress simultaneously.

Electronic Mail

Electronic mail is a means of exchanging messages by computer rather than by telephone or memo. Intelligent use of E-mail can help reduce telephone tag and ensure that important information is accessible at all times.

It works like this. Wine company executive Michael Rose types into his computer the name "Jim Jacobson" and Jim's "address" (code number). He then types, "Where's the 1,000-case shipment due from California Thursday?" Jim, who checks his mailbox every few hours, types back, "Rail snafu misrouted shipment to Montreal. Will arrive tomorrow." No phones, no interruptions, no lost message slips.

The same message can be sent simultaneously to five or ten or twenty people, or, for that matter, to everyone on the E-mail system. So, for example, if ten people need to see the agenda for an upcoming conference, a few keystrokes will send the agenda to each of them. If you wish a response, you can use the "return receipt" function to indicate the date by which a response is needed. Once you have confirmation of delivery, you can either delete the message, move it to your calendar on the day you specified for a response as a reminder for you, or archive it to a hard disk or floppy disk.

On most E-mail systems, you can set up individual "file folders" with the names of the people with whom you communicate most often, saving both incoming and outgoing messages. This enables you to keep track of communications with those individuals. Folders can also be set up by project, by date, or by whatever category you like.

With a computer and a modem, you can subscribe to a commercial E-mail service, such as MCI Mail, AT&T Mail, and EasyLink, which allows subscribers to send and receive E-mail and faxes through a central clearinghouse. You can even communicate through commercial E-mail with a low-tech individual who has neither fax nor computer. Send a message in the usual way to your E-mail service, and the service will send it, for a price, to someone's office or home.

Getting Organized the Electronic Way

Using the TRAF System Electronically

The good news about paper, as you might remember from Chapter 2, is that there are really only four and a half things you can do with it: *T*oss it away, *R*efer it to someone else, *A*ct on it, or *F*ile it—and the half, read it. These four choices form the acronym TRAF. Adding a second F, for the all-important *F*ollow-up, gives us TRAFF.

The decision-making process represented by the TRAF, or TRAFF, acronym can be enlarged to include the computer, and—more good news—the computer's special abilities can extend your TRAFing reach. (To start, you'll need a definition, somewhat simplified here, of the word "file" in computerese. Every letter, memo, report, or other document typed into the computer is a separate file that must be assigned a name. Thus a "file directory" or a "file list" is simply a list of documents.)

Toss. A hard disk can get cluttered just as a desktop can if it is a depository for too much stuff that should be thrown away. To toss a piece of paper means to throw it into the wastebasket. To toss a computer document means to delete it. Simple keystrokes do the trick. So keep your hard disk files current by regularly deleting any part of that day's production that doesn't need to be retained, especially if you print out "hard copy" (that is, paper copies) as well.

On a longer-term basis, a very worthwhile project is to "clean out" your computer files to free up hard disk space and unclutter your file lists.

To start the file deletion project, first print out your file directory, then pull each file up on the screen, and handle it in one of three ways:

1 *Delete.* Delete those files that are no longer needed. As each file is deleted, cross it off the paper list.
2 *Refer.* Just as with paper, some of your files might best be referred on to others. Mark each referral on your list with an R. (See the discussion of the referral process on the next page.)
3 *Store on floppy disks.* As an alternative to actually discarding files, simply transfer unneeded files to a floppy disk and then delete them from the hard disk. Label and store the disk in a storage disk file box.

A WORD ABOUT BACKUP. It is said that the world is divided into two groups of people: those who have lost data, and those who are about to. Backing up your files electronically— that is, copying the material on your hard disk onto floppy disks—is *essential.* If you don't have complete backup disks or tapes, the entire contents of your hard disk could be lost. If you have backups, in the event of a hard disk failure you can simply copy your backups onto a new or repaired hard disk.

Other good rules: Stop periodically during a long work session and save your work, and back up your work files on floppy disk each time you leave the computer for any length of time.

REFER. To "refer" a piece of paper means to pass it on to someone else, either through putting it in your out box, dropping it off on someone else's desk, or using a referral folder. What are the electronic equivalents of these processes? These referral techniques have their computerized analogies but, because of the computer's capabilities, across a much vaster range. In what situations would you use them? Here are six different ways to refer by computer:

1 *Paper referral.* Print out the document you wish to refer and pass it along as you would any other piece of paper.

2 *E-mail.* The electronic equivalent of the out box is, of course, E-mail (see page 301), through which you can send a message to one person, or to everyone in the system.

3 *Fax referral.* Letitia Martin uses her computer's fax modem to fax the monthly operations meeting schedule to her colleagues in the operations group who aren't covered by electronic mail. *Tip:* When documents are scheduled for distribution at a meeting, why not predistribute them through E-mail or fax?

4 *Disk referral.* Copy a document onto a floppy disk, attach an explanatory note or tag, and put it into your out box.

5 *Computerized individual referral files.* Say, for example, that you confer frequently with Len. Create a "Len" file in the program you use most often, and whenever a Len issue comes up, type it in. Prepare for your next confab

with Len by printing out your "Len" file and, *voilà,* an instant agenda. *Tip:* When you send Len an E-mail message, copy that into Len's file as well if it requires further discussion or follow-up.

6 *Copying and transferring.* You can expand the whole concept of referral by copying files from one computer to another via floppy disk or network. The same effect can be achieved between electronic organizers and computers with the appropriate cable connections. For example, Scott Marino, a salesman for an electronics firm, was able to copy the price list from his hand-held organizer into the organizers of several colleagues who had been away when the latest price update was issued.

Letitia Martin particularly appreciates the ease of personal coordination. So that her new husband would know all her friends, she copied her personal phone list into her husband's organizer. Letitia and her husband also download their travel schedules into each other's organizers. At the office, Letitia passed on her "important numbers" list to her secretary.

ACT. To "act" means that you do it yourself. For example, suppose a speaker you have engaged for a seminar requests a testimonial letter. Either you type that letter into the computer yourself or you dictate it into a dictating machine for your secretary to transcribe. Your secretary can, if your computers are linked, type the letter into his or her machine, and you can call it up on yours to review.

Another example: Your boss has approved your proposal. Now you have to prepare an action plan. Then, if your computer is linked to others in a group, you can "refer" it by sending it electronically to your colleagues for their review.

Computers can also provide a very useful backup to encourage you to process your daily stack of paperwork. Greg Innis, for example, a human-resources manager, found it easy enough to TRAF papers into his action stack but not so easy to get down to dealing with them. So he used a computer to help him keep his paperwork on track. He created a computer file called PP, for "priority papers." After TRAFing his incoming papers daily in the normal way, printing out and adding to the stack any important E-mail messages, faxes, etc., he would flip through the stack quickly and select the three top items he wanted to make sure to complete that day. Greg then listed those three tasks in the PP file.

Then every day at 4:30, Greg checked the PP file, completed any of the three tasks still outstanding, and deleted them as he finished them. Reaching "blank screen mode," as he called it, at the end of each day, his chief tasks accomplished and deleted, ensured that the jobs got done and also gave him a feeling of real satisfaction.

FILE.   One of the great conveniences offered by the computer is, of course, automatic filing, sorting and classifying by any categories that seem useful. But filing documents for ready retrieval, which seems easy on a computer, since every document is listed on the file directory, can be a test of the art of filing. What was very easy to enter can prove to be very difficult to retrieve if the file names have become meaningless to you.

Say, for example, that you're looking at an old file entry that reads "SWAT." What in the world is that? When naming new files, a good rule is to apply the "three-months test": three months from now, will you know what this file name means?

To set up a retrieval system for your computer files, think of your computer's hard disk as a huge file cabinet. A long computer file directory with documents haphazardly named is like a file cabinet full of unordered file folders assigned overprecise names that you can't recall. Finding anything becomes an ordeal.

The same basic file logic that applies to your paper files— using broad headings with obvious names—can help make sense of your computer files as well.

For detailed information on computer filing techniques, interested readers should consult a range of books and manuals. Four basic filing methods that have proved useful, used either alone or in combination, are the "key word" method, setting up subdirectories, cross-referencing, and using file extensions.

1 *Key word.* Commence each file pertaining to a certain topic or correspondent with a common word. If, for example, you write occasionally to Rose Widgets, identify each letter by the name "Rose," and add something that distinguishes that particular document—like the date. Key words work well for up to fifteen, even twenty listings. Beyond that, the same problem—too many files to keep track of—occurs again.

2 *Subdirectories.* Just as you can insert dividers in a file drawer to mark major divisions, you can put your computer files into subdirectories. For example, Sara Fisher, an independent TV writer and screenwriter, divided her numerous files into four main categories: query letters to producers, proposals of story ideas, actual scripts, and general correspondence. Since names for subdirectories on her IBM-compatible personal computer cannot be longer than eight characters without an extension (see below), she named her subdirectories QUERIES, PROPS, SCRIPTS, and GENLETS. These subdirecto-

ries themselves contained a great many files, so she subdivided each one further, creating subordinate subdirectories. Thus she divided her SCRIPTS subdirectory into three groups—scripts she was currently working on, scripts that had already been produced, and scripts that had not yet been produced. She named these sub-subdirectories DRAFTS, PROD, and UNPROD.

3. *Cross-reference.* Since it is very easy to copy files from one subdirectory to another and to rename files, you can duplicate files in any way that you find useful. For example, Eileen Logan, an international-marketing specialist, had created a file for her report on cosmetics-buying trends in France, given it the title COSMETIC, and put it in a subdirectory named FRANCE. However, she also had subdirectories for cosmetics trends year by year. So she copied the file to her subdirectory COSM96 and renamed the file there FRANCE96.

4. *File extensions.* In the MS-DOS file system used by most IBM-compatible computers, file names, like subdirectory names, can be no more than eight letters long, unless they have extensions—a period followed by up to three letters. One might have several files for which the name FRANCE96 was appropriate—a report, a schedule of promotional events, a sales projection, and so on. These could be given titles such as FRANCE96.RPT, FRANCE96.PR, and FRANCE96.SP. Not only are all files pertaining to "France in 1996" identifiable, but the extensions allow one to identify and collect all files of a certain class. To prepare a report on sales projections in all of Western Europe one would start by calling up the files FRANCE96.SP, ITALY96.SP, GBRIT96.SP, and so on.

The Contacts and Business Card File

One vexing filing issue for which no one seems able to come up with a satisfactory solution is that of accumulated business cards. But with the magic of computers, business cards, and contacts of any sort, can be transformed from an annoying irritant to a real gold mine of professional and personal resources.

This transformation occurs by means of the "contact manager" (which can go by different names depending on the software) in your organizing software.* When you call up a contact manager, a form will come up on your screen on which you can record the name, title, and address of the person and any information that might prove useful. Here are two examples from the contacts files of an independent management consultant:

> **George Prescott.** Met at Martin Eberhard's dinner party 11/30. Financial planner. Summer home on Cape Cod.
> **Thelma Stoneman.** Agent for graphics designers. Met at Women's Entrepreneur Conference 6/16. Knows Sheila Stetson.

With entries like this, and software with versatile search features so that you can search your contacts file by name, key words, date, etc., you have a wealth of resources at your command. If, for example, future endeavors suggest the need for a graphics designer, or you become interested in buying a property on Cape Cod, enter those words and these entries will

---

*If you have heavy contact management requirements, you might want to consider separate contact-management software specifically intended for that purpose, such as Act! or TeleMagic. This software—most useful for people whose "contacts are their life," such as writers who want to track their contacts with editors, executive search specialists, etc.—will permit the entry of virtually unlimited information concerning your contacts, including discussions, negotiations, or whatever your interests may be.

come up. For another example, one foundation organizes its current list of fund-raising prospects by industry category. Under "Health Services," for instance, there appeared the names of pharmaceutical company, a manufacturer of surgical equipment, and other prospective contributors, ready to be tapped when an appropriate project came up. The same prospects were also organized by geographic area.

However, do not discard your manual business-card files, which are a valuable resource. Mark on the card the date and occasion of your meeting and the names of mutual contacts. Then file it. When you expect fairly regular contact, staple it to an address-file card. Or set up a separate system using 3×5 index cards, organized by name or professional category.

When instant access isn't critical, the easiest method is to keep business cards in a file folder with closed sides labeled "Names" or "Contacts." Alternatively, add them to an appropriate file in your regular system.

Organizing Time the Electronic Way

In adopting the four-point time management program recommended in *The Organized Executive,* you may find that computerizing your program can markedly increase the ease and flexibility of time management. To recap, the four-point program is:

1 Create a Master List of all tasks of every description in a single location.
2 Pull out your Daily List from your Master List and other sources.
3 Set priorities.
4 Whenever feasible, schedule your tasks according to your personal energy timeframe.

There are numerous organization/time management programs on the market, ranging from high-powered software that will enable you to monitor complex projects to simpler programs oriented toward your personal time and task management. A number of programs are listed in the Office Appendix. Palmtops and hand-held organizers generally come equipped with organization and time management capabilities, making it unnecessary to buy separate software. In this section, we take a general approach that will apply to all or most of the software programs.

As a rule of thumb, if a usual day consists of running from appointment to meeting to business lunch to sales call, then the palm-top or organizer, which can be kept in your pocket, handbag, or briefcase and pulled out with the same ease as a traditional calendar/planner such as Filofax, will most likely be your time management tool of choice.

If, however, most of your working day is spent at your desk, and/or you regularly monitor complex projects, then a PC time management program such as Lotus Agenda, Borland's Sidekick, or Who-What-When by Chronos will probably serve you best. You will still need a notebook or an organizer, however, on which to jot down notes, tasks, and follow-ups that come up when you are not at your computer, to be incorporated later. See the box below for a brief description of some organization/time management program features. Not every program offers every feature, but this list will help identify features most useful to you.

CREATING A MASTER LIST.   As if you had a blank notebook in your hand on which you started writing in tasks as they occurred to you—that is, creating a Master List—the blank screen of your organizer or time management program is your notebook.

FEATURES OF ORGANIZATION/TIME MANAGEMENT
SOFTWARE

- Datebook/appointment calendar.
- Task "notepad" for to-do lists. (Basic feature)
- Pop-up calendar that can display by day, week, month, and quarter.
- Priority settings.
- Alarm or beeper to alert you to start a task.
- Visual prompt to indicate a deadline. Some prompts can be set to alert you a few hours or a few days before the actual deadline.
- "Note" or "index-card" feature which permits the addition of back-up information to a task listing.
- Contact manager. A "form" appears on the screen on which you can type not only name and address information, but also comments and notes about that contact.
- "Project manager" application, for complex projects.
- "People manager" application. A people manager is a performance review feature that involves setting long-term objectives, etc.
- Expense account feature.

Start your computerized Master List by creating a file in your organizing program called "Master List." Type everything from your current paper-based Master List into it. As with the paper Master List, review and update the computer Master List daily, entering tasks accumulated while you were away from the computer in a notebook, organizer, and/or a pocket dictating machine.

The advantage of such an organizer or program over a paper notebook is that you can move the items on your Master List around and sort and retrieve them in a variety of ways. For example, type in a client's name or initials, along with any information you want to enter. The next time that client calls, punch in his or her name or initials and all references to that person will appear. You'll know at once the current question on the table, whether you have a lunch date, or if there is anything you promised to send.

Code every entry to correspond with the categories you would like to recall—by priority, by colleagues you need to discuss the task with, by date, by key word, and by type or category of task. Categories of task or activity can be identified and retrieved by a common word. So, for example, note in your organizer, "Call Jeannie for contract info," "Call Bill re materials," as various calls occur to you. *Tip:* Enter the phone number too.

Okay, now you've got fifteen or twenty minutes between appointments. With your organizer in recall mode, type "Call," and all the calls you've entered will appear on the screen to be dealt with in a zip-zip-zip fashion. After the call is made, delete the reference, enter a follow-up date, or add new information as you wish.

A nice touch in some personal organizer programs is the capacity to insert detailed information about one of your tasks for review when you want to call it up. Say, for example, that a Master List entry reads, "Proofread proofs of journal article." Indicate with a symbol that you've typed in additional information. That information might be: "The production people say that the proofs have to be cut up and pasted on 8½ × 11 sheets of paper to leave room for the compositor's marks. Pain in the neck!" The main Master List will show only the short entry "Proofread proofs of journal article," until you choose to call up the backup information.

Some organizing programs express a similar concept with an "index card" feature that allows you to establish topic headings, and then type in as much material as you need under each heading.

Remember to establish start dates and deadlines for each task on your computer Master List. As you establish a start date for each task, move that task to the appropriate calendar day of your time management program. Once the start or due date of an item is entered, an electronic prompt—a visual reminder on the screen, or a beep or alarm—will be triggered when the date arrives. Some time management programs have a useful feature which enables you to start the prompt some days in advance of the deadline, so you can allocate your time appropriately. Note: Since the electronic ticklers are pegged to your computer's internal clock, don't forget to adjust the clock for standard or daylight time, and also according to different time zones when you travel.

MANAGING YOUR DAILY LIST.   When your calendar for a particular date comes up on the screen, all the items that you have assigned to that date will appear. This is your Daily List.

On the more casually styled organizer, giving a due date to each item creates an automatic rough-and-ready Daily List. For a more precise approach, the organizer's "calendar pages" headed by the date and year offer a handy site for locating a Daily List. Some people prefer to use the organizer calendar pages for this purpose rather than as an actual appointment calendar. Feeling that the small organizer screen is inconvenient for scheduling, they stay with the traditional paper calendar for appointments and scheduling.

SETTING PRIORITIES. Most time management programs recommend a symbol such as an asterisk to denote priority tasks. However, if you want a more precise priority setting plan—defining 1, 2, and 3 priorities (described in Chapter 5)—add the appropriate priority code to each item in your Daily List.

Setting priorities using an organizer might work as follows: Taking the example of the manufacturer discussed in Chapter 5, say the task "draft policy memo" is a 1 priority that the manufacturer needs to discuss with his colleague Jerry Westheimer, and he wants to have some resolution by June 15. Right after the final word, "memo," he would enter "#1" (for 1 priority), "JW" (Jerry Westheimer's initials), and "6/15" for the June 15 due date.

Now in recall mode, "#1" is typed. All the 1 priorities will appear on the screen. If there are too many to fit on the organizer's small screen, it can be scrolled forward. When the manufacturer types "JW," all tasks, discussion points, and anything else to which Jerry Westheimer's initials have been attached will appear. Typing "6/15" will bring up all other tasks scheduled for that day.

SCHEDULING TASKS. Use your computer in two ways. First, fortify your intention to take advantage of your personal energy time frame by scheduling 1 priority tasks in your prime working time. Set your private time off in your schedule with a bar graph, which many programs have. This is especially helpful if your calendar is on a network, because it will prevent your colleagues from scheduling meetings with you during your private time. And second, set your computer alarm or beeper to alert you to the "start time" for important tasks.

Here is how Harrison Josten, an advertising executive at a magazine, put the whole process together. First, Josten transferred his Master List from his notebook to his computer. Here are three of the items:

Schedule meeting with Jonathan Braddock to discuss ideas for new phone system.

Plan dates for business trip to Chicago and Los Angeles offices.

Prepare speech for sales conference on October 1st.

Next, Josten added details to his entry concerning the Braddock meeting: "Schedule meeting with J. Braddock to discuss new phone system 2:30–3:30 P.M., my office. Materials needed are workspace configurations, cost analysis, vendor bids."

On the morning of the day to which Harrison had assigned the Braddock scheduling, when he brought up his time management program, the touch of a key accessed everything he had scheduled for that day with a very abbreviated description, "Schedule meeting . . ." Another keystroke brought up the details.

Then, after the meeting had been scheduled, Harrison shifted the same text to the meeting day.

If Harrison wishes to see his schedule for the full month of August, he can pull up the calendar template for the month, which will show indicators for every August day on which something has been scheduled. He can, if he likes, schedule months or years ahead on the perpetual calendar.

Another task on Harrison's Master List, "Prepare speech for sales conference," is a 1 priority. Coding it "#1," he moved it to July 30 as a start date, blocking out his calendar from 9:30 to 11:00 to get a good start.

People: Calendaring, Communicating, and Sharing Data with Your Colleagues

Harrison Josten's office is on a network, so his secretary can inform him of his daily schedule, and he in turn can E-mail any instructions to his secretary. On a network, your secretary can maintain your calendar and schedule for you, you can do it yourself, or you can arrange some combination of the two. Making your calendar and schedule available to your secretary in both Read and Write modes enables him or her to use it just as you would. Your secretary can make tentative appointments for you, or remind you of important events through your shared computer alarm. Suggestion: Make your calendar available in Read Only mode to key staff for their general reference.

MONITORING ASSIGNMENTS AND PROJECT MANAGEMENT. The Master List will probably be adequate for keeping track of staffers' day-to-day activities. For purposes of complex project management, however, and staff performance review, look for a "project manager" or "people manager" application in your organization/time management program that will permit the establishment of more complex employee objectives, project stages and phases, and task and objective follow-up.

You might want to create permanent assignment lists for key staff people. This is simply done by creating a list called "assignments" under the "things to do" heading in your time management program.

After you and your staff have consulted and worked out deadlines, start dates, and benchmark dates, key your staffers' due dates into the calendar just as you would your own. The organizing software will notify you as the date draws closer and will let you know when the deadline has arrived. An alternative method is to create an individual assignments list for each person reporting to you.

As due dates draw nearer, why not E-mail one or more reminders to those involved? In general, gentle interim reminders to staffers, whether by E-mail, memo, or in person, serve the salutary effect of not only reminding the person of the task, but reinforcing your own commitment to it.

Note: Like any other type of computer file, your time management files *must* be backed up—either with the network system files, or on floppy disks. The latter is best.

SHARING DATA.   If you are on a network, you probably have the option of working "on the network" or "locally." Working on the network means that you can store your files on the computer's main file server, and your colleagues can call the documents up on their own screens. Working locally means that your files stay in your individual computer for your private use, until such time as you transfer them in whole or in part onto the network. You might find that some combination of the two works best. For example, Chuck Schwartz develops corporate proposals for a Big Eight accounting firm. Much of his work requires a high degree of security and confidentiality, so he stores his proposals on his own hard disk. However, he places a synopsis file with the same name on the network, minus the confidential information, so his colleagues can see the proposal's status at any given time.

MANAGING MEETINGS ELECTRONICALLY.   Russell Martin chairs the weekly meetings of the operations committee of his corporate division. He had become dissatisfied with the draggy pace at which committee members accomplished their assignments. Often they blamed delays on the fact that by the time Russell's secretary typed up the written summary of assignments and sent them out, it was midweek.

So Martin used a computer to compress the process of meeting follow-through. Martin's assistant, Richard Tolkien, brought his notebook computer to the meetings and typed in assignments and follow-ups as they came up, storing them on his notebook's floppy disk. For example, Stacy was asked to look into some productivity issues, scheduling conflicts were to be reviewed by Conrad, and the like.

As soon as each meeting ended, Richard returned to his office, copied the floppy disk from the meeting onto his desktop hard disk, and E-mailed the assignment and follow-up sheet to all participants, usually within the half-hour.

This brisk pace stimulated everyone's impulse to respond in kind, and that sense of dragginess was virtually eliminated.

Traveling Electronically

The benefits of computer-based organization and time management are particularly apparent when you are traveling. Useful electronic-organizing techniques include scheduling appointments/alarms, using a modem to access important documents on the network, faxing meeting notes and other documents back to your secretary, and communicating via E-mail. A portable computer will permit you to be as fully organized on the road as at home if you copy your organization and time management files from your desktop computer to your portable computer's hard disk. If you equip your portable with a modem or fax modem, you really *will* have your office in your briefcase.

With your portable computer and modem, your base office is as close as the nearest telephone modular jack. You can send and receive files from your office computer, exchange E-mail messages with colleagues and staff, transmit meeting memos and your own notes to your secretary, transmit instructions, and monitor schedule changes whether you are in the next town or halfway around the world. *Tip:* Computerized communication can be a money saver too, cutting down, for example, on overnight courier services.

This equipment is especially useful if you like to work at night or anytime out of office hours, particularly when you are traveling to another time zone. It eliminates the worry about time-zone differences. For instance, it's 8:00 A.M. and you're having breakfast; is your staff having lunch, or have they gone for the day? And on a more personal note, why not keep your preplanned packing lists and itinerary in your computer or organizer?

In addition, a fax modem or E-mail service can put you in touch with people other than those in your office, even if they are not on computer.

After each trip, it is wise to routinely transfer files from your portable to your desktop computer. There are two ways to accomplish this. The somewhat more cumbersome method is to copy the portable's files onto a floppy disk, and then copy the disk onto your desktop computer's hard disk. The more efficient method is to transfer files through software like Laplink, which, via a connector cable, copies files directly from one computer to another.

Also consider this handy device: a traveling answering machine. If you are likely to receive numerous calls at your hotel room while you are out, a miniaturized portable answering machine will be a boon. (You'll probably need a special double jack adapter and an alligator clip.)

13

Phones, Faxes, and Dictation Equipment

Telephone Technologies and Tactics

Cellular Telephones

Once upon a time, if you saw people talking to themselves in the street you deduced they had a problem. But now it's commonplace to see people walking down the streets or sitting in their cars, telephone in hand. These ubiquitous portable phones—called "cellular" because their signals are transmitted via "cells" (microwave dishes) set up at intervals all over the country—allow you to make and receive calls anywhere.

Some cellular services offer nationwide coverage, others more limited coverage. You select your coverage depending on how far you would like your telephonic reach to extend. Look for these features on a cellular phone: voice-activated dialing, memory dialing, last-number redial, and speakerphone.

To cellular or not to cellular? Certainly there are some people who must constantly be on call: doctors, lawyers, service representatives, some executives. The key is to determine whether demands on your time and decision-making authority make it essential for you to make and receive calls anytime anywhere. (In addition to having a cellular phone, you may want to consider installing a fax in your car.)

If you need to be available for a limited period only, you could rent a cellular phone. Some of the major car rental companies now offer both portable and in-car telephones at many airport locations to permit ready availability on the road.

Note that cellular telephones and cordless telephones are not the same thing. A cordless phone, which is essentially a radio, works within a close radius to the antenna base. So cordless phones are generally used as portable phones within your home or just outside, though some newer technologies can extend a cordless phone's range to as far as half a mile. Also note that many cellular phones do not work indoors.

The inevitable telephone interruptions can get completely out of hand if you have a cellular telephone and can be reached at any time. Pagers can be responded to at your convenience, but those messages can become burdensome too.

Two simple defensive measures will help to minimize these claims on your time and attention. First—a wise policy anyway—maintain a high degree of communication between you and your secretary and staff, so they are clear on what responsibilities they may shoulder for you. Make sure they understand when you should be interrupted and when you shouldn't.

Also, be judicious about giving out your cellular phone number or pager number, limiting access, say, to your manager, your spouse, and your secretary, who can inform you if you need to get back to someone right away.

Tip: Schedule one or two intervals during the day to reply to accumulated calls and pages.

Beepers and Pagers

To page or beep you, the person trying to contact you calls a special telephone number assigned by your paging service. The service then sends an electronic signal to the small, lightweight paging device which you keep on your person. The Dick Tracy–style wristwatch pager is becoming available, in addition to the traditional clip-on pocket pager.

Depending on your pager, the message you receive can range from a simple beep, requiring you to call your service for the message, to a display of the caller's phone number, to the display of an actual text message. You will probably want to answer a beeper page right away, since it could be an emergency, but the display messages can be stored and returned at your convenience.

Unlike cellular phones, most beepers and pagers are limited to a particular geographic range.

Electronic Phone Books and Phone Dialers

These light pocket tools store names and phone numbers and can call up one or two lines of text on a tiny screen. Some models can dial the telephone number by emulating a telephone's digital tones into the receiver. They are sort of an electronic version of the little black book.

Call Waiting, Call Answering, Call Forwarding, and Conference Calling

Call waiting is a service offered by your telephone company for single-line residential and small-business phones which allows you to put a caller on hold and take a second call. Call forwarding transfers calls coming to your phone to any other number you designate. So, for example, if you are spending the day at a client's office, your calls can be switched over to your client's number. Most voice-mail systems also have a call-forwarding feature.

Call answering—that is, voice mail for the one-line phone ("Press 1 for Jim, 2 for Jane," etc.)—is now available through your phone company. It works through your phone and can be used in lieu of an answering machine.

The conference-calling option allows three or more people to hold a meeting by phone.

Voice Mail

Voice mail is on the bare-bones level an office-wide answering machine. But it is an extraordinarily clever and flexible answering machine that can answer a phone when it's busy, can forward messages from one location to another or from one employee to another, and can broadcast messages to several people at the same time.

Says one executive in Birmingham, Alabama, "Our voice-mail system has almost eliminated telephone tag. If I am busy or out of the office, I can send all of my calls to my voice-mail box, and include a message to the caller that will reroute the 'must handle now' call to an associate. In addition, I can retrieve messages at any time from any location in a matter of minutes."

But there are some problems with voice mail. Its great strength—making it possible to conduct business by exchanging and forwarding messages at each party's convenience—also makes it a very isolating technology. Says Neil S. Sachnoff, a management consultant in the field of telecommunications, "Too often, employees use voice mail as a screen.

They stop answering their phones, forcing all callers to leave messages, returning only those calls they feel like returning. This is bad for business."*

Mr. Sachnoff suggests, first, establishing strict policies on the appropriateness of voice mail, and second, always giving the name of an alternative person who can answer calls for the person who is away.

There is anecdotal evidence that it has been very hard in recent years to reach a human being at IBM. And IBM's business difficulties are certainly widely known. Coincidence? Or indicative of an isolation from customers?

Two suggestions for getting the benefits of this useful technology while avoiding its drawbacks are, first, to *limit its use* to your one or two hours of private time and when you are out of the office, and second, to *scrupulously return every call,* either yourself or by way of an assistant. Many corporate chieftains, such as John Sculley of Apple, for example, are known for their insistence that every call that comes into their office be responded to. Robert Crandall, chief of AMR, parent company of American Airlines, stays in his office, sometimes until 9:00 P.M., until he has returned every call made to him that day.

Rolodexes and Address Books

"Don't always assume the computer is the ideal way to achieve better organization,"† states LaMar Pugh, executive director of the International Computer Virus Institute, who like many programmers still finds a manual Rolodex the best way to organize his addresses and telephone numbers.

Boardroom Reports, July 15, 1991.
†*Portable Office,* February 1991.

The chief advantage of the traditional movable card-file system, such as the popular Rolodex, named after its principal manufacturer, is its fingertip availability and flexibility: names can be added and deleted easily, and cards can be arranged to suit your particular needs, whether alphabetically or in "classified" sections (by profession or type of service).

One prominent physician, active in public affairs, has sections on "media," "outpatient services," and "women therapists" intermixed with straight alphabetical listings. She uses yellow cards to set off her "yellow pages."

An interior designer who had too many listings for one system now maintains two files: a straight alphabetical "name" file, and a classified "category" file for furniture refinishers, appraisers, and so on. One writer organized his system by subjects like China, medicine, and politics, and lists on each card the magazines and/or editors interested in that subject.

Address-card files come in various sizes and shapes, but I generally recommend the flat-tray rather than the roller type because it's easy to maneuver and the cards can't fall out. I also recommend using 3 × 5 cards, which provide enough room to add additional information beyond name, address, and phone number. One executive, who entertains clients frequently, uses the cards to note birthdays, food preferences, and which people shouldn't be seated next to which others at dinner parties. You can staple business cards right on cards of this size.

Although many executives turn their address file over to their secretaries, keeping at their own desks only a few essential numbers, others prefer to maintain duplicate sets.

An electronic address and telephone directory, on the other hand, either in your computer or in a separate electronic device, has some strong arguments in its favor. A computerized address directory can be used by both secretary and manager if their computers are linked. The secretary doesn't have to tell her manager that Virginia Smith has a new phone number; she simply enters it, and it's now available for them both.

Names are, of course, more easily found. If you can't remember the person's last name but remember the first name, company, city, or even state, the computer can quickly find the name for you. Try that when you're spinning your regular Rolodex in hopes of finding John What's-his-name.

Planning travel visits can also be enhanced by the computer's electronic sorting capabilities. Prepare for your upcoming trip to Denver, say, by listing all your Denver connections in order to decide whom to contact.

With an office address file, you may or may not wish to carry an address book. A public health official carries an address listing of about one hundred names printed out from his computer in a reduced size to fit his loose-leaf calendar/planner. He updates the entries by hand, and when the listings get messy, his secretary incorporates the changes into the computer and prints out fresh copy.

You can also set up a separate address book for travel. One salesman divides his book into sales territories. And an investment banker who travels abroad a great deal has sections for each of the countries she visits most often.

Faxes

The fax machine is both a boon and a burden. Instant transmission is great, but the sight of your fax pouring out papers—much of it probably junk faxes—can try your patience. Here are several thoughts about faxing that might make it work a little better for you.

Limit Your Faxing

Avoid fax bottlenecks at your end and at your recipient's end by reserving faxing, as a general rule, for documents that really are urgent—especially lengthy documents. And when someone is faxing to you, ask how many pages are coming. Mail or courier services might turn out to be better options.

Though faxing seems like the fastest and most efficient option, it often isn't when you factor in the cost of fax paper (if you don't use a plain paper copier) and the time and money spent copying and collating incoming faxes.

To brake excessive faxing and junk faxing, do not put your fax number on your business card or letterhead, unless it is used for special purposes such as taking orders. If that seems too drastic, you can at least print your fax number in smaller and lighter type than your phone number.

Tips to Help Fax More Efficiently

- Number pages to be faxed: "Page 1 of 1," "Page 2 of 2," etc.
- Make sure your fax has enough memory if it should run out of paper.
- Look for these features: automatic document feeder and cutter, automatic dialing, delayed transmission so that the fax can be sent later when the phone rates are lower, and an activity report that will register all faxes sent and received.
- Consider, in lieu of a separate fax machine, a fax modem for your PC. This will allow you to see your messages on the screen so you don't have to print them out unless you choose to, and makes it easy to transmit multiple faxes to others.

Is a Fax Always Appropriate?

Organizer Stephanie Schur observed that prospective clients rarely responded positively to her faxed sales materials, whereas they were much more apt to respond when the same materials were mailed. This is one example of the fact that sometimes faxing doesn't convey the "look" that you would prefer.

It is also important to be aware of "fax etiquette," and refrain from sending unsolicited faxes. Also, as mentioned above, try to avoid faxing long documents if possible.

Dictation Equipment

Not so long ago, the term "office technology" referred primarily not to computers but to dictating machines. Dictation equipment, which substituted for the traditional "boss dictating to secretary" relationship, provided the first real office revolution.

Today, "high-end" dictation equipment makes it possible to telephone letters and memos in to your secretary's desk at any time of the day or night from across the street or across the world. One executive who travels the world regularly telephones in his notes on meetings with clients, and any other relevant information, from any available phone, at his convenience.

His secretary types his dictation upon arriving in the morning and faxes it to his notebook portable, which has been set up to receive the correspondence. He reviews it and faxes back any revisions. Either he himself or his secretary can then E-mail or fax these texts to colleagues.

The two primary manufacturers of sophisticated dictation equipment are Dictaphone and Norelco.

But dazzling high-end dictation routines should not blind us to the very real benefits of pocket-size microcassette recorders. These handy devices are great for capturing "things to do" or instructions to your secretary while you're waiting for an elevator or in a taxicab. Brands include Lanier, Olympus, and Panasonic.

The trick to managing a pocket recorder successfully is to keep track of the microcassettes, which tend to be pesky, elusive little creatures. Four tips that have proved useful are:

1 Group the papers referred to in the microcassette, and Scotch-tape the cassette on top of the stack.
2 Taking a folder with pockets, put the papers in the left pocket and the microcassette in the right pocket. Use a single folder for each microcassette and the relevant papers.
3 Number each cassette with a Post-It, and put the same number, circled, on each backup document.
4 For dictation out of the office, make up a cassette kit. Stock a small pouch with several cassettes and glassine envelopes. Put a small Post-It inside each envelope. When finished with a cassette, drop the tape into one of the glassine envelopes, noting on the Post-It for identification purposes one or two high points. Turn tapes over to your secretary upon returning to the office.

Tip: Jack Gallaway, president of the Tropicana Hotel in Atlantic City, leaves thirty seconds blank at the beginning of each letter or memo. Then, if he makes a change, he saves his secretary considerable time and bother by going back to the beginning to explain that a change has been made. For example, "When you get to the paragraph about vendor specs, change the references to Mr. Williams to 'Dick Williams.'"

Computer and
Electronics Appendix

Glossary of Basic Computer Terms

Boot or **boot up**   To turn on your computer, which automatically readies your operating system for use.

Bulletin board   A bulletin board is a central information exchange on which individuals post messages and contribute to ongoing discussions. Subjects covered can range from baseball to Bach. Bulletin boards are accessible by modem. To learn what bulletin boards are available and how to join them, get the magazine *Boardwatch* at a computer store or large magazine store.

CD-ROM   An acronym for Compact Disk–Read Only Memory. These disks, which look like music compact disks, store huge amounts of reading material such as encyclopedias and trade directories. They are used for reading only and the information on them cannot be manipulated, but you can print them out. They can be accessed on your computer if it has a CD-ROM drive. Check current copyright laws for use of electronically published material.

DOS or **MS-DOS**   Every computer—every piece of hardware—requires a fundamental program that allows it to run other programs. The generic term for this kind of fundamental program is "operating system." The software called DOS, an acronym for Disk Operating System, or, interchangeably, MS-DOS, for its manufacturer, Microsoft, was adopted by the IBM PC, and subsequently by most IBM-compatible PCs. As of this writing, DOS 6.0 is the most up-to-date version.

Other operating systems include Unix, Xenix, and OS/2. Macintosh computers use yet another operating system. In general, all machines running the same operating system are compatible with one another, meaning, for example, that all machines using DOS can run the same programs. PC and Macintosh software is not compatible, though some Macintosh computers can run DOS software with the addition of interface software.

Download   To transfer data and/or files from another computer to your own, via a modem.

Disk drive   Disks are used for the storage of data. There are two types of disks: hard, or fixed, disks, and floppy disks. The hard disk drive—that is, the mechanism that controls the disk—is in the computer housing and is not visible from the outside. On most PCs, when you boot up the designation "C:/" will appear on the screen, which simply means that the C drive—the hard disk drive—is ready to go.

E-mail   Software that allows individuals to communicate with one another via computer. See page 301.

Floppy disk   A floppy disk is a disk of magnetic material in a square cover. It is inserted into your floppy disk drive. Files are stored on floppy disks and recovered from them. In contrast to the hard disk, which is permanently in place, floppy disks are removed after use and reinserted to be worked with again.

On-line service　An on-line service is an information collection accessible by modem. It may be a service to which you subscribe and pay for usage time, such as CompuServe and Prodigy, or it may be a free service offered by some libraries and government offices.

Program　See **Software.**

Read Only mode　Files in Read Only mode can be read and in some cases printed out, but they cannot be "written to"— i.e., changed.

Read/Write mode　Files in Read/Write mode can be not only read but changed.

Reading index　Some organizer programs offer an indexing application that can help you call up references in your CD-ROM and E-mail files by journal name, company, or key word, such as, for example, information about recent mergers.

Software　A program containing the electronic material necessary to perform specific tasks on your computer. WordPerfect, Lotus 1-2-3, and Windows are all examples of software. Software is purchased on floppy disks and then copied to a computer's hard disk.

Upload　To transfer data and/or files from your computer to another via a modem over telephone lines.

Windows　A very popular "operating environment" used on MS-DOS computers. As mentioned in the discussion of DOS, every computer requires a fundamental program, called an operating system, that allows it to run other programs. Two operating systems have dominated the PC world for a number of years: MS-DOS (the system for IBM and IBM-compatibles) and Macintosh.

The Macintosh system—felt by many to be much easier to use—is operated by moving a little arrow about the screen, using a device called a "mouse," or alternatively a trackball. You point the arrow at tiny icon indicators of function, such as a little drawing (icon) of a typewriter to indicate a word processing program, etc., and then click a button on the mouse or trackball to indicate you want to use the function. One can have several files or even several programs on the screen at the same time, each occupying its own "window."

The Macintosh system became so popular that the Microsoft Corporation, which manufactures the MS-DOS program for IBM and IBM-compatibles, designed a new program called Windows, which emulates in many respects the Macintosh method.

Microsoft Windows is not an operating system. Like all IBM and IBM-compatible programs, it runs on DOS. It has been dubbed a "graphic user interface" (GUI) or "operating environment" to distinguish it from a true operating system. Windows has become so popular that other programs, like Lotus 1-2-3, for example, have been made available in versions that are compatible with it and share its visual style and icons.

Portable Computer Features and Accessories

AC ADAPTER. The adapter allows your computer to work on any standard electrical outlet and also serves as a battery charger. Try to find the least bulky adapter.

AUTORESUME. Some portable models offer a convenience feature that allows you to turn the computer off, and then pick up exactly where you left off when you turn it back on again without having to boot up again.

BATTERIES. Portable computers are powered by rechargeable batteries—the traditional nickel-cadmium (NiCad) batteries, or the newer, lighter nickel-metal-hydride (NiMH) batteries. The AC adapter also serves as the battery's charger.

Despite rapid advances in the capabilities of portables, battery capacities have a very long way to go. One good battery ("good" defined as lasting three or more hours) will barely get you from New York to Houston. Battery-gauge software is available which, by means of an icon in a corner of your screen, indicates how much power your battery has left.

Carry a spare fully charged battery with you. Also, when buying a portable computer, consider the length of time it takes the battery to recharge. Some batteries can take several hours, or even overnight, to recharge.

Power-saving features include automatic screen dimming and automatic "power down" of the hard disk after a specified period of nonuse. *Tip:* You may want to power down your portable before going through airport customs so you can "wake up" your computer at a touch if security personnel wish to check it.

FLOPPY DISK DRIVE. Most laptop/notebook computers include a 1.44-megabyte internal floppy disk drive. If you need to transfer data often, the lack of an internal floppy disk drive will be annoying.

HARD DISK DRIVE. Hard drives for portables are usually in the 60- to 80-megabyte range, though 120-megabyte and larger drives are available. Some hard drives can be quite noisy. Check for loudness.

KEYBOARD. The more writing and editing you do on your computer, the more important a good keyboard will be. Does your handspan fit comfortably on the keys, or do you feel constrained? Are the keys comfortable to the touch? Do the keys have give when you depress them, or is their "travel" hard and short? Does the layout seem normal, or have function keys (F keys) been rearranged to fit in the tight space? Are there dedicated keys for Home, Page Up, Page Down, and End, or are you forced to use a special function key in combination with the cursor-arrow keys?

If your computing leans more heavily toward number crunching, then your priority is a separate numeric pad that can be plugged into one of your computer's accessory ports. (Notebook keyboards designate certain letter keys to function as number keys when the "numeric lock" key is depressed, but this is not very convenient for heavy use.)

MODEM/FAX MODEM. A modem is a device, either internal or external, which permits the transfer of data over telephone lines from one computer to another.

If a portable has an internal modem there is a phone jack on its side, usually labeled "line." When you are transmitting data, one end of a standard telephone modular cord plugs into the "line" jack and the other end plugs into a standard telephone jack in the wall.

Many computers are not prefitted with internal modems, but have internal modem expansion slots into which you can fit an independent modem unit. Not every internal modem fits every computer. You can also equip your portable computer with a fax modem which will allow you to transmit a document created on your computer to any fax machine.

Some external modems for laptops and notebooks are about the size of a cigarette packet. Generally speaking, external modems can be used with any computer.

PORTABLE PRINTERS. Printers come in small, lightweight models, about the size of a notebook computer, or even smaller, and print with near-laser quality. They can weigh as little as two or three pounds. Manufacturers of portable printers include Kodak, Epson, IBM, Hewlett-Packard, and Canon.

SCREEN/MONITOR DISPLAY. Portable computer screens are either monochrome or color. Monochrome screens have one basic foreground and one basic background color, with shades in between which make up to some extent for the absence of color. A reasonably crisp and clear display can mean the difference between a productive business trip and one that sends you home with severe eyestrain. A top-of-the-line color screen is the ideal, and they have come down dramatically in price. However, a first-rate monochrome display will be sharp and clear, and will save considerably in price. You can expect any portable of notebook size or larger to have a backlit or sidelit VGA display, but screens do vary in brightness and clarity, and only you can determine if a particular screen will do for you. Check out as many displays as possible before you buy. Does the screen tilt at a comfortable viewing angle? Be sure the brightness and contrast controls are convenient.

TRACKBALL (MOUSE SUBSTITUTE). It is hard to use a mouse while traveling without encroaching on your neighbor's seat space. Some manufacturers of portables have dealt cleverly with this problem by installing a trackball—a mouse substitute—on the keyboard. The Macintosh PowerBook is noted for this feature. Clip-on trackballs are available for other small portables.

WEIGHT. The claimed weight for a portable computer is sometimes deceptive, since it doesn't usually take add-ons or the carrying case into account. A computer that alone may weigh seven pounds can weigh fifteen pounds with all its gear. These two steps will help you get a better sense of a portable computer's true weight:

1 Some peripherals, like floppy disk drive or modem/fax modem, can be either internal or external. If they are internal, assume they are included in the stated weight. If they are external, roughly estimate their weight and add that on.

2 Add seven or eight pounds to the stated weight for the gear that supports the computer: extra battery pack, AC adapter, power cord, manual or quick reference guide, fast charger, portable printer, paper and accessories, and carrying case.

Computer, Copier, and Fax Supplies

Computers and printers

AC adapters for portables

Batteries for portables

Cleaning supplies for screen and keys (surfaces)

Compressed-air canister to blow dust out from between keys and around the disk slots (available at computer stores and camera stores)

Diskettes

Document clip to hold paper upright

Dustcovers for keyboard and printer

Mouse pad (rubber)

Printers, dot matrix: continuous-feed paper, ribbons, single-sheet feed option

Printers, ink jet: plain paper, ink cartridges

Printers, laser: compatible paper, ink cartridges

Screen wipers

Storage boxes for diskettes

Surge suppressor

Copiers
Paper
Toner

Fax machines
Ink cartridges
Paper: "fax paper," or plain paper

Schedules Appendix

Here are nine schedules designed for clients, with a brief explanation of each schedule.

SCHEDULE I. NANCY DARCY

	MONDAY	TUESDAY	WEDNESDAY	THURSDAY	FRIDAY
9:00	*Private work session:* Paperwork Planning/writing reports				Review the week; plan for the next
10:00			↑	↑	
11:00	Dept. staff meeting	Meeting—D.L.	Meeting—S.J.P.	Meeting—R.M.D.	Meeting—A.B.L.
Noon	Lunch/cafeteria	Reading/lunch	Business lunch	Business lunch	Lunch/cafeteria
1:00	Open house	Private work session	Open house	Private work session	Open house
2:00					
2:30	Appt: Bill Smith	Appt: Stan Wright	Appt: Steve King	Appt: Sue Wilkins	Appt: Alice Crane
3:00					
4:00	Personnel Evaluations	Phone calls & appts.	Phone calls & appts.	Personnel Evaluations	Phone calls & appts.
4:45	Wrap-up: Marcy				
5:00		↑			

Darcy's conflict was the need to reconcile two contradictory job elements: dealing with paperwork and projects, and working with staff and others. Darcy scheduled a "private" early-morning block from 9:00 to 11:00 A.M. Her "public" time began at 11:00 A.M. every day, with a staff meeting. Other meetings, visitors, and appointments were consolidated into an afternoon block. "Open house" time was from 1:00 to 2:30 P.M. Monday, Wednesday, and Friday, leaving the later afternoon for lesser-priority projects, other appointments, and phone calls.

SCHEDULE II. PATRICK HICKOK

	MONDAY	TUESDAY	WEDNESDAY	THURSDAY	FRIDAY
9:00	Reserved for London calls & other phoning	→	→	→	→
10:00	Marketing meeting; brief session with Rose [secretary]	Process mail, etc., with Rose			
11:00	Be available to people—calls, meetings, appointments, etc.	→	→	→	→
Noon	Lunch	Lunch	Lunch	Lunch	Lunch
1:00	Open time	Open time	Open time	Private work session: planning, writing letters & reports, etc.	Open time
2:00					
3:00					
4:00					
5:00					

Hickok, a senior vice president with an investment house, needed a fairly flexible schedule because so much of his work involved responding to late-breaking or last-minute events in the financial community. Therefore, we planned his mornings around the one fixed point in his schedule—the daily calls to London that had to be made at 9:00 A.M. because of the time difference—and left his afternoons open. To give him even greater flexibility, we blocked out one full afternoon a week for reflective and conceptual work, rather than trying to allocate some time each day for these responsibilities.

SCHEDULE III. CRAIG MARSHALL

	MONDAY	TUESDAY	WEDNESDAY	THURSDAY	FRIDAY
8:00	Private work session: planning, writing, etc.				
9:00					
10:00					
11:00	Process mail with Rosalie [secretary]; return calls				
Noon					
1:00	Lunch	Lunch	Lunch	Lunch	Lunch
2:00	Flexible time: outside appts., private work, returning calls, etc.	George	Martha	John	Flexible time
3:00		Ron	Alan	Joan	
4:00		Carol	Bill	"Open" time	
5:00	Review follow-ups; plan for tomorrow				
5:30					

This young corporate vice president heads a fairly large department, and maintaining contact with his staff takes up a sizable chunk of his time. But these meetings were haphazard, and too many matters were being brought to his attention at the last minute—resulting in a sharp rise in time-consuming troubleshooting. So Marshall and I reorganized his schedule to meet his dual needs for greater supervisory involvement and private time.

Schedule IV. Winston Reynolds

	MONDAY	TUESDAY	WEDNESDAY	THURSDAY	FRIDAY
9:00	Meeting	Meetings	Paperwork	Meetings	Staff meeting/weekly wrap-up
9:30	Paperwork		Meetings		
10:00	Paperwork		Meetings		Paperwork
10:30	Return calls		Meetings		Meetings
11:00	Return calls		Meetings		Meetings
11:30	Meet with secretary—plan week		Meetings		Meetings
Noon					
1:00	Lunch	Lunch	Lunch	Lunch	Lunch
2:00	Meetings	Meetings	Return calls	Meetings	Meetings
3:00	Meetings	Meetings	Meetings	Meetings	Meetings
4:00		Return calls		Return calls	Return calls
5:00					

Reynolds, a senior corporate executive, spends the bulk of his time attending meetings: board meetings, directors' meetings, committee meetings, government hearings in Washington. He has little straight paperwork—but what there is wasn't getting done. Reynolds himself devised an imaginative plan to make the the office time he needed. The following comments are extracted from my report to him:

Your schedule is volatile, and that's the way you like it. I endorse your idea of blocking one half hour for paperwork on Monday, Wednesday, and Friday mornings, plus a block each day to return phone calls. The idea is to "play the percentages;" some work blocks will be canceled, but others won't, giving you a fighting chance of accomplishing your paperwork.

SCHEDULE V. PATRICIA WORKMAN

	MONDAY	TUESDAY	WEDNESDAY	THURSDAY	FRIDAY
9:00	Telephoning	Meetings	Private work session: projects, writing, etc.	Meetings	Private work session: projects, writing, etc.
10:00	Process paperwork/mail				
11:00		Process paperwork	Process paperwork	Process paperwork	Process paperwork
Noon					
1:00	Lunch	Lunch	Lunch	Lunch	Lunch
2:00	Telephoning	Meetings	Private work session	Meetings	Weekly wrap-up: check to make sure all routine work—papers, calls, etc.—have been processed
3:00					
4:00					
5:00					

Workman is a junior corporate manager with administrative responsibilities whose schedule broke down into weekly blocks rather than a daily routine. To help her keep this schedule, I recommended the following tactics (as quoted from my report):

To keep routine paperwork from piling up, process at 11:00 every day. At the beginning of each week, I suggest that you enter the appropriate "block" into your calendar (i.e., on Monday, write "phoning" and so forth). It might be wise to block out your calendar a few weeks in advance.

Schedule VI. Stuart Baker

	MONDAY	TUESDAY	WEDNESDAY	THURSDAY	FRIDAY
9:00	Check in-box & calendar. Do all routine tasks (2's & 3's), follow-ups, etc. List at least 2 but no more than 5 substantive tasks for afternoon.				
10:00					
11:00	Appointments	"Open house"	"Open house"	Appointments	"Open house"
Noon	Lunch	Lunch	Lunch	Lunch	Lunch
1:00					
2:00	Private work session for priority tasks on morning's list				
3:00	Meet with secretary				
4:00	Daily wrap-up: return calls, tie up loose ends				
5:00					

Baker, a young executive with a national corporation, carried a heavy project load and was responsible for producing a great many policy papers and reports. But he had gotten himself into a bind because he was trying to do his most concentrated work in the mornings—the "low" part of his day. We devised a more realistic schedule that allowed him to take advantage of his personal peak time, afternoon.

SCHEDULE VII. MARCIA SURREY

	MONDAY	TUESDAY	WEDNESDAY	THURSDAY	FRIDAY
9:00	Write up story ideas	Copy editing	Write up story ideas	Write up story ideas	Copy editing
10:00	Make calls		Calls	Calls	
11:00	Process mail/action box (with Angela); check ticklers		Process mail/action box; check ticklers, etc.	Process mail/action box; check ticklers, etc.	
Noon					
1:00	Lunch	Lunch	Lunch	Lunch	Lunch
2:00	Action box; appointments	Copy editing	Action box; appointments	Action box; staff "open house" hours	Copy editing
3:00					
4:00	Reading		Reading	Reading	
5:00					

Surrey is assignments editor for a major metropolitan newspaper, and her job breaks down into two main areas—copy editing and what she calls "everything else," which includes paperwork, reading, and generating story ideas. We blocked out two days a week for copy editing only, and devised a fairly precise program for non-copy editing days to ensure that she had the time for "everything else."

SCHEDULE VIII. JOHN McDONOUGH

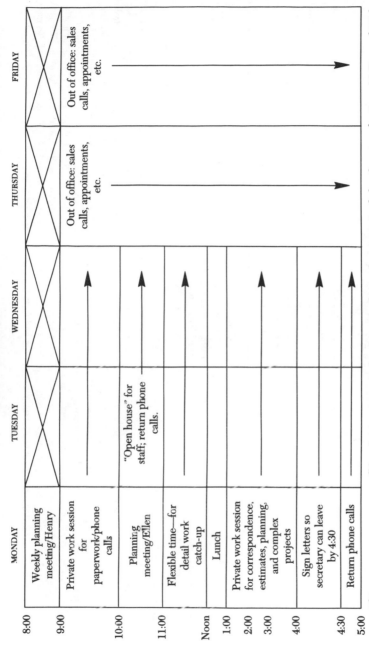

	MONDAY	TUESDAY	WEDNESDAY	THURSDAY	FRIDAY
8:00	Weekly planning meeting/Henry				
9:00	Private work session for paperwork/phone calls			Out of office: sales calls, appointments, etc.	Out of office: sales calls, appointments, etc.
10:00	Planning meeting/Ellen	"Open house" for staff; return phone calls.			
11:00	Flexible time—for detail work catch-up				
Noon	Lunch				
1:00					
2:00	Private work session for correspondence, estimates, planning, and complex projects				
3:00					
4:00	Sign letters so secretary can leave by 4:30				
4:30	Return phone calls				
5:00					

This entrepreneur owns a small but thriving company that designs and manufactures stained glass for art applications. McDonough's job involves a great deal of detail, and he found it difficult to keep up with this work and make time for his many out-of-the-office sales calls and trips. We worked out a fairly rigid daily schedule with not one but *three* daily private work blocks, to compensate for the many days he was out of the office.

Schedule IX. Martin Garner

	MONDAY	TUESDAY	WEDNESDAY	THURSDAY	FRIDAY
9:00	Paperwork		Paperwork		Paperwork
10:00	Private work session: planning			Phones	Phone work
11:00		Sales calls	In-office appointments		
Noon	Working lunch with sales reps				
1:00			Lunch	Lunch	Lunch
2:00			Flexible time (catching up on reading, planning, troubleshooting, appointments, etc.)	Sales calls	Phone work
3:00	Private work session: budget/sales planning; action box				
4:00					
5:00					Weekly review

Garner owns a fire-damage restoration service and, like many small business owners, has virtually sole responsibility for a variety of functions, including financial management, staff management, operations, and sales. His initial daily task list ran to eight pages, so our first job was to bring that list down to manageable proportions. Garner began by dividing it into three categories: high pay-off tasks (those he liked or did best), "must-do's," and "everything else." Then he concentrated on the latter category, eliminating and delegating as many tasks as possible. His final task list was more workable and included processing mail and paperwork, covering the phones, priority projects (budgeting and sales planning), outside sales calls and estimates, and reading.

That accomplished, we turned to Garner's chief problem—reconciling his in-office time needs with the amount of time he had to spend out of the office. We blocked out his time on a weekly basis, giving him at least three and a half days in the office. We also outfitted him with a traveling briefcase, a cellular phone, and a fax in his car, from which he could handle paperwork and dictation between calls—saving him a lot of wasted time driving back and forth between calls and the office.

Office Appendix

Office Supplies Checklist

The following list indicates the range of supplies you might
need for optimum office efficiency.

Address book and/or Rolodex.
Bulletin board or several squares of stick-on cork.
Business cards.
Calculator.
Calendar/planner
Clipboard.
Clock.
Computer, copier, and fax supplies: see page 340.
Desk blotter.
Desk lamp.
Dictation machine(s) and cassettes.
Dictionary and other references: airline guide, company
policies manual, interest tables, etc.
File folders.
File rack for desktop files. Styles include "expandable"
plastic racks, onto which additional sections can be

clipped as needed, or sturdier metal racks with fixed compartments.

In-box and out-box.

Letter opener.

Marking pens.

Pads: personalized memo pads; notepads with carbon attachments; plain, small pads for odd notes; Post-It stick-ons; larger legal- or letter-size pads.

Paper clips: regular and oversized.

Pencil sharpener.

Pencils and pens.

Routing and referral slips; other office forms (Chapter 3).

Rubber bands: mixed sizes.

Ruler.

Scissors.

Scotch tape and dispenser.

Specialized equipment: graphics tools, etc.

Spiral or looseleaf bound notebook(s) for Master List.

Stapler, staples, and staple remover.

Stationery and envelopes. Keep on hand a supply of full-sized (8½″ × 11″) letterhead stationery, matching business-size (#10) envelopes, and smaller notepaper for handwritten notes.

Telephone.

Telephone directory (Rolodex).

Telephone message holder: old-fashioned desk needle; box; small, compartmentalized metal rack.

TRAF-system equipment: "action" box/folder, "to file" box/folder, referral folders for staff and colleagues.

Typewriter or memory typewriter and related supplies: ribbons, correction paper, correction fluid ("white-out").

Office Deployment Checklist

Desk. Useful features include:

Surface shallow enough to reach outer edge easily, and deep enough to keep file rack and stacking boxes out of your immediate work area.

Fairly shallow desk drawers.

Central drawer for paper clips and small supplies.

Drawers that slide easily.

Matte desk surface. Surfaces made of glass or other reflecting materials can cause eyestrain.

Pullouts for extra work space.

Front panel to block legs from view.

Side extension or "ell" for equipment.

Locking mechanism (if you have confidential material).

Some desk deployment guidelines are:

Have you opened up ample work space?

Can you process (TRAF) papers in an easy flow?

Can you swivel to any piece of equipment you might need?

Is the equipment used most frequently easily accessible?

Are the objects on your desk used often enough to warrant the space they take up?

In general: Can you find things easily, use equipment comfortably?

Chair. Should be comfortable, be height-adjustable, and have wheels and a swivel mechanism. If you type, the chair should not have arm rests, although retractable arm rests are fine. More expensive models have neck rests and adjust to a reclining position.

Other seating. At least two visitors' chairs and/or couch. Should be comfortable, but not too low or soft.

Lighting. Proper lighting can materially affect concentration. Position the head of an adjustable desk lamp (gooseneck or jointed variety) for optimal lighting on your work area. If feasible, position your desk near the window for access to natural light.

Other facilities. Small conference table and chairs, coffee machine and accoutrements, small refrigerator, credenza, bookcases and/or shelving.

Office Products and Equipment

The listing below represents only a partial selection of products available and where information can be obtained. None of the equipment is guaranteed or represented by the author.

Answering machines
AT&T, Small Business Network, General Business Systems, 32 Avenue of the Americas, New York, NY 10013 (800)247-7000 or (212)387-5400
Code-a-Phone, 16277 S.E. 130th Street, Clackamas, OR 97015 (503)655-8940
Panasonic Company, 1 Panasonic Way, Secaucus, NJ 07094 (201)348-7000
PhoneMate, 20665 Manhattan Place, Torrance, CA 90501 (310)618-9910
Sony Corporation, 1 Sony Drive, Mail Drop T1-11, Park Ridge, NJ 07656 (800)222-7669 or (201)368-9272

Calendars/diaries/organizers/planners
Day Runner, Inc., 3562 Eastham Drive, Culver City, CA 90232 (800)232-9786 or (213)837-6900

Day-Timers, Inc., Post Office Box 2368, Allentown, PA 18001 (215)395-5884

The Economist Diaries, Post Office Box 302, Nashville, TN 37202 (800) 628-0677 or (615)254-4724

Executive ScanCard System, The Executive Gallery, Inc., 380 Dublin Avenue, Columbus, OH 43215 (800)848-2618 or (614)469-3100

Filofax Inc., 500 West Avenue, Stamford, CT 06902 (800)345-6798 or (203)353-9777

Franklin Day Planner, Post Office Box 25127, Salt Lake City, UT 84125 (800)654-1776 or (801)975-1776

Keith Clark ("At-a-Glance"), 101 O'Neil Road, Sidney, NY 13838 (607) 563-9411

Letts of London, 104 Parkway Drive South, Hauppauge, NY 11788 (516) 864-3000

Time/Design, 11835 West Olympic Boulevard, Suite 450, Los Angeles, CA 90064 (800)637-9942 or (213)312-0288

Cellular and cordless telephones

AT&T Small Business Network, General Business Systems, 32 Avenue of the Americas, New York, NY 10013 (800)247-7000 or (212)387-5400

Mitsubishi Electronics, 800 Biermann Court, Mount Prospect, IL 60056 (708)298-9223

Motorola Corporation, Cellular Division, 600 N. Highway 45, Libertyville, IL 60048 (800)331-6456 or (708)523-5000

NEC America, 8 Old Sod Farm Road, Melville, NY 11747 (800)225-5664 or (516)753-7000

Panasonic Company, 1 Panasonic Way, Secaucus, NJ 07094 (201)348-7000

Sony Corporation, 1 Sony Drive, Mail Drop T1-11, Park Ridge, NJ 07656 (800)222-7669 or (201)368-9272

Computer product supplies

American Computer Supply, 2828 Forest Lane, Dallas, TX 75234 (800) 527-0832 or (214)241-3388

Inmac, 2465 Augustine Drive, Santa Clara, CA 95054 (800)547-5444 or (408)727-1970

Moore Business Products, 701 Woodlands Parkway, Vernon Hills, IL 60061 (800)323-6230 or (708)913-3200

Computer programs, organizing & time management: see *Software—Organizing & time management programs*

Computers *(desktop and portable)*

AST Research, 16215 Alton Parkway, Irvine, CA 92718 (800)876-4278

Compaq Computer Corporation, 20555 State Highway 249, Houston, TX 77070 (800)345-1518 or (713)370-0670

Dell Computer Corporation, 9505 Arboretum Boulevard, Austin, TX 78759 (800)289-3355 or (512)388-4400

Gateway 2000, 210 Gateway Drive, P.O. Box 2000, North Sioux City, SD 57049-2000 (800)846-2065 or (605)232-2000.

Hewlett-Packard Corporation, 1000 N.E. Circle Blvd., Corvallis, OR 97330 (503)757-2000

IBM Personal Computer Company, Route 100, Post Office Box 100, Somers, NY 10589 (914)766-1900

Macintosh, Apple Computer, Inc., 20525 Mariani Avenue, Cupertino, CA 95014 (800)446-3000 or (408)996-1010

NCR Corporation, 1700 S. Patterson Blvd., Dayton, OH 45479 (800)225-5627 or (513)445-5000

NEC America, 8 Old Sod Farm Road, Melville, NY 11747 (800)632-4636 or (516)753-7000

Poqet Computer Corp., 650 N. Mary Avenue, Sunnyvale, CA 94086 (408)737-8100

Sharp Electronics Corporation, Sharp Plaza, Mahwah, NJ 07430 (800) 732-8221/2 or (201)529-8200

Tandy Corporation (Radio Shack), 1800 One Tandy Center, Fort Worth, TX 76102 (817)390-3011

Toshiba America, Computer Systems Div., 9740 Irvine Blvd., Irvine, CA 92718 (800)334-3445 or (714)583-3000

Zeos International, Ltd., 530 Fifth Avenue N.W., St. Paul, MN 55112 (800)423-5891 or (612)633-5877

Copiers

Canon USA, Inc., Home Office Products Division, One Canon Plaza, Lake Success, NY 11042 (800)432-1467 or (516)488-6700

Mita Copiers, 149 W. 51st Street, New York, NY 10019 (800)222-6482 or (212)554-2679

Panasonic Company, 1 Panasonic Way, Secaucus, NJ 07094 (800)843-0080 or (201)348-7000

Sharp Electronics Corporation, Sharp Plaza, Mahwah, NJ 07430 (800) 237-4277 or (201)529-8200

Xerox Corporation, Xerox Square, Rochester, NY 14644 (800)832-6979 or (716)423-5090

Dictation machines

Dictaphone Corporation, 3191 Broadbridge Ave., Stratford, CT 06497 (800)447-7749 or (203)381-7000

Lanier Voice Products, Post Office Box 3064, Cedar Rapids, IA 52406 (800)241-1706 or (319)365-8404

Norelco, Philips Business Systems, 365 Crossways Park Drive, Woodbury, NY 11797 (516)921-9310

Olympus Corporation, 145 Crossways Park Drive, Woodbury, NY 11797 (800)221-3000 or (516)364-3000

Panasonic Company, 1 Panasonic Way, Secaucus, NJ 07094 (800)843-0080 or (201)348-7000

E-mail services

AT&T Mail, AT&T Corporation, New Brunswick, NJ (800)367-7225

EasyLink, Western Union Corporation, Dallas, TX (800)527-5184

MCI Mail, MCI International Corporation, Washington, DC (800)444-6245

Fax machines

Canon USA, Inc., Home Office Products Division, One Canon Plaza, Lake Success, NY 11042 (800)652-2666 or (516)488-6700

dex Business Systems, Inc., 301 Lee Farm Corporate Park, Danbury, CT 06810 (800)243-7046 or (203)796-5400

NEC America, 8 Old Sod Farm Road, Melville, NY 11747 (800)632-4636 or (516)753-7000

Panasonic Company, 1 Panasonic Way, Secaucus, NJ 07094 (800)843-0080 ext. 4016 or (201)348-7000

Sharp Electronics Corporation, Sharp Plaza, Mahwah, NJ 07430 (800) 237-4277 or (201)529-8200

Xerox Corporation, Xerox Square, Rochester, NY 14644 (800)832-6979 or (716)423-5090

Office products/office furniture/file & storage systems/desk accessories
Business & Institutional Furniture Company, 611 N. Broadway, Milwaukee, WI 53202 (800)558-8662 or (414)272-6080. Will meet or beat any price.
Foster Manufacturing Company, 414 N. 13th Street, Philadelphia, PA 19108 (800)523-4855 or (215)625-0500. Graphic arts equipment and storage systems.
Global Business Furniture, 63 Hemlock Drive, Hempstead, NY 11550. (800)645-1232 or (516)759-6001. Features a wide selection of furniture and equipment.
Oxford (Esselte Pendaflex Corporation), Clinton Road, Garden City, NY 11530 (516)741-3200. Extensive variety of filing products.
Reliable HomeOffice, 1001 West Van Buren, Chicago, IL 60680 (800) 621-4344 or (312)666-1800. Handsome, high-style products such as electronic organizers, telephones, desktop accessories, office furniture, etc.
Rolodex Corporation, 245 Secaucus Road, Secaucus, NJ 07094. (201)348-3939. The most widely known brand of card files and directories. Rolodex also manufactures electronic address directories and organizers.
The Sharper Image, 650 Davis St., San Francisco, CA 94111. (800)344-4444 (415)445-6000. Trendy, high-tech, top of the gadgetry line.
Steelcase Inc., 901 44th Street S.E., Grand Rapids, MI 49508 (616)247-2710. Filing & storage cabinets.

Organizers/planners (electronic "personal information managers"). See also Software—Organizing and time management programs
Atari Portfolio, Atari Computer, 1196 Borregas Avenue, Sunnyvale, CA 94088 (800)443-8020 or (408)745-2000
Casio B.O.S.S., Casio Inc., Post Office Box 7000, Dover, NJ 07801 (800) 272-0272 or (201)891-9466
Sharp Wizard, Sharp Electronics Corp., Sharp Plaza, Mahwah, NJ 07430 (800)732-8221/2 or (201)529-8200

Organizing and time management software: see Software—Organizing and time management programs

Pagers

Motorola Corporation, Pager Div., 1000 Mittel Drive, Wood Dale, IL 60191 (800)247-2346 or (708)616-4600

Printers

Canon, Canon USA, Inc., One Canon Plaza, Lake Success, NY 11042 (800)848-4123 or (516)488-6700

Epson, Epson America, Inc., 20770 Madrona Avenue, Torrance, CA 90509 (800)289-3776 or (310)782-0770

Hewlett-Packard, 1000 N.E. Circle Blvd., Corvallis, OR 97330 (800)527-3753 or (503)757-2000

IBM Personal Computer Company, Route 100, Post Office Box 100, Somers, NY 10589 (914)766-1900

Kodak (Eastman Kodak), 910 Elm Grove Road, Rochester, NY 14653 (800)255-3434 or (716)724-4000

Panasonic Company, 1 Panasonic Way, Secaucus, NJ 07094 (800)742-8086 or (201)348-7000

Software—Contact managers

Act! Contact Software International, 1840 Hutton Drive, #200, Carrollton, TX 75006 (800)365-0606 or (214)418-1866

TeleMagic, Remote Control International, 5928 Pascal Court, Carlsbad, CA 92008 (619)431-4000

Software—Organizing and time management programs

IBM Current, IBM Desktop Software, 472 Wheelers Farms Road, Milford, CT 06460 (800)426-7699 ext. 294 or (203)783-7000

InfoSelect, MicroLogic Corp., 100 Second Street, Post Office Box 70, Hackensack, NJ 07602 (800)342-5930 or (201)342-6518

Info-XL, Valor Software Corporation, 4840 Pebble Glen Drive, San José, CA 95129 (408) 559-1100

Lotus Agenda, Lotus Development Corp., 55 Cambridge Parkway, Cambridge, MA (800)343-5414 or (617)577-8500

Lotus Organizer. Same address as above.

Office PC (a desktop manager for WordPerfect users), WordPerfect Corp., 1555 N. Technology Way, Orem, UT 84057 (800)321-4566 or (801)225-5000

PackRat, Polaris Software, 1820 S. Escondido, Suite 102, Escondido, CA 92025 (800)338-5943 or (619)674-6500

Schedule Plus, Microsoft Corp., 1 Microsoft Way, Redmond, WA 98052 (800)426-9400 or (206)882-8080

SideKick, Borland International, 1800 Green Hills Road, Post Office Box 660001, Scotts Valley, CA 95066 (800)331-0877 or (408)438-8400

Who-What-When, Chronos Software Inc., 555 Dettaro Street, Suite 240, San Francisco, CA 94107 (800)777-7907 or (415)626-4244

Software—Project management programs

Microsoft Project for Windows, Microsoft Corp., 1 Microsoft Way, Redmond, WA 98052 (800)426-9400 or (206)882-8080

Project Scheduler 4, Scitor Corp., 393 Vintage Park Drive, Suite 140, Foster City, CA 94404 (415)570-7700

Time Line, Symantec Corp., 10201 Torre Avenue, Cupertino, CA 95014 (800)441-7234 or (408)253-9600

Software—Utility programs

Battery Watch, Traveling Software Inc., 18702 N. Creek Parkway, Bothell, WA 98011 (800)662-2652 or (206)483-8088. A battery "fuel gauge" that pops up on your screen to show how much more time is left on your battery.

Laplink, Traveling Software Inc., see above for address and telephone. This utility program allows files to pass readily back and forth between portable and desktop PCs.

XTree Gold, XTree Company, 4330 Santa Fe Road. San Luis Obispo, CA 93401 (800)388-3949 or (805)541-0604. A "file manager" program which allows you to organize, move, delete, copy, and rename files without having to master the DOS commands.

Wall planning systems and charts

Caddylak Systems Inc., 131 Heartland Blvd., Brentwood, NY 11717 (516)333-8221

Memindex Wall Planning Guides, Memindex, Inc., 149 Carter Street, Rochester, NY 14601 (800)828-5885 or (716)342-7890

Re-Markable, Remarkable Products, Inc., 157 Veterans Drive, Northvale, NJ 07647 (201)784-0900

A note on products: One of the most comprehensive guides to organizing products and services, both traditional and computerized, that we have seen is Susan Silver's book *Organized to Be the Best!* (see bibliography). You might also check your local library for the *Buyers Laboratory* subscription service, which compares and recommends models of business products in much the same way that *Consumer Reports* reviews consumer products.

Also consider the periodical *What to Buy for Business*, which is an independent consumer guide to buying business equipment such as computers, fax machines, copiers, etc. Its offices are located at 350 Theodore Fremd Ave., Rye, NY 10580 (800)247-2185 or (914)925-2566.

Bibliography

The books and articles marked with an asterisk are those the author consulted in writing *The Organized Executive*. These publications, as well as those without an asterisk, are recommended for further reading.

GENERAL MANAGEMENT

*Drucker, Peter F. *The Practice of Management*. New York: HarperCollins, 1986.
*———. *The Effective Executive*. New York: HarperCollins, 1985.
*———. *Management*. Abridged and rev. New York: HarperCollins, 1985.
———. *Managing in Turbulent Times*. New York: HarperCollins, 1985.
*Edelston, Martin, and Buhagiar, Marion. *"I" Power: The Secrets of Great Business in Bad Times*. Fort Lee, NJ: Barricade Books, 1992. Dist. by Publishers Group West, Emeryville, CA 94608.
Grove, Andrew S. *High Output Management*. New York: Vintage, 1985.
Kotter, John. *The General Managers*. New York: Macmillan, 1982.
Marden, Orison Swett. *Do It to a Finish*. New York: Crowell, 1909. A charming and very sound older book on some practical traits that serve managers well.
Peters, Tom. *Liberation Management*. New York: Knopf, 1992.
———. *Thriving on Chaos: Handbook for a Management Revolution*. New York: Knopf, 1987.

*Schoenberg, Robert J. *The Art of Being a Boss.* New York: HarperCollins, 1988.

Townsend, Robert. *Further Up the Organization.* New York: HarperCollins, 1988.

———. *Up the Organization.* New York: Fawcett, 1970.

TIME AND TASK MANAGEMENT

Blanchard, Kenneth, and Johnson, Spencer. *The One-Minute Manager.* New York: Morrow, 1982.

*Bliss, Edwin C. *Getting Things Done: The ABC's of Time Management.* Rev. ed. New York: Macmillan, 1991.

———. *Doing It Now: A Twelve-Step Program for Curing Procrastination and Achieving Your Goals.* New York: Bantam, 1984.

Boardroom Reports. "On the Road: Business Travel" is based on the text of an interview with Stephanie Winston published in *Boardroom Reports,* October 20, 1979. Adapted with permission.

Culp, Stephanie. *Conquering the Paper Pile-up.* Cincinnati: Writer's Digest Books, 1990.

———. *How to Get Organized When You Don't Have the Time.* Cincinnati: Writer's Digest Books, 1986.

*Davidson, Jim. *Effective Time Management: A Practical Workbook.* New York: Human Sciences Press, 1978.

———. *How to Plan Your Life.* Rev. ed. New York: Pelican, 1986.

Eisenberg, Ronni, with Kelly, Kate. *Organize Yourself!* New York: Collier Books/Macmillan, 1986.

*Grossman, Lee. *Fat Paper.* New York: McGraw-Hill, 1976.

Hedrick, Lucy H. *Five Days to an Organized Life.* New York: Dell, 1990.

Hemphill, Barbara. *Taming the Paper Tiger: Organizing the Paper in Your Life.* 3rd ed. Washington, DC: Kiplinger Books, 1992.

Kiechel, Walter III. "Overscheduled, and Not Loving It." *Fortune,* April 8, 1991.

———. "Getting Organized." *Fortune,* March 3, 1986.

Klein, Ruth. *Where Did the Time Go? The Working Woman's Guide to Creative Time Management* (Rocklin, CA: Prima Publishing, 1993).

*Kobert, Norman. *Managing Time.* New York: Boardroom Books, 1980.

*Lakein, Alan. *How to Get Control of Your Time and Your Life.* New York: New American Library, 1973, 1989. The time-management classic.

LeBoeuf, Michael. *Working Smart: How to Accomplish More in Half the Time.* New York: Warner Books, 1980, 1988.

*Mackenzie, Alec. *The Time Trap: The New Version of the 20-Year Classic on Time Management.* New York: AMACOM, 1990, 1991.

Mayer, Jeffrey J. *If You Haven't Got the Time to Do It Right, When Will You Find the Time to Do It Over?* New York: Simon & Schuster, 1990.

Schlenger, Sunny, and Roesch, Roberta. *How to Be Organized in Spite of Yourself.* New York: New American Library, 1989.

Silver, Susan. *Organized to Be the Best!* Los Angeles: Adams-Hall Publishing, 1989, 1991.

*Tennov, Dorothy. "How to Be More Efficient Every Hour of the Day." *Family Circle,* November 15, 1977. Interesting elaboration of the concept of planning one's work schedule around personal rhythms.

Winston, Stephanie. *Getting Organized: The Easy Way to Put Your Life in Order.* Rev. ed. New York: Warner, 1991.

OFFICE PLANNING AND DESIGN (INCLUDING HOME OFFICE)

Alvarez, Mark. *The Home Office Book: How to Set Up an Efficient Personal Workspace in the Computer Age.* Woodbury, CT: Goodwood Press, 1990.

Conran, Sir Terence. *Design Guides: Home Office.* New York: Van Nostrand Reinhold, 1990.

Dartford, James. *Office Spaces.* New York: Van Nostrand Reinhold, 1990.

Edwards, Paul and Sarah. *Working from Home: Everything You Need to Know About Living and Working Under the Same Roof.* 3rd ed. Los Angeles: Jeremy P. Tarcher, 1990.

9 to 5 Fact Sheets. Series of fact sheets on office design of special interest to computer workers. 9 to 5 National Association of Working Women, 614 Superior Avenue NW, Cleveland, OH 44113.

Szenasy, Susan. *Office Furniture.* New York: Facts on File, 1985.

COMPUTERS/OFFICE TECHNOLOGY

Books

Boone, Mary E. *Leadership and the Computer: Top Executives Reveal How They Personally Use Computers to Communicate, Coach, Convince and Compete.* Rocklin, CA: Prima Publishing, 1991.

Gookin, Dan. *How to Understand and Buy Computers.* 4th ed. San Diego: Computer Publishing Enterprises, 1991.

Haynes, Colin. *Portable Computing: Work on the Go.* New York: AMA-COM, 1990.

Kraynak, Joe. *The Plain English Computer Dictionary.* Englewood Cliffs, NJ: Sams/a unit of the Simon & Schuster Business & Professional Group, 1992.

Seymour, Jim. *Jim Seymour's PC Productivity Bible.* New York: Brady Computer Books/a unit of the Simon & Schuster Business & Professional Group, 1991.

———. *Jim Seymour's On the Road—The Portable Computing Bible.* New York: Brady Computer Books/a unit of the Simon & Schuster Business & Professional Group, 1992.

Periodicals

Boardwatch Magazine. 7586 West Jewell Ave., Suite 200, Lakewood, CO 80232 (800) 933-6038.

Byte, 1 Phoenix Mill Lane, Peterborough, NH 03458 (603)924-9281

Compute, 324 W. Wendover Avenue, Suite 200, Greensboro, NC 27408 (919)275-9809

Home Office Computing, 730 Broadway, New York, NY 10003 (212)505-3580.

MacUser, P.O. Box 52461, Boulder, CO 80321 (303)447-9330.

New York Times. Weekly columns by Peter H. Lewis: "Personal Computers" (Tuesday) and "The Executive Computer" (Sunday).

Office Technology Adviser. An annual special issue of *Inc. Magazine* concentrating on office technology. 38 Commercial Wharf, Boston, MA 02110, (617)248-8000.

PC Computing. Ziff-Davis Publishing Company, Box 50253, Boulder, CO 80321 (800)365-2770.

PC Magazine, One Park Avenue, New York, NY 10016-5802 (212)503-5255.

PC Novice. 120 West Harvest Drive, Post Office Box 85380, Lincoln, NE 68501 (800)848-1478.

PC World. 501 Second Street, San Francisco, CA 94107 (415)243-0500.

Books discussing operating systems such as DOS and OS/2 and also Windows are available, as well as books on Lotus 1-2-3, WordPerfect, Excel, and other software.

Digests of business books and articles

Newstrack Executive Tape Service. ManagersEdge Corporation, Box 1347, Englewood, CO 80150. Taped extracts of major newspaper and magazine articles related to business. By subscription.
Soundview Executive Book Summaries. 5 Main Street, Bristol, VT 05443. Summaries of current business books. By subscription.

Videotapes

John Cleese series of organizing & time management videos: "Meetings, Bloody Meetings," (1976), "More Bloody Meetings," (1986), "The Unorganized Manager" (1988). Video Arts, Inc., Northbrook Tech Center, 4088 Commercial Avenue, Northbrook, IL 60062, (800)553-0091 or (708)291-1008.
"How to Get Control of Your Time and Your Job." Designed by Alan Lakein, 1983. Cally Curtis Company, 1111 North Las Palmas Avenue, Hollywood, CA 90038 (213)467-1101.
"Smart Solutions for Managing Your Time." Inc. Magazine, 1992. Business Resources, Wilkes-Barre, PA.
"Time Management for Managers," hosted by Christopher Reeve, 1980. Time-Life Video, 1271 Avenue of the Americas, New York, NY 10020 (212)484-5940.
"Time Management for Managers and Professionals" (12-part course), 1979. William Oncken Corp., Deltak, Inc., East-West Technological Center, 1751 Diehl Road, Naperville, IL 60566 (708)369-3000.
"Time Management: Mark McCormack," 1991. Quiet Advantage, 1949 South Manchester St. 34, Anaheim, CA 92802 (714)748-1840.

Audiotapes

Epstein, Bee. *How to Create Balance at Work, at Home, in Your Life.* 6 cassettes. Los Angeles: Adams-Hall.
Winston, Stephanie. *The Organized Executive.* New York: Simon and Schuster Sound Ideas, 1987.

————. *Getting Organized: The Easy Way to Put Your Life in Order.* New York: Simon and Schuster Sound Ideas, 1986.

GENERAL INFORMATION

American Management Associations, 135 W. 50th Street, New York, NY 10020. The AMA serves as a clearinghouse for management information, offering extensive book lists, courses, seminars, and materials on many aspects of management, including organization and time management.

Index